iPad
For Seniors

12th Edition

by Dwight Spivey

for
dummies®
A Wiley Brand

iPad For Seniors For Dummies®, 12th Edition

Published by: John Wiley & Sons, Inc., 111 River Street, Hoboken, NJ 07030-5774, www.wiley.com

Copyright © 2020 by John Wiley & Sons, Inc., Hoboken, New Jersey

Published simultaneously in Canada

For general information on our other products and services, please contact our Customer Care Department within the U.S. at 877-762-2974, outside the U.S. at 317-572-3993, or fax 317-572-4002. For technical support, please visit www.wiley.com/techsupport.

Wiley publishes in a variety of print and electronic formats and by print-on-demand. Some material included with standard print versions of this book may not be included in e-books or in print-on-demand. If this book refers to media such as a CD or DVD that is not included in the version you purchased, you may download this material at http://booksupport.wiley.com. For more information about Wiley products, visit www.wiley.com.

Library of Congress Control Number: 2020931671

ISBN 978-1-119-60792-2 (pbk); ISBN 978-1-119-60795-3 (ebk); ISBN 978-1-119-60801-1

Manufactured in the United States of America

V10017681_022120

Contents at a Glance

Table of Contents

Introduction

I f you bought this book (or are even thinking about buying it), you've probably already made the decision to buy an iPad. The iPad is designed to be easy to use, but you can still spend hours exploring the preinstalled apps, configuring settings, and learning out how to sync the device to your computer or through iCloud. I've invested those hours so that you don't have to — and I've added advice and tips for getting the most from your iPad.

This book helps you get going with your iPad quickly and painlessly so that you can move directly to the fun part.

About This Book

This book is specifically written for mature people like you, folks who may be relatively new to using a tablet and want to discover the basics of buying an iPad, working with its preinstalled apps, getting on the Internet, and using social media. In writing this book, I've tried to consider the types of activities that might interest someone who is 50 years old or older and picking up an iPad for the first time.

Foolish Assumptions

This book is organized by sets of tasks. These tasks start from the beginning, assuming that you've never laid your hands on an iPad, and guide you through basic steps using nontechnical language.

This book covers going online using either a Wi-Fi or cellular connection, browsing the web (Chapter 10), and checking email (Chapter 11). I'm also assuming that you'll want to use the Apple Books e-reader app, so I cover its features in Chapter 13. I also assume that you might be interested in getting to know Apple's personal assistant, Siri, so I give you an overview of it in Chapter 6. Not to mention covering other great things you can do with your iPad, such as monitoring use of your iPad and its apps (Chapter 4), taking and sharing your photos and videos (Chapters 15 and 16, respectively), getting the latest news (Chapter 20), and much more!

Icons Used in This Book

Icons are tiny pictures in the margin of pages that call your attention to special advice or information, such as

TIP

These brief pieces of advice help you to take a skill further or provide alternative ways of getting things done.

WARNING

Heads up! This may be difficult or expensive to undo.

REMEMBER

This is information that's so useful it's worth keeping in your head, not just on your bookshelf.

TECHNICAL STUFF

Maybe this isn't essential information, but it's neat to know.

Beyond the Book

Like every *For Dummies* book, this one comes with a free Cheat Sheet that brings together some of the most commonly needed information for people learning to use, in this case, the iPad. To get the Cheat Sheet, head for www.dummies.com and enter *iPad For Seniors For Dummies Cheat Sheet* in the Search box.

Where to Go from Here

You can work through this book from beginning to end or simply open a chapter to solve a problem or acquire a specific new skill whenever you need it. The steps in every task quickly get you to where you want to go, without a lot of technical explanation.

At the time I wrote this book, all the information it contained was accurate for the 12.9-inch iPad Pro (1st, 2nd, and 3rd generations), 11-inch iPad Pro, 10.5-inch iPad Pro, 9.7-inch iPad Pro, 9.7-inch iPad (6th generation, a.k.a. "iPad 2018"), iPad Air 2, iPad Air (3rd generation), iPad (5th, 6th, and 7th generations), iPad mini (5th generation), iPad mini 4, version 13 of iPadOS (the operating system used by the iPad), and version 12.9 or later of iTunes. Apple may introduce new iPad models and new versions of iOS and iTunes between book editions. If you've bought a new iPad and found that its hardware, user interface, or the version of iTunes on your computer looks a little different, be sure to check out what Apple has to say at www.apple.com/iPad. You'll no doubt find updates there on the company's latest releases.

1

Getting to Know Your iPad

IN THIS PART . . .

Starting out with your iPad

Navigating the home screen

Updating and synchronizing your iPad

Discovering preinstalled apps

Activating special features

Seeing how your iPad is being used

IN THIS CHAPTER

» Discovering what's new in
  iPads and iPadOS 13

» Choosing the right iPad for you

» Understanding what you need
  to use your iPad

» Exploring what's in the box

» Taking a look at the gadget

Chapter **1**

Buying Your iPad

You've read about it. You've seen the lines at Apple Stores on the day a new version of the iPad is released. You're so intrigued that you've decided to get your own iPad. This device offers lots of fun apps, such as games and exercise trackers; allows you to explore the online world; lets you read e-books, magazines, and other periodicals; allows you to take and organize photos and videos; plays music and movies, and a lot more.

Trust me: You've made a good decision, because the iPad redefines the mobile computing experience in an exciting way. It's also an absolutely perfect fit for seniors.

In this chapter, you learn about the advantages of the iPad, as well as where to buy this little gem and associated data plans from providers for iPads that support cellular data. After you have one in your hands, I help you explore what's in the box and get an overview of the little buttons and slots you'll encounter — luckily, the iPad has very few of them.

Discover the Newest iPads and iPadOS 13

Apple's iPad gets its features from a combination of hardware and its software operating system (called *iOS;* the term is short for iPad operating system). The most current version of the operating system is iPadOS 13. It's helpful to understand which features the newest iPad models and iPadOS 13 bring to the table (all of which are covered in more detail in this book).

The iPad is currently available in various sizes, depending on the version of iPad. Here are the five basic sizes, by iPad type:

» **iPad:** The seventh-generation iPad features a touchscreen that measures 10.2 inches diagonally and sports a super-fast 64-bit desktop-class A10 Fusion processor.

» **iPad Air:** The third-generation iPad Air employs a touchscreen measuring 10.5 inches diagonally and features a 64-bit A12 Bionic processor.

» **iPad mini:** The iPad mini 5's screen measures 7.9 inches diagonally and uses a 64-bit A12 Bionic processor to do the behind-the-scenes work.

» **iPad Pro:** The two iPad Pro models are the fastest of the bunch. One measures 11 inches diagonally, and the other is 12.9 inches; they both come with blazing fast A12X Bionic processors.

TECHNICAL
STUFF

Dimensions of devices are typically shown in the units of measurement commonly used in a region. This means, for example, that the basic iPad is shown on Apple's U.S. site as being 9.8 inches (250.6mm) high and 6.8 inches (174.1mm) wide. In metric-system countries, both dimensions are given, but the order is reversed. When it comes to screen sizes, however, the dimensions are given in inches.

In addition to the features of previous iPads, the latest iPad models offer

» **Screen resolution:** In addition to screen size, screen resolution has evolved so that Apple's *Retina display,* which supports very high-resolution graphics, now appears across the line. The name derives from the concept that individual pixels on the screen are so small that at normal viewing distance, they can't be distinguished.

» **Apple Pencil:** Originally designed exclusively for use with iPad Pro models, the Apple Pencil now works with all of the latest iPad models. (Be sure to check which version of Apple Pencil will work with your iPad by visiting www.apple.com/apple-pencil.) Apple Pencil lets you draw and write on the screen with a familiar pencil-style tool rather than with your finger. The Apple Pencil contains a battery and sophisticated processing powers that make the experience of using it very much like (and sometimes better than) traditional pencils. Third-party pencils and drawing tools exist, but Apple's integration of Apple Pencil is remarkably smooth; the product has taken off quickly among graphic artists, illustrators, and designers. As other people have discovered its usability for marking up documents, it is becoming more and more common in business environments.

» **Faster motion coprocessor:** This coprocessor processes game features, such as the gyroscope and accelerometer. The iPad Air, both iPad Pro models, and the iPad mini all feature the M12 coprocessor, while the iPad sports an M10.

» **Touch ID:** This security feature is included on all newer iPad models. Sensors in the Home button allow you to train the iPad to recognize your fingerprint and grant you access with a finger press. Touch ID also allows you to use the Apple Pay feature to buy items without having to enter your payment information every time.

» **Facial recognition:** Touch ID is replaced on the latest iPad Pro models with Face ID. Using Face ID and the front-facing camera, your iPad Pro model unlocks when it recognizes your face.

» **Barometric sensor:** On all iPad models, this sensor makes it possible for your iPad to sense air pressure around you. This feature is especially cool when you're hiking a mountain, where the weather may change as you climb. Perhaps more to the point, the changes in barometric pressure can be sensed on a smaller scale so that elevation can be sensed and measured as you move normally.

» **More keyboard options:** The iPad Pro has a full-size onscreen keyboard. Because the screen has more space, the top of the keyboard can contain extra commands for filling in passwords and using more advanced input techniques.

» **Smart Connector for Smart Keyboard:** Additionally, you can use a Smart Connector to hook up a Smart Keyboard, which makes getting complex work done much easier.

» **Live photos:** Using the 3D Touch feature, you can press a photo on the screen to make it play like a short video. The Camera app captures 1.5 seconds on either side of the moment when you capture the photo, so anything moving in the image you photographed, such as water flowing in a stream, seems to move when you press the still photo.

The iPadOS 13 update to the operating system adds many features, including (but definitely not limited to)

» **Performance enhancements:** Apple promises that iPadOS 13 will increase the speed and performance of your iPad, including older models going back as far as iPad Air 2. From apps to keyboards to taking pictures, everything gets a speed upgrade.

» **Siri improvements:** Siri just keeps getting better. Siri can now speak in more natural tones and cadence, thanks to new software rendering capabilities. Siri can also give you more personalized information, including being able to find event information and reminders in other apps. And Siri can now play audio files from third-party app providers.

» **Dark Mode has arrived:** With iOS 13, you have the option of using Dark Mode, which shifts the iOS color scheme from light to dark. Dark Mode is especially helpful in low-light situations, or when you don't want to disturb others with the bright light from your iPad's screen.

- » **Accessibility enhancements:** Voice Control allows you to control your iPhone entirely with your voice, dictation is much more accurate, processing of voice commands happens right on your iPhone (as opposed to being transmitted to an online location and then returned to your iPhone), Numbers and Grids help to make more accurate selections, and the list goes on.

- » **Upgrades to Photos:** The Photos app receives some love in iPadOS 13, allowing for faster and more accurate searches of your Photos Library, better organization, better filters, enhanced and non-destructive video editing, and other features make this a great update.

- » **Built-in apps have been updated:** iPadOS 13 provides performance enhancements and interface upgrades for all of the apps that come pre-installed with it.

TIP

Don't need or use all the built-in apps? If so, you can remove them from your Home screen. When you remove a built-in app from your Home screen, you aren't deleting it — you're hiding it. This is due to security reasons that are beyond the scope of this book. However, the built-in apps take up very little of your iPad's storage space, and you can easily add them back to your Home screen by searching for them in the App Store and tapping the Get button.

These are but a very few of the improvements made to the latest version of iPadOS. I highly suggest visiting www.apple.com/ipados to find out more.

Choose the Right iPad for You

The most obvious differences among iPad models are their thickness and weight, with the Pro being biggest, followed by iPad Air, then iPad (shown along with a few Apple accessories in **Figure 1-1**), and finally the smallest, iPad mini. All three models come in space gray and silver, and the iPad Air, iPad, and iPad mini offer a third option, gold.

Image courtesy of Apple, Inc.

FIGURE 1-1

All four models come in Wi–Fi only for accessing a Wi–Fi network for Internet access, or Wi–Fi + Cellular for connecting to the Internet through Wi–Fi or a cellular network (as your cellphone does). The iPad models also differ slightly in available memory and price based on that memory (prices are accurate as of this writing and are subject to change):

» **iPad Pro 11-inch:** Wi-Fi models come in 64GB for $799, 256GB for $949, 512GB for $1,149, and 1TB for $1,349; Wi-Fi + Cellular models come in 64GB for $949, 256GB for $1,099, 512GB for $1,299, and 1TB for $1,499.

» **iPad Pro 12.9-inch:** Wi-Fi models come in 64GB for $999, 256GB for $1,149, 512GB for $1,349, and 1TB for $1,549; Wi-Fi + Cellular models come in 64GB for $1,149, 256GB for $1,299, 512GB for $1,499, and 1TB for $1,699.

» **iPad Air:** Wi-Fi models come in 64GB for $499 and 256GB for $649; Wi-Fi + Cellular models come in 64GB for $629 and 256GB for $779.

» **iPad:** Wi-Fi models come in 32GB for $329 and 128GB for $429; Wi-Fi + Cellular models come in 32GB for $459 and 128GB for $559.

» **iPad mini:** The Wi-Fi model comes in 64GB for $399 and 256GB for $549, and the Wi-Fi + Cellular model comes in 64GB for $529 and 256GB for $679.

Finally, the iPad models vary in screen quality and resolution, camera quality, and so on. Logically, the bigger the iPad, the bigger the price and higher the quality.

Decide How Much Storage Is Enough

Storage is a measure of how much information — for example, movies, photos, and software applications (apps) — you can store on a computing device. Storage can also affect your iPad's performance when handling such tasks as streaming favorite TV shows from the World Wide Web or downloading music.

TIP

Streaming refers to playing video or music content from the web (or from other devices) rather than playing a file stored on your iPad. You can enjoy a lot of material online without ever downloading its full content to your iPad.

Your storage options with the various iPad models range from 32 gigabytes (GB) to 1 terabyte (TB), which is equivalent to 1,000GB. You must choose the right amount of storage because you can't open the unit and add more as you typically can with a desktop computer. However, Apple has thoughtfully provided iCloud, a service you can use to back up content to the Internet. (You can read more about iCloud in Chapter 3.)

How much storage is enough for your iPad? Here's a guideline:

» If you like lots of media, such as movies or TV shows, you may need at least 256GB.

» For most people who manage a reasonable number of photos, download some music, and watch heavy-duty media, such as movies online, 128GB is probably sufficient.

» If you simply want to check email, browse the web, and write short notes to yourself, 32GB likely is plenty.

Know What Else You May Need: Internet and Computer

Although you can use your iPad on its own without any Internet or Wi-Fi access and without a computer to pair it with, it's easier if you have Internet access and a computer that you can (occasionally) use with your iPad.

Use basic Internet access for your iPad

You need to be able to connect to the Internet to take advantage of most iPad features. If you have an Apple ID, you can have an iCloud account, Apple's online storage service, to store and share content online, and you can use a computer to download photos, music, or applications from non-Apple online sources (such as stores, sharing sites, or your local library) and transfer them to your iPad through a process called *syncing*. You can also use a computer or iCloud to register your iPad the first time you start it, although you can have the folks at the Apple Store handle registration for you if you have an Apple Store nearby. If you don't have a store nearby, visit www.apple.com/shop/help for assistance.

You can set up your iPad without an Internet connection and without going to an Apple Store: The best way to find out more information is to contact http://support.apple.com through an Internet connection on another device or at a public library or Internet cafe.

Can you use your iPad without owning a computer and just use public Wi-Fi hotspots to go online (or a cellular connection, if you have such a model)? Yes. To go online using a Wi-Fi–only iPad and to use many of its built-in features at home, however, you need to have a home Wi-Fi network available.

Pair your iPad with a computer

For syncing with a computer, Apple's iPad User Guide recommends that you have

» A Mac or PC with a USB port and one of the following operating systems:

  • macOS X version 10.9 or later

  • Windows 7 or later

» iTunes 12.8 or newer on a Mac running macOS El Capitan (10.11.6) through macOS Mojave (10.14.6), the Finder on Mac's running macOS Catalina (10.15), and iTunes 12.9 or newer on a PC, available at www.itunes.com/download

» An Apple ID and iTunes Store account

» Internet access

» An iCloud account

Apple has set up its iTunes software and the iCloud service to give you two ways to manage content for your iPad — including movies, music, or photos you've downloaded — and specify how to sync your calendar and contact information.

There are a lot of tech terms to absorb here (iCloud, iTunes, syncing, and so on). Don't worry: Chapters 2 and 3 cover those settings in more detail.

Choose Wi-Fi Only or Wi-Fi + Cellular

You use Wi-Fi to connect to a wireless network at home or at locations such as an Internet cafe, a library, a grocery store, or a bus, train, plane, or airport that offers Wi-Fi. This type of network uses short-range radio to connect to the Internet; its range is reasonably limited, so if you leave home or walk out of the coffee shop, you can't use it anymore. (These limitations may change, however, as some towns are installing community-wide Wi-Fi networks.)

The cellular technologies allow an iPad to connect to the Internet via a widespread cellular network. You use it in much the same way that you make calls from just about anywhere with your cellphone. A Wi-Fi + Cellular iPad costs additional money when compared to the basic Wi-Fi–only model, but it also includes GPS (Global Positioning System) service, which pinpoints your location so that you can get more accurate driving directions.

Also, to use your cellular network in the United States, you must pay a monthly fee. The good news is that no carrier requires a long-term contract, which you probably had to have when you bought your cellphone and its service plan. You can pay for a connection during the month you visit your grandkids, for example, and get rid of it when you arrive home. Features, data allowance (which relates to accessing email or downloading items from the Internet, for example), and prices vary by carrier and could change at any time, so visit each carrier's website (see the following tip) to see what it offers. Note that if you intend to stream videos (watch them on your iPad from the Internet), you can eat through your data plan allowance quickly.

How do you choose? If you want to wander around the woods or town — or take long drives with your iPad continually connected to the Internet to get step-by-step navigation info from the Maps app — get Wi-Fi + Cellular and pay the additional costs. If you'll use your iPad mainly at home or via a Wi-Fi *hotspot* (a location where Wi-Fi access to the Internet is available, such as a local coffee shop or book store), don't bother with cellular. Frankly, you can find *lots* of hotspots at libraries, restaurants, hotels, airports, and other locations.

If you have a Wi-Fi–only iPad, you can use the hotspot feature on a smartphone, which allows the iPad to use your phone's cellular connection to go online if you have a data-use plan that supports hotspot use with your phone service carrier. Check out the features of your phone to turn on the hotspot feature.

Consider iPad Accessories

At present, Apple offers a few accessories that you may want to check out when you purchase your iPad, including

» **iPad Smart Case/Smart Cover:** Your iPad isn't cheap, and unlike a laptop computer, it has a constantly exposed screen that can be damaged if you drop or scratch it. Investing in the iPad Smart Case or Smart Cover is a good idea if you intend to take your iPad out of your house.

» **Printers:** Several HP, Brother, Canon, and Epson printers support the wireless AirPrint feature. At this writing, prices range from $129 to $399, and discounts are often available.

» **Smart Keyboard:** You can buy an attachable keyboard for your iPad Pro for $169, which will make working with productivity apps much easier. This keyboard connects to your iPad to provide power and transmit data between the devices. Also, the Magic Keyboard from Apple costs $99 and uses Bluetooth to connect to your iPad, a Mac, an iPhone, or any other device that works with a Bluetooth keyboard.

» **Apple Pencil:** For $99 (first generation) or $129 (second generation), you can buy the highly sophisticated stylus for use with the iPad. The Apple Pencil makes it easy to draw on your iPad screen or manage complex interactions more precisely.

» **Apple Digital AV Adapter:** To connect devices to output high-definition media, you can buy this adapter for about $40 and use it with an HDMI cable. More and more devices that use this technology are coming out, such as projectors and TVs. But remember that wireless connections such as Bluetooth and Wi-Fi are less expensive and can eliminate all those cables and cords. In some circumstances, a wired connection is faster and more effective than wireless.

Explore What's in the Box

After you fork over your hard-earned money for your iPad, you'll be holding one box. Besides your iPad and a small documentation package, here's a rundown of what you'll find when you take off the shrink wrap and open it up:

» **iPad:** Your iPad is covered in a thick plastic sleeve-film that you can take off and toss (unless you think there's a chance that you'll return the device, in which case you may want to keep all packaging for 14 days — Apple's standard return period).

» **Documentation:** Under the iPad itself is a small, white envelope about the size of a half-dozen index cards. Open it and you'll find some Apple stickers and some very brief instructions on how to use your iPad. Apple feels that using an iPad should be so intuitive that you don't really need instructions. But this book exists and folks are buying it (thanks!), so they may not be right about that.

» **A USB-C cable or Lightning-to-USB cable (which one you have depends on your iPad model):** Use this cord to connect the iPad to your computer or use it with the last item in the box: the USB power adapter.

» **USB power adapter:** The power adapter attaches to the cable so that you can plug it into the wall and charge the battery.

That's it. That's all you'll find in the box. It's kind of a study in Zen-like simplicity.

Take a First Look at the Gadget

The little card contained in the documentation that comes with your iPad gives you a picture of the iPad with callouts to the buttons you'll find on it. In this task, I give you a bit more information about those buttons and other physical features of the iPad. **Figure 1-2** shows you the layout for the two iPad Pro models, while **Figure 1-3** gives you the rundown for features pertaining to the iPad Air, iPad, and iPad mini (the only exception being that the iPad mini doesn't support the Smart Connector).

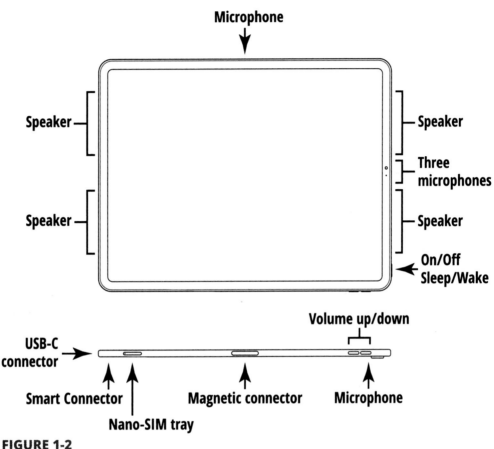

FIGURE 1-2

Here's the rundown on what the various hardware features are and what they do:

>> **Home/Touch ID button:** On the iPad, press this button to go back to the Home screen to find just about anything. The Home screen displays all your installed and preinstalled apps and gives you access to your iPad settings. No matter where you are or what you're doing, press the Home button, and you're back at home base. You can also double-press the Home button to pull up a scrolling list of apps so that you can quickly move from

one app to another. (Apple refers to this as multitasking.) If you press and hold the Home button, you open Siri, the iPhone voice assistant. Finally, on the newest iPads, the Home button contains a fingerprint reader used with the Touch ID feature.

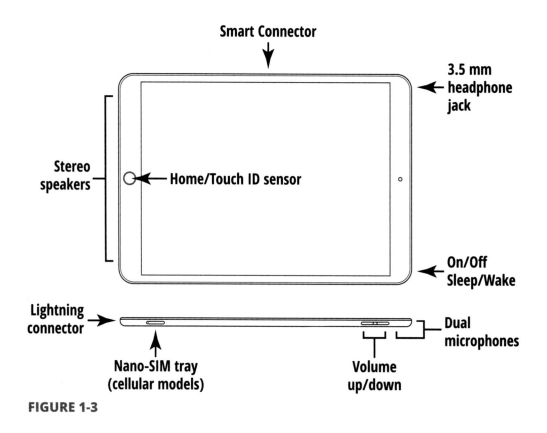

FIGURE 1-3

» **Sleep/Wake button:** You can use this button (whose functionality I cover in more detail in Chapter 2) to power up your iPad, put it in Sleep mode, wake it up, or power it down.

» **Lightning/USB-C Connector slot:** Plug in the Lightning or USB-C connector (depending on your iPad model) at the USB end to the power adapter to charge your battery or use it without the power adapter to sync your iPad with your computer (which you find out more about in Chapter 3).

» **Cameras:** iPads (except for the original iPad) offer front- and rear-facing cameras, which you can use to shoot photos or video. The rear one is on the top-right corner (if you're looking at the front of the iPad), and you need to be careful not to put your thumb over it when taking shots. (I have several very nice photos of my fingers already.)

» **Smart Connector:** iPad Air and iPad include this feature to support accessories such as the Smart Keyboard.

» **(Tiny, mighty) speakers:** One nice surprise when I first got my iPad was hearing what a great little stereo sound system it has and how much sound can come from these tiny speakers. The speakers are located along one side of the iPad Air 2 and iPad mini 4. With iPad Pro, you get four speakers, two on either side, which provide the best sound of all the models.

» **Volume:** Tap the volume switch, called a *rocker,* up for more volume and down for less. You can use this rocker as a camera shutter button when the camera is activated.

» **Headphone jack and microphone(s):** If you want to listen to your music in private, you can plug in a 3.5mm mini-jack head-phone (including an iPhone headset, if you have one, which gives you bidirectional sound). A tiny microphone makes it possible to speak into your iPad to deliver commands or enter content using the Siri personal-assistant feature. Using Siri, you can do things such as make phone calls using the Internet, use video-calling services, dictate your keyboard input, or work with other apps that accept audio input.

IN THIS CHAPTER

» See what's needed to use your iPad

» Turn on your iPad and use the multitouch screen

» Display and use the keyboard

» Switch between apps and adjust views

» Discover the Control Center

» Get to know the apps that are already installed

Chapter **2**

Exploring Your iPad

Good news! Getting anything done on the iPad is simple, when you know the ropes. In fact, using your fingers to do things is a very intuitive way to communicate with your computing device, which is just what iPad is.

In this chapter, you turn on your iPad and then take your first look at the Home screen. You also practice using the onscreen keyboard, see how to interact with the touchscreen in various ways, get pointers on working with cameras, get an overview of built-in applications (more commonly referred to as apps), and more.

See What You Need to Use iPad

You need to be able, at a minimum, to connect to the Internet to take advantage of most iPad features, which you can do using a Wi-Fi network (a network that you set up in your own home or access in a public place such as a library) or a cellular data connection from your cellular provider (if your iPad model supports cellular data).

You may want to have a computer so that you can connect your iPad to it to download photos, videos, music, or applications and transfer them to or from your iPad through a process called *syncing* (see Chapter 3 for more about syncing). An Apple service called iCloud syncs content from all your Apple iOS devices (such as the iPad or iPhone), so anything you buy on your iPhone that can be run on an iPad, for example, will automatically be pushed to your iPad. In addition, you can sync without connecting a cable to a computer using a wireless Wi-Fi connection to your computer.

Your iPad will probably arrive registered and activated, or if you buy it in a store, the person helping you can handle that procedure.

Turn On iPad for the First Time

When you're ready to get going with your new toy, be sure you're within range of a Wi-Fi network that you can connect with and then hold the iPad with one hand on either side, oriented like a pad of paper. Plug the Lightning-to-USB or USB-C cable (depending on the iPad model you have) that came with your device into your iPad and plug the other end into a USB port on your computer just in case you lose your battery charge during the setup process.

Now follow these steps to set up and register your iPad:

1. Press and hold the Sleep/Wake button on the top of your iPad until the Apple logo appears. In another moment, a screen appears with a cheery Hello on it.

2. Slide your finger to the right on the screen where it says Slide to Set Up.

3. Follow the series of prompts to make choices about your language and location, using iCloud (Apple's online sharing service), and so on.

4. After you deal with all the setup screens, a Welcome to iPad screen appears; tap Get Started to display the Home screen.

TIP

If you set up iCloud when registering or after registering (see Chapter 3), updates to your operating system will be downloaded to your iPad without plugging it into a computer running iTunes. Apple refers to this feature as *PC Free*, simply meaning that your device has been liberated from having to use a physical connection to a computer to get upgrades.

TIP

You can choose to have personal items transferred to your iPad from your computer when you sync the two devices using iTunes, including music, videos, downloaded apps, audiobooks, e-books, podcasts, and browser bookmarks. Contacts and Calendars are downloaded via iCloud, or (if you're moving to iPad from an Android phone) you can download an app from the Google Play Store called Move to iOS (developed by Apple) to copy your current Android settings to your iPad (see this support article from Apple for more info: https://support.apple.com/en-us/HT201196). You can also transfer to your computer any content you download directly to your iPad by using iTunes, the App Store, or non-Apple stores.

Meet the Multitouch Screen

When the iPad Home screen appears (see **Figure 2-1**), you see a pretty background and two sets of icons.

One set of icons appears in the Dock, along the bottom of the screen. The *Dock* contains the Messages, Safari, Music, Mail, and File app icons by default, though you can swap out one app for another. The Dock appears on every Home screen and can even be accessed from within apps. You can add new apps to your iPad to populate as many as 10 additional Home screens for a total of 11 Home screens.

Other icons appear above the Dock and are closer to the top of the screen. I cover all these icons in the "Take Inventory of Preinstalled Apps" task, later in this chapter. Different icons appear in this area on each Home screen. You can also nest apps in folders, which almost gives you the possibility of storing limitless apps on your iPad. You are, in fact, limited — but only by your iPad's memory.

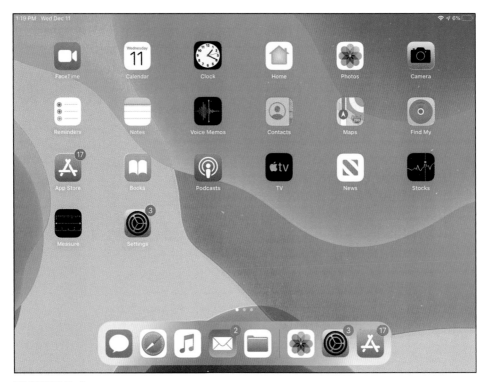

FIGURE 2-1

TIP

Treat the iPad screen carefully. It's made of glass and it will break if an unreasonable amount of force is applied, if dropped, or if the kids in your life throw it against the wall (yes, that's actually happened in our house).

The iPad uses *touchscreen technology:* When you swipe your finger across the screen or tap it, you're providing input to the device just as you do to a computer using a mouse or keyboard. You hear more about the touchscreen in the next task, but for now, go ahead and play with it for a few minutes — really, you can't hurt anything. Use the pads of your fingertips (not your fingernails) and try these tasks:

» **Tap the Settings icon.** The various settings (which you read more about throughout this book) appear, as shown in **Figure 2-2**.

1:56 PM   Wed Dec 11   14%

Settings   General

✈ Airplane Mode	⭘	Software Update >
📶 Wi-Fi	computer	
⭐ Bluetooth	On	AirDrop >
		Handoff >
🔲 Notifications		Multitasking & Dock >
🔊 Sounds		
🌙 Do Not Disturb		iPad Storage >
⏳ Screen Time		Background App Refresh >
⚙ General		Date & Time >
🎛 Control Center		Keyboard >
Ⓐ Display & Brightness		Fonts >
ⓘ Accessibility		Language & Region >
🌸 Wallpaper		Dictionary >
🔍 Siri & Search		
		VPN Not Connected >

FIGURE 2-2

REMEMBER

To return to the Home screen, press the Home button for iPad Air, iPad, and iPad mini. For iPad Pro models, swipe up from the very bottom of the screen.

>> **Swipe a finger from right to left on the Home screen.** This action moves you to the next Home screen.

The little white dots at the bottom of the screen, above the Dock icons, indicate which Home screen is displayed.

TIP

>> **To experience the screen rotation feature, hold the iPad firmly while turning it sideways.** The screen flips to the horizontal orientation, if the app you're in supports it.

To flip the screen back, just turn the device so that it's oriented like a pad of paper again. (Some apps force iPad to stay in one orientation or the other.)

>> **Drag your finger down from the very top edge of the screen to reveal the Notification Center items, such as reminders and calendar entries.** (Notification Center is covered in Chapter 18.) Drag up from the very bottom edge of the Home screen to hide Notification Center and then drag up to display Control Center (containing commonly used controls and tools and discussed later in this chapter).

TIP

You can customize the Home screen by changing its *wallpaper* (background picture) and brightness. You can read about making these changes in Chapter 5.

Although the iPad's screen has been treated to repel oils, you're about to deposit a ton of fingerprints on your iPad — one downside of a touchscreen device. A soft cloth, like the one you might use to clean your eyeglasses, is usually all you'll need to clean things up, though. Having said that, there are third-party cleaners and screen protectors available should you opt to use them; just be sure they're compatible with your particular iPad model, as materials used in each model may vary.

Say Hello to Tap and Swipe

You can use several methods for getting around and getting things done in iPad using its multitouch screen, including

>> **Tap once.** To open an app, choose a field (such as a search box), choose an item in a list, use an arrow to move back or forward one screen, or follow an online link, simply tap the item once with your finger.

>> **Tap twice.** Use this method to enlarge or reduce the display of a web page (see Chapter 10 for more about using the Safari web browser) or to zoom in or out in the Maps app.

» **Pinch.** As an alternative to the tap-twice method, you can pinch your fingers together or move them apart on the screen (see **Figure 2-3**) when you're looking at photos, maps, web pages, or email messages to quickly reduce or enlarge them, respectively. This method allows you to grow or contract the screen to a variety of sizes rather than a fixed size, as with the double-tap method.

FIGURE 2-3

 TIP

You can use the three-finger tap to zoom your screen to be even larger or use multitasking gestures to swipe with four or five fingers. This method is handy if you have vision challenges. Go to Chapter 5 to discover how to turn on this feature using Accessibility settings.

» **Drag to scroll (known as _swiping_).** When you touch your finger to the screen and drag to the right or left, the screen moves (see **Figure 2-4**). Swiping to the left on the Home screen, for example, moves you to the next Home screen. Swiping down while reading an online newspaper moves you down the page; swiping up moves you back up the page.

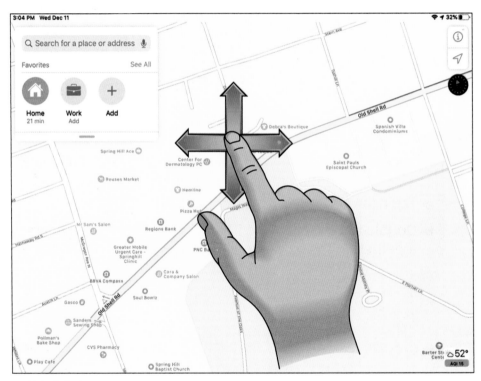

FIGURE 2-4

» **Flick.** To scroll more quickly on a page, quickly flick your finger on the screen in the direction you want to move.

» **Tap the Status bar.** To move quickly to the top of a list, web page, or email message, tap the Status bar at the top of the iPad screen. (For some sites, you have to tap the Status bar twice to get this to work.)

» **Press and hold.** If you're using Notes or Mail or any other application that lets you select text, or if you're on a web page, pressing and holding text selects a word and displays editing tools that you can use to select, cut, or copy and paste the text.

When you rock your iPad backward or forward, the background moves as well (a feature called *parallax).* You can disable this feature if it makes you nauseous. From the Home screen, tap Settings⇨Accessibility⇨Motion and then tap and turn on the Reduce Motion setting by tapping the toggle switch (it turns green when the option is enabled).

TIP

You can try these methods now:

» Tap the Safari button in the Dock at the bottom of any iPad Home screen to display the web browser.

» Tap a link to move to another page.

» Double-tap the page to enlarge it; then pinch your fingers together on the screen to reduce its size.

» Drag one finger up and down the page to scroll.

» Flick your finger quickly up or down on the page to scroll more quickly.

» Press and hold your finger on a word that isn't a link (links take you to another location on the web).

The word is selected, and the Copy/Look Up/Share tool is displayed, as shown in **Figure 2-5**. (You can use this tool to either get a definition of a word or copy it.)

» Press and hold your finger on a link or an image.

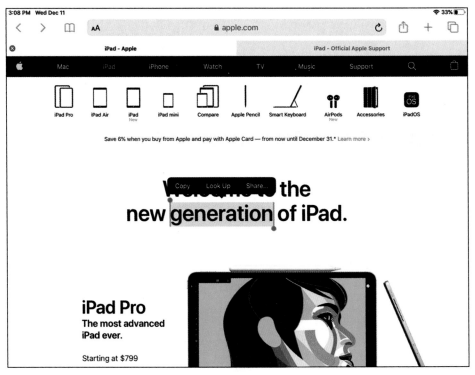

FIGURE 2-5

A menu appears (shown in **Figure 2-6**) with commands that you select to open the link or picture, open it in a new tab or window, download a linked file, add it to your Reading List, copy it, or share it. If you press and hold an unlinked image, the menu also offers the Add to Photos command.

Tap outside of the menu to close it without making a selection.

» Position your fingers slightly apart on the screen and then pinch your fingers together to reduce the page; with your fingers already pinched together on the screen, move them apart to enlarge the page.

» Press the Home button to go back to the Home screen.

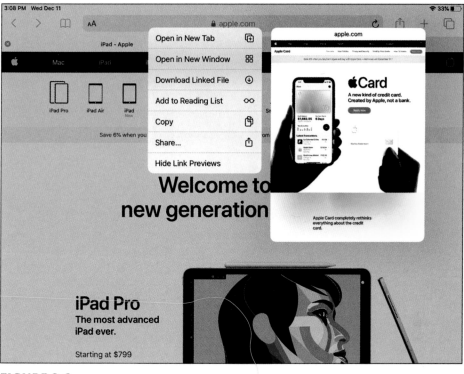

FIGURE 2-6

The Dock

The Dock at the bottom of your iPad's screen houses apps you use most often. You can remove or add apps from it simply by dragging-and-dropping their icons in or out of the Dock. You can also reorder icons within the dock using the same drag-and-drop method. To drag-and-drop, tap and hold an app icon until it pulsates (essentially tagging it to your finger) and then drag to a new location and drop it by removing your finger from the screen.

You'll note that the Dock is divided between left and right sides by a thin gray line. The icons on the right side of the Dock are for those you use often, but don't keep in the Dock at all times. This makes it easier to access these apps while you're using them more heavily. You can enable or disable this behavior by opening the Settings app and going to General⇨Multitasking & Dock and toggling the Show Suggested and Recent Apps switch On (green) or Off.

Display and Use the Onscreen Keyboard

The built-in iPad keyboard appears whenever you're in a text-entry location, such as a search field or a text message. Follow these steps to display and use the keyboard:

1. Tap the Notes icon on the Home screen to open the Notes app.

2. Open a note to work in:

- Tap the note page.
- If you've already created some notes, tap one to display the page and then tap anywhere on the note.

3. Type a few words using the keyboard, as shown in **Figure 2-7.**

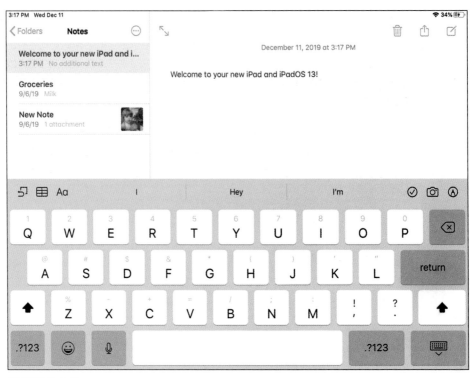

FIGURE 2-7

To make the keyboard display as wide as possible, rotate your iPad to landscape (horizontal) orientation. (If you've locked the screen orientation in Control Center, you have to unlock the screen to do this.)

QuickType provides suggestions above the keyboard as you type. You can turn this feature off or on by tapping and holding either the Emoji (the smiley face) or International icon (looks like a globe) on the keyboard to display a menu. Tap Keyboard Settings and toggle the Predictive switch to turn the feature Off or On (green). To quickly return to Notes from Keyboard Settings, tap the word Notes in the upper-left of your screen.

After you open the keyboard, you're ready to use it for editing text.

You'll find a number of shortcuts for editing text:

» If you make a mistake while using the keyboard — and you will, especially when you first use it — tap the Delete key (it's near the *p* key, with the little *x* on it) to delete text to the left of the insertion point.

To type a period and space, just double-tap the spacebar.

» To create a new paragraph, tap the Return button (just like the keyboard on a Mac, or the Enter key on a PC's keyboard).

» To type numbers and symbols, tap the number key (labeled .?123) on the left side of the spacebar (refer to Figure 2-7). The characters on the keyboard change (see **Figure 2-8**).

If you type a number and then tap the spacebar, the keyboard returns to the letter keyboard automatically. To return to the letter keyboard at any time, simply tap the key labeled ABC on the left side of the spacebar.

You can easily access an alternative character on a key by tapping-and-dragging down on the key. For example, if you need an exclamation mark (!), simply tap-and-drag the comma (,) key downward, and an exclamation mark will be inserted (since it's the alternate character on the comma key).

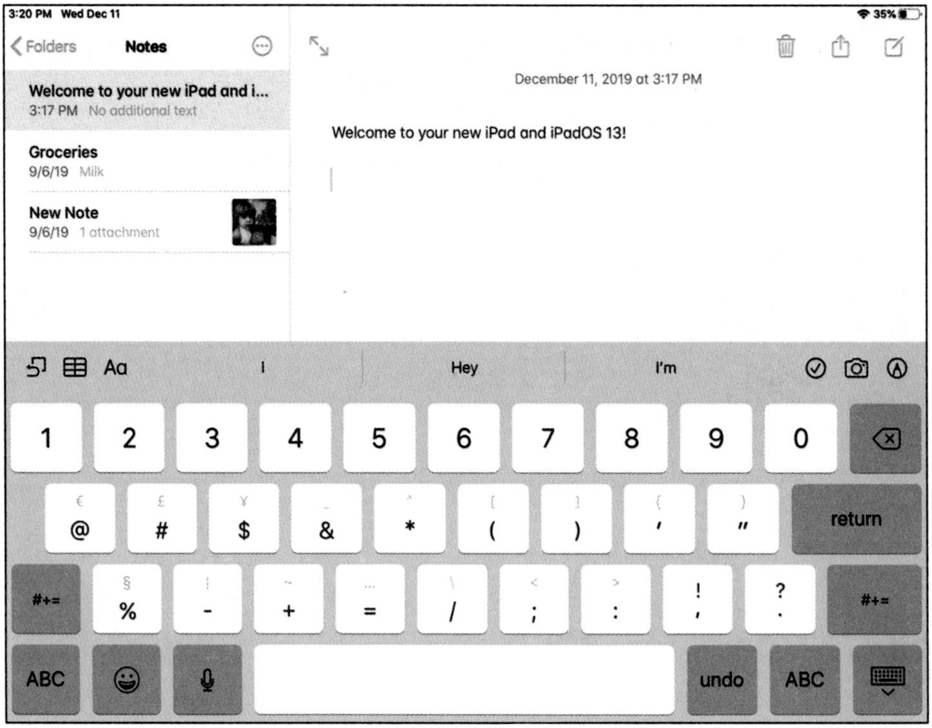

FIGURE 2-8

» Use the Shift button (it's a wide, upward-facing arrow in the lower-left corner of the keyboard) to type capital letters:

- Tapping the Shift button once causes only the next letter you type to be capitalized.

- Double-tap (rapidly tap twice) the Shift key to turn on the Caps Lock feature so that all letters you type are capitalized until you turn the feature off.

- Tap the Shift key once to turn off Caps Lock.

  You can control whether Caps Lock is enabled by opening the Settings app, tapping General and then Keyboard, and toggling the switch called Enable Caps Lock.

» To type a variation on a symbol or letter (for example, to see alternative presentations for the letter *A* when you press the A button on the keyboard), hold down the key; a set of alternative letters/symbols appears (see **Figure 2-9**).

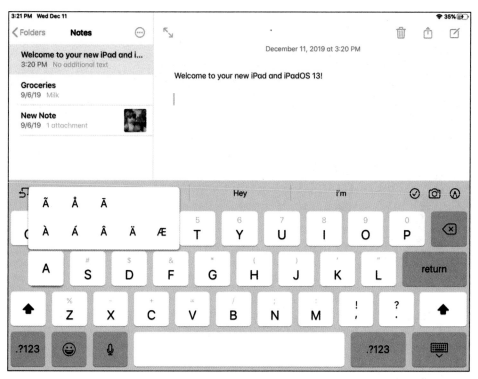

FIGURE 2-9

TECHNICAL
STUFF

This trick works with only certain letters and symbols.

» Tap the smiley-faced Emoji button to display the Emoji keyboard containing symbols that you can insert, including numerical, symbol, and arrow keys, as well as a row of symbol sets along the bottom of the screen.

Tapping one of these displays a portfolio of icons from smiley faces and hearts to pumpkins, cats, and more. Tap the ABC button to close the Emoji keyboard and return to the letter keyboard.

TIP A small globe symbol will appear instead of the Emoji button on the keyboard if you've enabled multilanguage functionality in iPad settings.

» Press the Home button or swipe up from the bottom of the screen (iPad Pro models only) to return to the Home screen.

TIP You can buy a Smart Keyboard Folio to go with iPad Pro models or a Smart Keyboard for iPad Air and iPad. This physical keyboard from Apple attaches to your iPad and allows both power and data exchange. The connection for your keyboard is magnetic, so it's a snap to put it and the iPad together.

QuickPath

QuickPath allows you to quickly zip your finger from key to key to quickly spell words without ever lifting it from the screen. For example, spell the word "path" by touching "p" on the keyboard and then quickly moving to "a" then "t" then "h." Tada! You've spelled "path" without leaving the screen.

Use the Small Keyboard

The *small keyboard* feature allows you to shrink the keyboard so that more of the rest of the screen is visible and to assist with one-handed typing. Open an application such as Notes in which you can use the onscreen keyboard and then follow these steps:

1. Tap an entry field or page to display the onscreen keyboard.

2. Spread two fingers apart, place them on the keyboard, and then quickly pinch your fingers together on the keyboard to shrink it, as shown in **Figure 2-10**. (This feature can be finicky, so you may have to try it a few times.)

FIGURE 2-10

3. Now hold the iPad with a hand on either side and practice using your thumbs to enter text. You may also move the small keyboard around the screen by tapping-and-dragging the dark gray handle at the bottom of the keyboard (under the spacebar).

4. To restore the original keyboard, pinch two fingers together, place them on the keyboard, and then quickly spread them apart.

Be sure to double-check that you didn't inadvertently type unnecessary characters in your text when pinching.

TIP

Flick to Search

The Spotlight Search feature in iPad helps you find suggestions from the web, Music, iTunes, and the App Store as well as suggestions for nearby locations and more. Here's how to use Spotlight Search:

1. Tap and swipe down on any area of any Home screen (except the far edges) to reveal the Search feature (see **Figure 2-11**).

FIGURE 2-11

2. Begin entering a search term.

    In the example in **Figure 2-12**, after I typed the word "coffee," the Search feature displayed maps and other search results. As you continue to type a search term or phrase, the results narrow to match it.

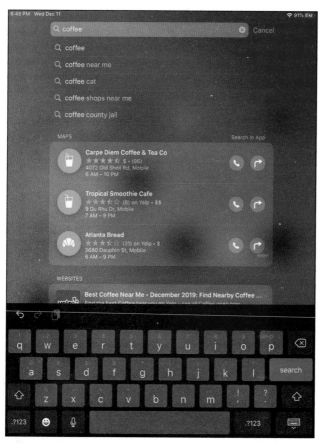

FIGURE 2-12

3. Scroll down to view more results.

4. Tap an item in the search results to open it in its appropriate app or player.

Easily Switch Between Apps

iPadOS 13 lets you easily switch from one app to another without clos-ing the first one and returning to the Home screen. With iPadOS 13, you accomplish this task by previewing all open apps and jumping from one to another; you quit an app by simply swiping upward. To find out the ropes of basic app switching, follow these steps:

1. Open the App Switcher by doing one of the following:

   - Press the Home button twice.
   - Swipe up from the bottom edge of on any screen with one finger, pause in the middle of the screen, and then lift your finger.

2. The App Switcher appears (see **Figure 2-13**).

FIGURE 2-13

3. To locate another app that you want to switch to, flick to scroll to the left or right.

4. Tap an app to open it.

TIP

Press the Home button once or swipe up from the bottom of the screen (iPad Pro models) to return to the app that you were working in.

Use Slide Over and Split View

iPadOS 13 allows you to be more productive than ever before with your iPad with features like Slide Over and Split View.

Slide Over lets you view one app in a floating panel, while viewing and working with other apps behind it. Split View allows two apps to share the screen between them, splitting the screen so that one app is on the left and the other is on the right. You can even adjust the amount of space each app is allocated by dragging a divider between them.

Starting with Slide Over

To use the Slide Over feature, follow these steps:

1. From within an app you're already using, swipe up from the bottom edge of the screen to open the Dock.

2. Touch the icon of the app in the Dock you'd like to slide over the app you're already working in, hold it for a brief moment, and then drag it above the Dock.

3. The second app will open "floating" above the first app; it's now in Slide Over mode, as illustrated with Notes and Safari in **Figure 2-14**.

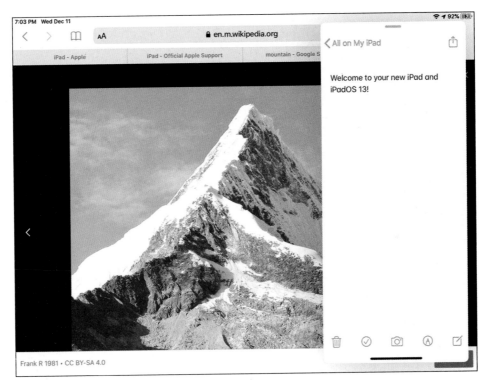

FIGURE 2-14

4. Simply tap the Home button or swipe up from the bottom of the
screen (iPad Pro models) to close Slide Over. You can also tap-and-
hold the top of the floating app and then slide it off the screen to the
right or left.

Moving to Split View

If you want to use both apps at the same time, you can move on to
Split View. With Slide Over open, tap and drag the small gray handle
at the top of the floating window toward the edge of the screen to
open Split View, as shown in **Figure 2-15**. Simply tap the Home button or swipe up on one of the apps to exit Split View.

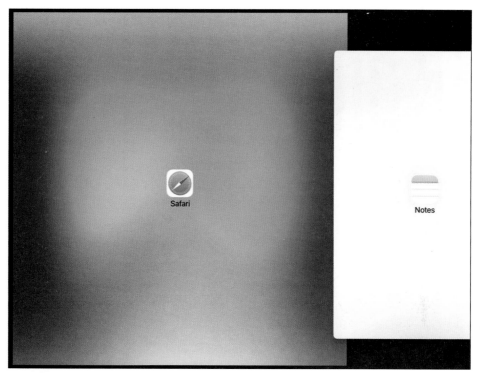

FIGURE 2-15

TIP

While you're in Split View, you can drag the heavy black divider (see **Figure 2-16**) left or right to change the sizes of the panes, or you can have equal space for both apps. Both apps are fully functional, although in some special cases, the app may not show certain noncritical elements to adjust to the narrower width of the split view when compared to the full screen.

TIP

You can drag-and-drop items between apps in Slide Over and Split View. For example, with Photos and Notes open, drag-and-drop a picture from Photos into a note in the Notes window. Another example might be dragging a link from a text document into the Safari web browser to open it.

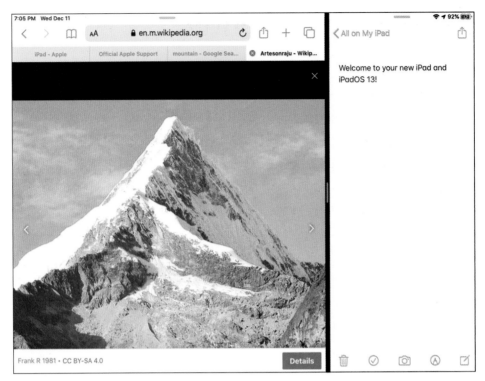

FIGURE 2-16

Examine the iPad Cameras

iPads have front- and back-facing cameras. You can use the cameras to take still photos (covered in more detail in Chapter 15) or shoot videos (covered in Chapter 16).

For now, take a quick look at your camera by tapping the Camera app icon on the Home screen. You can use the controls on the screen to take pictures and video, switch between front and rear cameras, turn the flash on and off, and so much more. See Chapters 15 and 16 for more detail about using the iPad cameras.

Discover Control Center

Control Center is a one-stop screen for common features and settings, such as connecting to a network, increasing screen brightness or volume, and more. Here's how to use it:

1. To display Control Center, swipe down from the upper-right corner of the screen. The Control Center screen appears to the right.

2. In the Control Center (highlighted in **Figure 2-17**), tap a button or tap and drag a slider to access or adjust a setting.

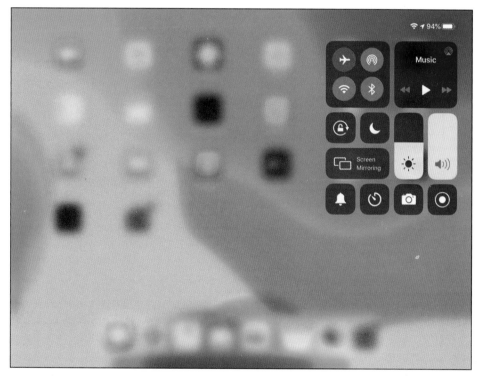

FIGURE 2-17

3. After you make a change, tap anywhere on the screen outside of the Control Center to exit it.

Some options in Control Center are hidden from initial view but may be accessed by tapping and holding a button in Control Center. For example, tap and hold on the Brightness slider to reveal the Dark Mode and Night Shift buttons (as shown in **Figure 2-18**).

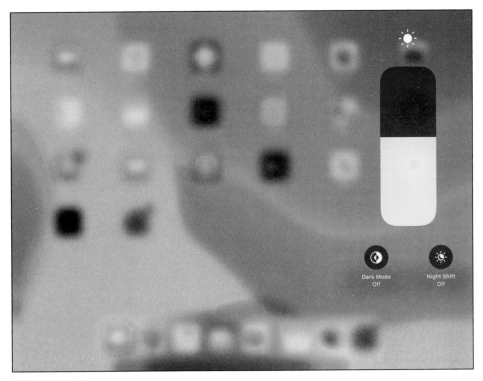

FIGURE 2-18

Try tapping-and-holding other buttons in Control Center to see what other options are waiting for you to discover. If you tap and hold an item and its icon just bounces, no further options are available for the item.

iPadOS 13 allows you to customize Control Center (a feature I love):

1. Tap Settings.

2. Tap Control Center and then tap Customize Controls to open the Customize screen (shown in **Figure 2-19**).

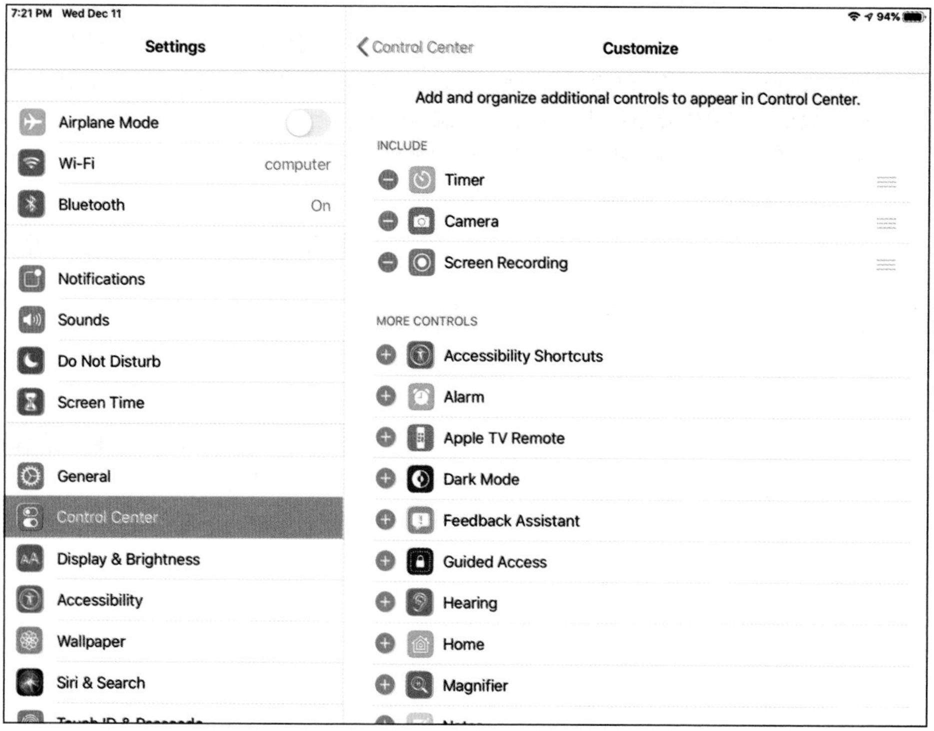

FIGURE 2-19

3. Remove items from Control Center by tapping the – to the left, and then tap the Remove button that appears to the right.

4. To add an item to Control Center, tap the + to the left. You'll see the item in Control Center the next time you visit it. Don't forget to use tap-and-hold to find any extras the item may afford.

Understand Touch ID

iPad Air, iPad, and iPad mini sport a feature called Touch ID, which allows you to unlock your iPad by touching the Home button. That button contains a sophisticated fingerprint sensor. Because your fingerprint is unique, this feature is one of the most foolproof ways to protect your data.

If you're going to use Touch ID (it's optional), you must educate the iPad about your fingerprint on your finger of choice by tapping Settings ⇨ Touch ID & Passcode, entering your passcode, and choosing what to use Touch ID for — for example, unlocking the iPad, using Apple Pay (Apple's electronic wallet service), or making purchases from the App Store and the iTunes Store. You can change these preferences any time you like.

Then, if you did not set up a fingerprint previously or want to add another one, tap Add a Fingerprint from inside Touch ID & Passcode. Follow the instructions and press your finger lightly on the Home button several times to allow Touch ID to sense and record your fingerprint. (You will be guided through this process and told when to touch and when to lift your finger.) With the iPad Unlock option turned on, press the power button to go to the lock screen and touch the Home button. The iPad unlocks. If you chose the option for using Touch ID with Apple Pay or purchasing an item in the Apple stores, you'll simply touch your finger to the Home button rather than entering your Apple ID and password to complete a purchase.

TIP

There's a difference between touching and tapping your iPad. It's the ordinary everyday difference: touching is a light touch without applying pressure. Tapping means you apply pressure — the same amount you would use in tapping people on their shoulder to get their attention.

Take a Look at Face ID

iPad Pro models don't have a Home button, so Touch ID isn't available. However, they do use a different — and very cool — method of authenticating a user: Face ID. Face ID uses your iPad Pro's built-in cameras and scanners to scan your face and save a profile of it. It then remembers the information and compares it to whoever is facing the iPad Pro. If the face doesn't match the profile, the person can't access the iPad Pro (unless they know and use your passcode, which you have to set up to use Face ID). Face ID is so advanced that it can even work in total darkness.

To set up Face ID:

1. Go to Settings and tap Face ID & Passcode.

2. Tap Set Up Face ID.

3. Hold the iPad Pro in front of your face (in portrait mode, not landscape).

4. Tap the Get Started button and then follow the prompts to slowly move your head in a complete circle. If you have difficulty moving your head, tap the Accessibility Options button at the bottom of the screen and follow the prompts from there.

5. Tap Continue and follow the prompts to perform the circle step again.

6. Tap Done when finished.

The next time you want to use your iPad Pro, simply hold it up in front of you, swipe up from the bottom of the screen when the lock icon unlocks, and you'll jump right into the Home screen or whatever app you were last using.

For more information on using Face ID and its capabilities, visit https://support.apple.com/en-us/HT208109.

Lock Screen Rotation

Sometimes you don't want your screen orientation to flip when you move your iPad around. Use these steps to lock the iPad into portrait orientation (narrow and tall, not low and wide):

1. Swipe down from the upper-right corner of any screen to open Control Center.

2. Tap the Lock Screen button. (It's the button in the top-right corner of Control Center.)

3. Tap anywhere on the screen outside of the Control Center to exit it.

Perform the steps again to unlock the screen, if desired.

Explore the Status Bar

Across the top of the iPad screen is the Status bar. Tiny icons in this area can provide useful information, such as the time, battery level, and wireless-connection status. **Table 2-1** lists some of the most common items you find on the Status bar.

TABLE 2-1 **Common Status Bar Icons**

Icon	Name	What It Indicates
	Wi-Fi	You're connected to a Wi-Fi network.
	Activity	A task is in progress — a web page is loading, for example.
2:30 PM	Time	You guessed it: You see the time.
	Screen Rotation Lock	The screen is locked in portrait orientation and doesn't rotate when you turn the iPad.
	Do Not Disturb	Your iPad's communications are disabled during scheduled times.
	Battery Life	This shows the charge percentage remaining in the battery. The indicator changes to a lightning bolt when the battery is charging.

TIP

If you have GPS, cellular (if your iPad supports it), Bluetooth service, or a connection to a virtual private network (VPN), a corresponding symbol appears on the Status bar whenever a feature is active. (If you don't already know what a virtual private network is, there's no need to worry about it.)

Take Inventory of Preinstalled Apps

The iPad comes with certain functionality and applications — or apps, for short — built in. When you look at the Home screen, you see icons for each app. This task gives you an overview of what each app does. (You can find out more about every one of them as you read different chapters in this book.)

By default, the following icons appear in the Dock at the bottom of every Home screen (refer to Figure 2-1), from left to right:

» **Messages:** For those who love to instant message, the Messages app comes to the rescue. The Messages app has been in iPad for quite some time. Now you can engage in live text- and image-based conversations with others on their phones or other devices that use email. You can also send video or audio messages.

» **Safari:** You use the Safari web browser to navigate on the Internet, create and save bookmarks of favorite sites, and add web clips to your Home screen so that you can quickly visit favorite sites from there. You may have used this web browser (or another, such as Google Chrome) on your desktop computer.

» **Mail:** Use this application to access email accounts that you have set up in iPad. Your email is then displayed without you having to browse to the site or sign in. You can use tools to move among a few preset mail folders, read and reply to email, and download attached photos to your iPad. Read more about email accounts in Chapter 11.

» **Music:** Music is the name of your media player. Though its main function is to play music, you can use it to play other audio files, like audiobooks, as well.

» **Files:** This app allows you to browse files that are stored not only on your iPad, but also files you may have stored on other services, such as iCloud Drive, Google Drive, Dropbox, and the like.

Apps with icons above the Dock on the Home screen include the following:

» **Calendar:** Use this handy onscreen daybook to set up appointments and send alerts to remind you about them.

» **Photos:** The Photos app in iPad helps you organize pictures in folders, send photos in email, use a photo as your iPad wallpaper, and assign pictures to contact records. You can also run slideshows of your photos, open albums, pinch or unpinch to shrink or expand photos, and scroll photos with a simple swipe.

» **FaceTime:** Use FaceTime to place phone calls using video of the sender and receiver to have a more personal conversation.

» **Camera:** The Camera app is Control Center for the still and video cameras built into the iPad.

» **Clock:** This app allows you to display clocks from around the world, set alarms, and use timer and stopwatch features.

» **Maps:** With this iPad mapping app, you can view classic maps or aerial views of addresses and find directions from one place to another whether traveling by car, foot, or public transportation (which requires installing a third-party app). You can even get your directions read aloud by a spoken narration feature.

» **TV:** This media player is similar to Music but specializes in playing videos and offers a few features specific to this type of media, such as chapter breakdowns and information about a movie's plot and cast.

» **Notes:** Enter text, format text, or cut and paste text and objects (such as images) from a website into this simple notepad app.

» **Contacts:** In this address-book feature, you can enter contact information (including photos, if you like, from your Photos or Cameras app) and share contact information by email. You can also use the search feature to find your contacts easily.

» **Reminders:** This useful app centralizes all your calendar entries, alerts to keep you on schedule, and allows you to create to-do lists.

» **News:** News is a customizable aggregator for stories from your favorite news sources.

» **iTunes Store:** Tapping this icon takes you to the iTunes store, where you can shop 'til you drop (or until your iPad battery runs out of juice) for music, movies, TV shows, and audiobooks and then download them directly to your iPad. (See Chapter 12 for more about how the iTunes Store works.)

» **App Store**: Here you can buy and download applications that do everything from enabling you to play games to building business presentations. Many of these apps and games are free!

» **Apple Books**: The Apple Books app (formerly known as iBooks) is bundled with the iPad out of the box. Because the iPad has been touted as being a good small screen e-reader — a device that enables you to read books on an electronic device, similar to the Amazon Kindle Fire HD — you should definitely check this one out. (To work with the Apple Books e-reader application itself, go to Chapter 13.)

» **Home**: Home helps you control most (if not all) of your home automation devices in one convenient app.

» **Podcasts:** Before iOS 8, you had to download the free Podcast app, but now it's built into your iPad. Use this app to find and listen to recorded informational programs.

» **Find My:** The Find My app combines the Find iPhone and Find Friends apps to help you locate Apple devices that you own (see Chapter 21 for more info) and track down friends who also own an Apple device.

» **Shortcuts**: This new app helps you string together multiple iPad actions into single Siri commands.

» **Settings**: Settings is the central location on the iPad where you can specify settings for various functions and do administrative tasks, such as set up email accounts or create a password.

Lock iPad, Turn It Off, or Unlock It

Sleep is a state in which the screen goes black, though you can quickly wake up the iPad. You can also turn off the power to give your new toy a rest.

Here are the procedures you use to put the iPad to sleep or turn it off:

TIP

» **Sleep:** Press the Sleep/Wake button, and the iPad goes to sleep. The screen goes black and is locked.

The iPad automatically enters Sleep mode after a brief period of inactivity. You can change the time interval at which it sleeps by adjusting the Auto-Lock feature in Settings ➪ Display & Brightness.

» **Power Off:** From any app or Home screen, press and hold the Sleep/Wake button until the Slide to Power Off bar appears at the top of the screen, and then swipe the bar. You've just turned off your iPad.

» **Force Off:** If the iPad becomes unresponsive, hold the Power and Home buttons simultaneously until the iPad shuts itself off. For iPad Pro models, press and hold both the top button and either Volume button to achieve the same result.

To wake the iPad up from Sleep mode, simply press the Home button once or tap the screen (iPad Pro models).

If you have the Passcode feature enabled, you'll need to enter your Passcode before proceeding to unlock your screen after pressing the Home button. However, if you have Touch ID enabled, you need to press the Home button only once and rest your finger on it for it to scan your fingerprints; the iPad will automatically unlock. If you have Face ID, your iPad will scan your face and unlock when you swipe up from the bottom of the screen.

TIP

Want a way to shut down your iPad without having to press buttons? Go to Settings ➪ General and scroll all the way to the bottom of the screen. Tap the Shut Down button, slide the Power Off slider, and your iPad will turn off.

Chapter **3**

Beyond the Basics

I n this chapter, I look at updating your iPad OS version (the operating system that your iPad uses) and making sure that your iPad's battery is charged.

Next, if you want to find free or paid content for your iPad from Apple, from movies to music to e-books to audiobooks, you'll need to have an iTunes account.

You can also use the wireless sync feature to exchange content between your computer and iPad over a wireless network.

Another feature you might take advantage of is the iCloud service from Apple to store and push all kinds of content and data to all your Apple devices — wirelessly. You can pick up where you left off from one device to another through iCloud Drive, an online storage service that enables sharing content among devices so that edits that you make to documents in iCloud are reflected on all of your iPadOS and iOS devices, and Macs running OS X Yosemite or later.

TECHNICAL STUFF

The operating system for Apple's Mac computers used to be called OS X. These days, it's referred to as macOS. The Mac operating system is mentioned a few times throughout this book, and you should know that OS X and macOS are different names for different versions of the same thing.

Update the Operating System to iPad OS 13

This book is based on the latest version of the iPad operating system at the time: iPad OS 13. To be sure that you have the latest and greatest features, update your iPad to the latest iPad OS now (and do so periodically to receive minor upgrades to iPad OS 13 or future versions of iPad OS). If you've set up an iCloud account on your iPad, you'll receive an alert and can choose to install the update or not, or you can update manually:

1. Tap Settings. (Be sure you have Wi-Fi enabled and that you're connected to a Wi-Fi network to perform these steps.)

2. Tap General.

3. Tap Software Update.

   Your iPad checks to find the latest iPad OS version and walks you through the updating procedure if an update is available.

TIP

You can also allow your iPad to perform automatic updates overnight. Go to Settings ➪ General ➪ Software Update ➪ Automatic Updates and toggle the switch to On (green). Your iPad must be connected to Wi-Fi and its charger to automatically update.

Charge the Battery

My iPad showed up in the box fully charged, and I hope yours did, too. Because all batteries run down eventually, one of your first priorities is to know how to recharge your iPad battery.

Gather your iPad and its Lightning-to-USB cable (earlier models have the Dock cable) and the Apple USB power adapter.

Here's how to charge your iPad:

1. Gently plug the Lightning connector end (the smaller of the two connectors) of the Lightning-to-USB cable into the iPad.

2. Plug the USB end of the Lightning-to-USB cable into the Apple USB power adapter.

3. Plug the adapter into an electric outlet.

Sign into an iTunes Account for Music, Movies, and More

The terms iTunes Account and Apple ID are interchangeable: Your Apple ID is your iTunes Account, but you'll need to be signed into iTunes with your Apple ID to download items from the iTunes Store.

TIP

If you've never set up an Apple ID or iTunes Account, please visit https://support.apple.com/en-us/HT204316 on your computer, iPhone, or iPad for help in doing so.

To be able to buy or download free items from the iTunes Store or the App Store on your iPad, you must open an iTunes account. Here's how to sign in to an account:

1. Tap Settings on your iPad.

2. Scroll down and tap iTunes & App Store. The screen shown in **Figure 3-1** appears.

Tap here

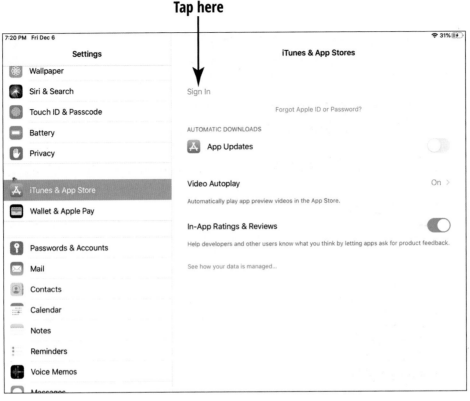

FIGURE 3-1

3. Tap Sign In (see **Figure 3-2**), enter your Apple ID and password, and then tap the Sign In button.

4. Tap Password Settings in the iTunes & App Store screen to bring up the screen shown in **Figure 3-3.**

5. Select whether you'd like your password to be requested every time a download is attempted (recommended) or to allow downloads for up to 15 minutes after the password has been entered without having to reenter it. Also, toggle the switch to On or Off (depending on whether you require your password to be entered when downloading free items). I recommend setting it to On, as even if an app is free, there may be some items that you just don't want loaded onto your iPad without your permission.

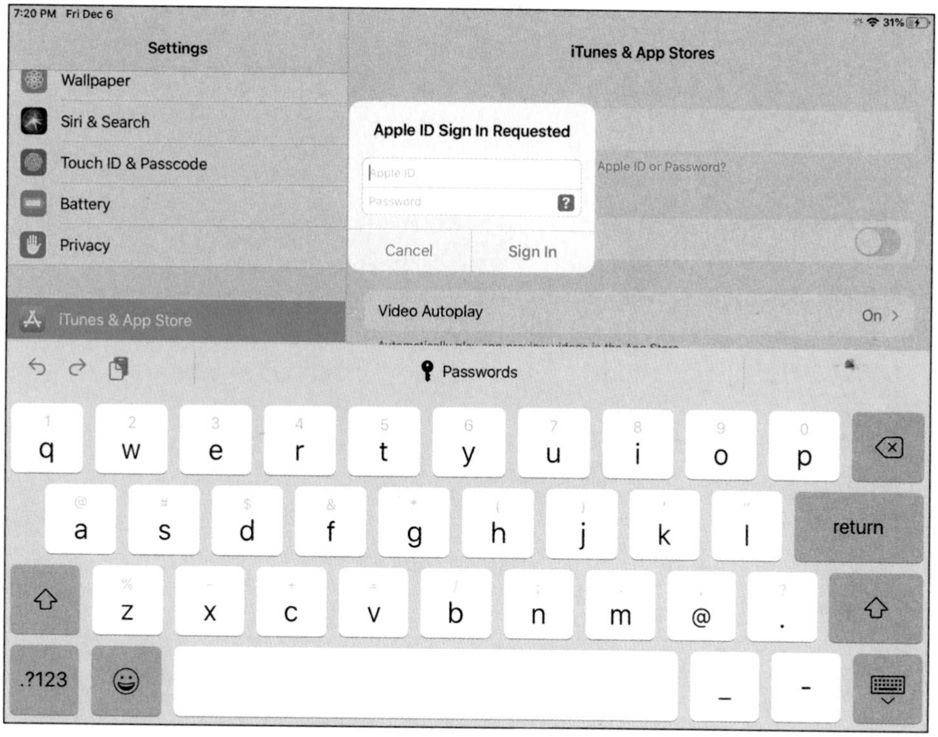

FIGURE 3-2

TIP

If you prefer not to leave your credit card info with Apple, one option is to buy an iTunes gift card and provide that as your payment information. You can replenish the card periodically through the Apple Store.

SIGN IN WITH APPLE

Sign in with Apple is new privacy feature in iPadOS 13 that allows you to use your Apple ID to sign in to many social media accounts or websites. This service provides a simple and secure way to sign in to accounts without having to remember a unique password for each one. Think of it as Apple's more secure replacement for Sign in with Google or Sign in with Facebook, both of which you've probably seen online. The Sign in with Apple button will show up in apps and websites when an account log in is required.

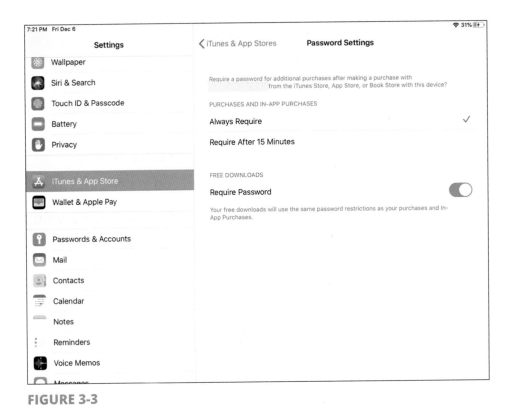

FIGURE 3-3

Sync Wirelessly

You can connect your iPad to a computer and use the tools there to sync content on your computer to your iPad. Also, with Wi-Fi turned on in Settings, use the iTunes Wi-Fi Sync setting to allow cordless syncing if you're within range of a Wi-Fi network that has a computer connected to it with iTunes installed and open.

There are a few steps you have to take with your iPad connected to your computer before you can perform a wireless sync with iTunes:

1. If you're charging with an electrical outlet, remove the power adapter.

2. Use the Lightning-to-USB cable to connect your iPad to your computer.

3. Open iTunes and then click the icon of an iPad that appears in the tools in the left corner of the screen.

4. Click the check box labeled Sync with this iPad over Wi-Fi.

You may need to scroll down a bit to see the Sync with this iPad over Wi-Fi option.

5. Click Apply in the lower-right corner of the iTunes window.

6. Disconnect your iPad from your computer.

You can click any item on the left side of the iTunes window to handle settings for syncing such items as Movies, Music, and Apps. In the Apps category, you can also choose to remove certain apps from your Home screens. You can also tap the list of items in the On My Device section on the left side to view and even play contents directly from your iPad.

After you complete the preceding steps, you'll be able to wirelessly sync your iPad with your computer. Follow these steps:

1. Back up your iPad. See Chapter 22 to find out how.

2. On the iPad, tap Settings ➪ General ➪ iTunes Wi-Fi Sync. The iTunes Wi-Fi Sync settings appear.

3. In the iTunes Wi-Fi Sync settings, tap Sync Now to sync with a computer connected to the same Wi-Fi network.

4. If you need to connect your iPad to a network, tap Settings ➪ Wi-Fi and then tap a network to join.

If you have your iPad set up to sync wirelessly to your Mac or PC and both are within range of the same Wi-Fi network, iPad will appear in your iTunes Devices list. This setup allows you to sync and manage syncing from within iTunes.

Your iPad will automatically sync with iTunes once a day if both are on the same Wi-Fi network, iTunes is running, and your iPad is charging.

Understand iCloud

There's an alternative to syncing content by using iTunes. iCloud is a service offered by Apple that allows you to back up most of your content to online storage. That content is then pushed automatically to all your Apple devices through a wireless connection. All you need to do is get an iCloud account, which is free (again, this is simply using your Apple ID), and make settings on your devices and in iTunes for which types of content you want pushed to each device. After you've done that, content that you create or purchase on one device — such as music, apps, and TV shows, as well as documents created in Apple's iWork apps (Pages, Keynote, and Numbers), photos, and so on — is synced among your devices automatically.

You can stick with iCloud's default storage capacity, or you can increase it if you need more capacity.

>> Your iCloud account includes 5GB of free storage. You may be fine with the free 5GB of storage.

Content that you purchase from Apple (such as apps, books, music, iTunes Match content, Photo Sharing contents, and TV shows) isn't counted against your storage.

>> If you want additional storage, you can buy an upgrade. Currently, 50GB costs only $0.99 per month, 200GB is $2.99 per month, and 2TB (which is an enormous amount of storage) is $9.99 per month. (All prices are in U.S. dollars.) Most likely, 50GB will satisfy the needs of folks who just like to take and share pictures, but if videos are your thing, you may eventually want to consider the larger capacities.

To upgrade your storage, go to Settings, tap your Apple ID at the top of the screen, go to iCloud ⇨ Manage Storage, and then tap Change Storage Plan next to iCloud Storage. On the next screen, tap the amount you need and then tap Buy (in the upper-right corner).

If you change your mind, you can get in touch with Apple within 15 days to cancel your upgrade.

TIP

Turn on iCloud Drive

iCloud Drive is the online storage space that comes free with iCloud (as covered in the preceding section).

Before you can use iCloud Drive, you need to be sure that iCloud Drive is turned on. Here's how to turn on iCloud Drive:

1. Tap Settings and then tap your Apple ID at the top of the screen.
2. Tap iCloud to open the iCloud screen.
3. Scroll down in the iCloud screen until you see iCloud Drive.
4. Tap the On/Off switch to turn on (green) iCloud Drive (see **Figure 3-4**).

FIGURE 3-4

Setup iCloud Sync

When you have an iCloud account up and running, you have to specify which type of content should be synced with your iPad by iCloud.
Follow these steps:

1. Tap Settings, tap your Apple ID at the top of the screen, and then tap
   iCloud.

2. In the iCloud settings shown in **Figure 3-5,** tap the On/Off switch for
   any item that's turned off that you want to turn on (or vice versa). You
   can sync Photos, Mail, Contacts, Calendars, Reminders, Safari, Notes,
   News, Wallet, Keychain (an app that stores all your passwords and
   even credit card numbers across all Apple devices), and more. The
   listing of apps on this screen isn't alphabetical, so scroll down if at first
   you don't see what you're looking for.

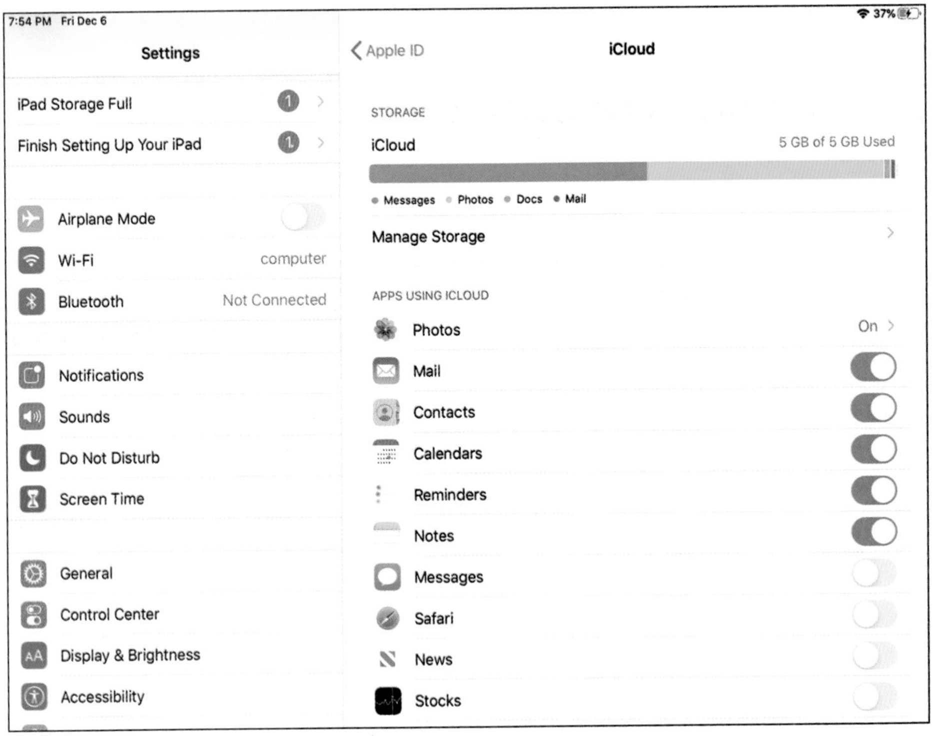

FIGURE 3-5

If you want to allow iCloud to provide a service for locating a lost or stolen iPad, tap your Apple ID in Settings, tap Find My, and then toggle the On/Off switch in the Find My iPad field to On (green) to activate it. This service helps you locate, send a message to, or delete content from your iPad if it falls into other hands.

3. To enable automatic downloads of iTunes-purchased music, apps, and books, return to the main Settings screen and then tap iTunes & App Store.

4. Tap the On/Off switch for Music, Apps, Books & Audiobooks, or Updates to set up automatic downloads of any of this content to your iPad by iCloud.

Consider turning off the Cellular Data option (if your iPad supports it), which you find in the Cellular section of Settings, to avoid having these downloads occur over your cellular connection, which can use up your data allowance. Wait until you're on a Wi-Fi connection to have iPad perform the updates.

Browse Your iPad's Files

Long-time iPad users have pined for a way to browse files stored on their devices, as opposed to being limited to finding documents and other files within the apps they're intended for or created by. iOS 11 introduced us to a new app called Files, which allows you to browse not only for files stored on your iPad, but also see the stuff you've stored on other online (cloud) services, such as Google Drive, Dropbox, and others.

You'll find the Files app in the Dock at the bottom of your screen, by default.

1. Tap the Files icon to open the app.

2. On the Browse screen (shown in **Figure 3-6**):

   • Tap the Search field to search for items by title.

   • Tap a source in the Locations or Favorites sections to browse a particular service or your iPad.

- Tap colors under Tags to search for files you've tagged according to categories.

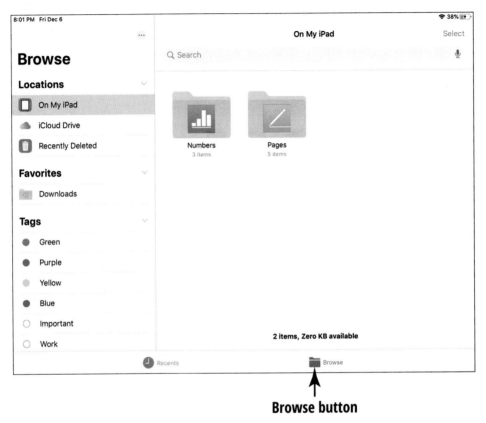

Browse button

FIGURE 3-6

3. Once in a source (see **Figure 3-7**), you may tap files to open or preview them, and you may tap folders to open them and view their contents.

4. Tap Select in the upper-right corner of the screen and then tap items to select them for an action. Available actions, found at the bottom of the screen, include

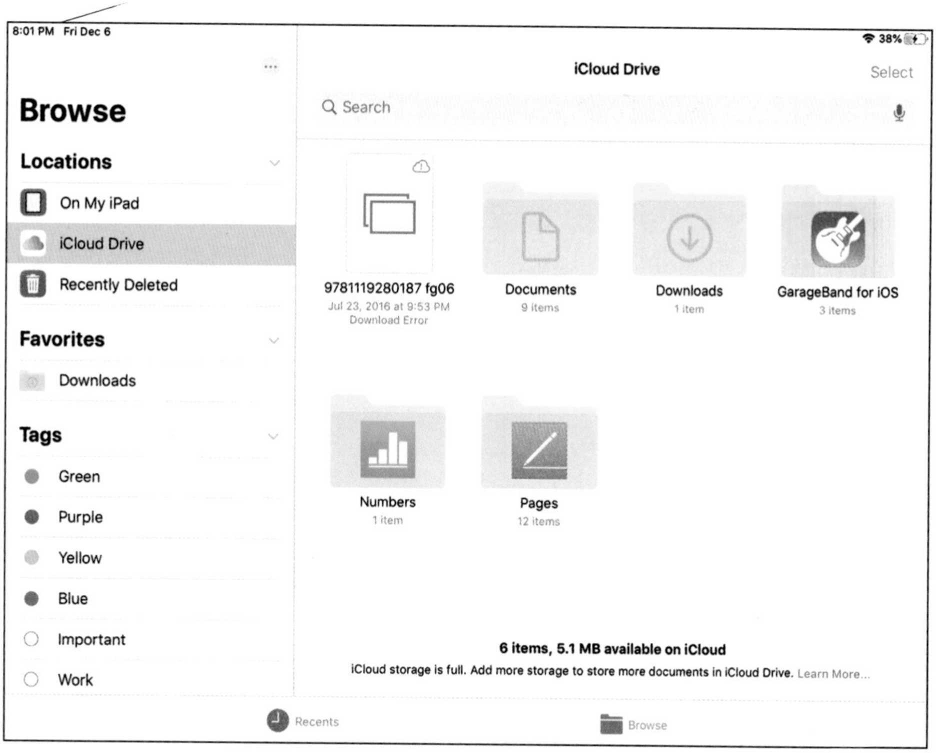

Browse

Locations

☐ On My iPad

☁ iCloud Drive

🗑 Recently Deleted

Favorites

▢ Downloads

Tags

● Green

● Purple

○ Yellow

● Blue

○ Important

○ Work

iCloud Drive   Select

🔍 Search

9781119280187 fg06   Documents   Downloads   GarageBand for iOS
Jul 23, 2016 at 9:53 PM   9 items   1 item   3 items
Download Error

Numbers   Pages
1 item   12 items

6 items, 5.1 MB available on iCloud
iCloud storage is full. Add more storage to store more documents in iCloud Drive. Learn More...

🕐 Recents   📁 Browse

FIGURE 3-7

- **Duplicating files:** Make copies of selected items.

- **Moving files:** Move files to other sources.

- **Sharing files:** Share files with other people in a variety of ways (Messages and Mail, for example), and you can even invite them to make edits, if you like.

- **Deleting files:** Trash files you no longer need.

TIP

If you need to retrieve a file you've deleted, go the Browse screen (if you're not already there) and tap Recently Deleted in the left toolbar. Tap Select in the upper-right corner, tap the file you'd like to retrieve, and tap the Recover button at the bottom of the screen. The file will be placed back in the location it was originally deleted from. Please note that some services may not allow you to retrieve a file you've deleted, so if you don't see the file you're looking for, contact that particular service for help.

USE EXTERNAL STORAGE

iPhone and iPad users have been asking Apple for quite the while to allow the use of external storage devices, such as SD cards, USB devices, or hard drives. You can connect such devices to your iPad now with iPadOS 13 using your iPad's Lightning port. You'll need to make sure your external device will connect to the Lightning port on your iPad, usually requiring an adapter. Apple has a Lightning-to-SD Card adapter that will enable you to use SD cards (from your camera, for example) with your iPad.

Every external storage device uses a file format, and Apple supports ExFAT, FAT32, HFS+, and APFS formats in the Files app. Be sure your external devices support one of those file formats before attempting to use them with your iPad. Also, some devices may need to be connected to an external power source. Again, check with the manufacturer of the device to find out if this is necessary.

IN THIS CHAPTER

» Understand Screen Time features

» Monitor how apps are used

» Create Downtime during your day

» Limit how long apps may be used

» Restrict access to certain websites

» Control privacy settings

Chapter **4**

Managing and Monitoring iPad Usage

The iPad you have will quickly become like an additional limb for you, if it hasn't become so already. And put one of these things down near a kid and you may likely not see it (or them) for a long time. Your iPad may well become one of your favorite tools, but your use of it really can get out of hand if you're not careful.

Apple understands this concern and has been one of the more active technology companies in helping resolve it. One of the most important additions to iOS in a while is Apple's response to the issue of spending too much time on our devices: Screen Time.

Screen Time is a feature that not only helps you monitor how much time you're spending on your iPad but also keep track ofwhich apps are consuming your days (and nights). It also can set time limits for app use, lock down your iPad after certain times, and even set content filters to help you or others in your sphere stay away from certain websites or apps.

Meet Screen Time

Screen Time isn't an app unto itself, but it is part of the Settings app. To find Screen Time:

1. On the Home screen, tap the Settings app icon to open it.

2. Swipe until you find the Screen Time options, shown in **Figure 4-1**, and tap to open it. If the Screen Time switch is Off (white), tap to turn it On (green).

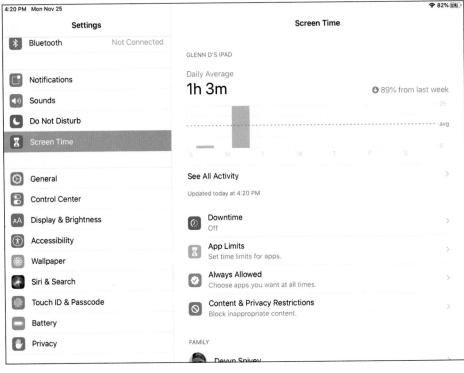

FIGURE 4-1

REMEMBER

You won't see much information in Screen Time if you've just enabled it for the first time, or if you've only had your iPad for a very short while.

3. You're greeted with a birds-eye view of your iPad usage. You'll see your iPad's name, as well as a quick glance at total usage time and a graph displaying the length of time you spent using apps of various categories.

4. Tap See All Activity to view the Screen Time details screen, which is a more detailed listing (see **Figure 4-2**) of your iPad activities, including a breakdown of how you used your apps throughout the day, which apps you used the most, and so on. In the Most Used section, tap Show Categories to see apps listed by category (such as Social Networking, Entertainment, Productivity, and more); tap Show Apps & Websites to return to the previous view.

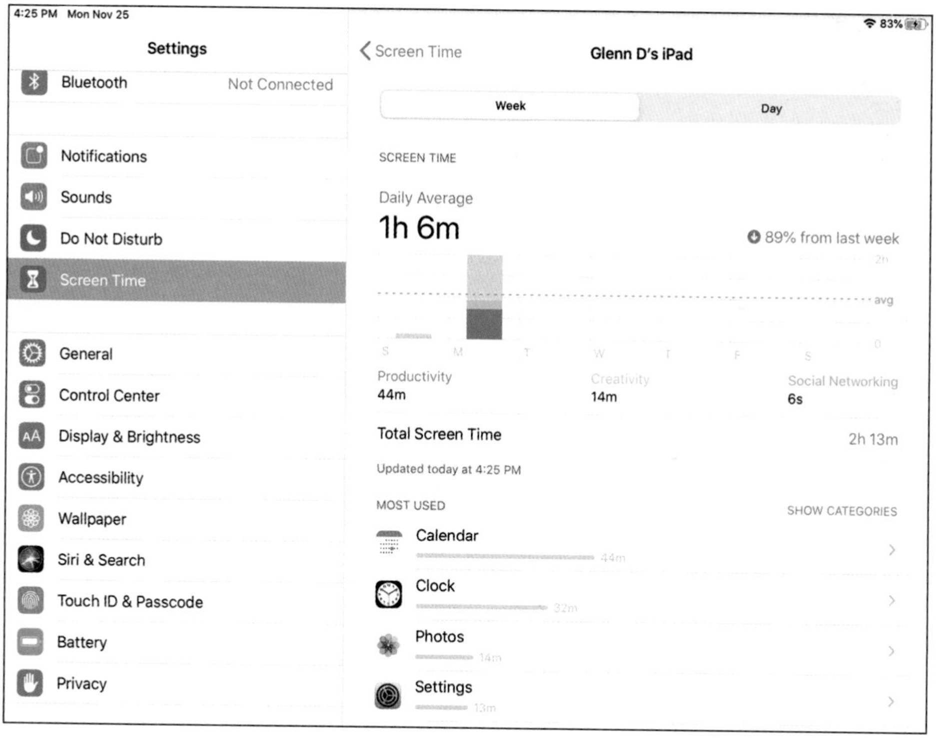

FIGURE 4-2

Tap a bar graph for a particular day (designated by S for Sunday, M for Monday, and so forth) to see even more detailed information about an activity for that day. Tap the same bar graph to return to the weekly information breakdown.

There are two tabs at the top of the page: one called Day and another called Week (see **Figure 4-2**). Tap the one you'd like to see displayed.

5. Tap an app under the Most Used section to see app-specific information, and then tap the back arrow in the upper-left corner to return to the previous screen.

6. Scroll down the page to see how many times you've picked up your iPad and when (see **Figure 4-3**), get an overview of how many notifications you've received, and which apps generated them.

Tap an app's name in the Notifications section to open the Notification settings for that app, should you want to make adjustments based on the activity reported for it.

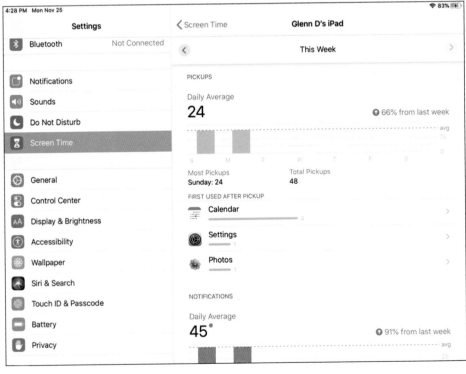

FIGURE 4-3

7. Tap the Sceen Time button in the upper-left corner to return to the main Screen Time settings.

8. Scroll down to Use Screen Time Passcode. If you'd like to use a passcode to keep your Screen Time settings secure (I recommend it), tap the option and provide a 4-digit passcode. This will prevent anyone else from changing your settings and also lets you allow users more time with apps when time limits have been set for them (more on that later in this chapter). If you prefer not to use a passcode, skip to the next step.

9. Toggle the Share Across Devices switch On or Off, depending on whether you'd like to view your Screen Time for this device on other iPadOS or iOS devices you may own.

10. Finally, Tap the Turn Off Screen Time button at the bottom of the options if you want to disable this awesome feature. Can you tell I very much like this new addition to iOS and can't imagine why you'd want to disable it?

Create Some Downtime

Screen Time's Downtime option lets you set aside some time during your day when you least use your iPad (or at least should use it the least). This feature would seem to be best used in the evening and during sleeping hours, but it could also be set up to discourage iPad use during other times, such as meals or while at work. When Downtime is on, the only apps that will be available are those you choose to allow (more on that in the next section).

To create some iPad downtime in your day:

1. Open the Screen Time options in the Settings app.

2. Tap Downtime and then toggle the Downtime switch to On (green) by tapping it, as shown in **Figure 4-4**.

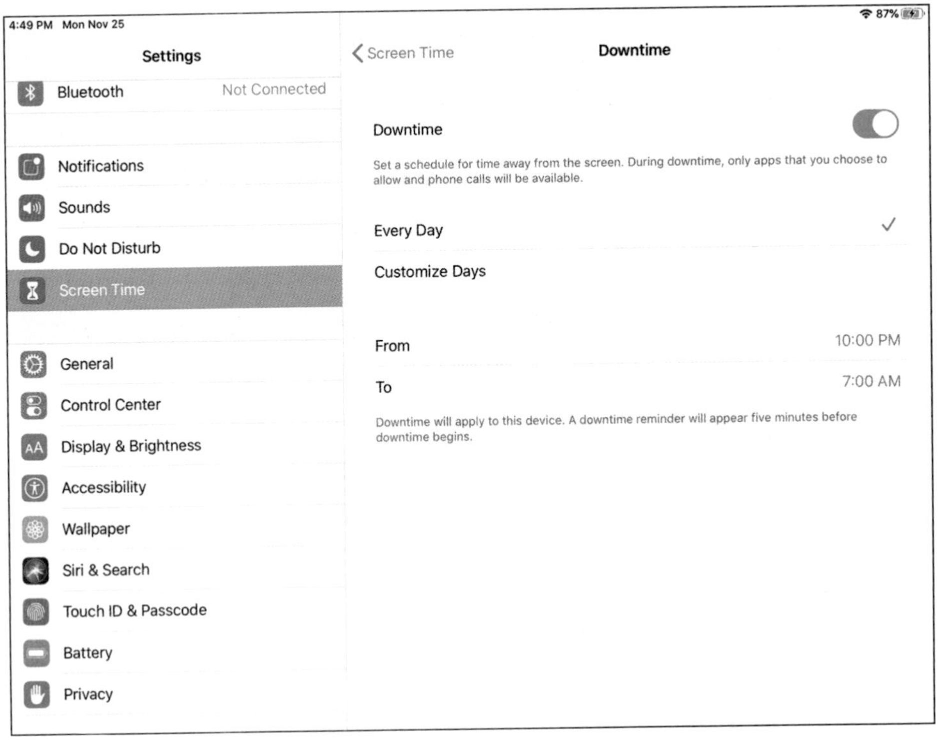

Settings		‹ Screen Time	**Downtime**

Bluetooth   Not Connected

Notifications

Sounds

Do Not Disturb

Screen Time

General

Control Center

Display & Brightness

Accessibility

Wallpaper

Siri & Search

Touch ID & Passcode

Battery

Privacy

Downtime ⬤

Set a schedule for time away from the screen. During downtime, only apps that you choose to allow and phone calls will be available.

Every Day ✓

Customize Days

From   10:00 PM

To   7:00 AM

Downtime will apply to this device. A downtime reminder will appear five minutes before downtime begins.

FIGURE 4-4

3. Tap From to select a time of day to begin your downtime, and then tap To to choose a time for downtime to stop.

TIP

If you have other iPadOS or iOS devices and are signed into iCloud using the same Apple ID as your iPad, the Downtime settings will apply for all of those devices (assuming iPadOS 13 or iOS 13 is installed on them).

Allow Certain Apps During Downtime

If you've decided to use Downtime, you may want certain apps to always be available, even during the Downtime period. The Phone app is always available, but you may allow others as you please.

1. Open Screen Time options in the Settings app.

2. Tap the Always Allowed option.

3. In the Allowed Apps section, you'll see a list of apps that are already enabled for use during Downtime by Apple (shown in **Figure 4-5**). These include Phone, Messages, FaceTime, and Maps. Note that Phone cannot be disabled.

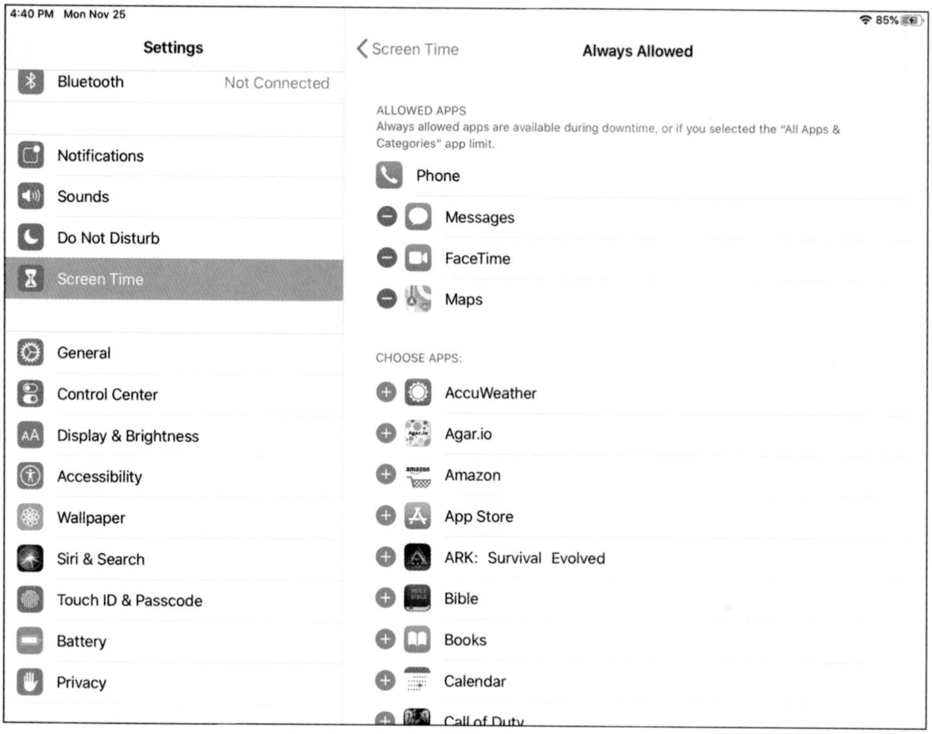

FIGURE 4-5

4. To allow other apps, scroll through the list in the Choose Apps section and tap the green plus sign (+) to the left of the app's name to add it to the Allowed Apps list.

5. To remove apps from the Allowed Apps list, tap the red minus sign (–) to the left of its name, and then tap the red Remove button that appears to its right.

If you're wondering which apps to allow, consider starting with those that may be used for contacting friends and family, as well as those that are used for medical monitoring and other health-related needs.

Set App Limits

App Limits is an ingenious feature of Screen Time that acts to help you curtail excessive use of apps that tend to consume most of your time. Let's face it: Sometimes we just get so engrossed in checking out social media and browsing the web that we end up wondering where half the day went. App Limits helps remind you when the time limit is up, but does allow you to have a bit of extra time or completely ignore the limit for the day if need be.

To create app limits based on app categories:

1. Open the Screen Time options in the Settings app.

2. Tap App Limits, and then tap the Add Limit button.

3. Tap the circle to the left of a category to select all apps in the category, as shown in **Figure 4-6**, or tap a category name and tap a circle next to a particular app to only select it (as opposed to selecting all apps in the category).

Tap All Apps & Categories to set limits for everything in one fell swoop.

4. Tap Next in the upper-right corner of the screen.

5. Use the scroll wheel to set time limits in terms of hours and minutes, shown in **Figure 4-7**. Tap Customize Days under the scroll wheel to set specific times for particular days.

FIGURE 4-6

FIGURE 4-7

6. Tap Add in the upper-right corner and the new limit appears in the App Limits list, as shown in **Figure 4-8**. Tap it to make changes to the allotted time or to delete it by tapping the red Delete Limit button, then tap Delete Limit again to confirm.

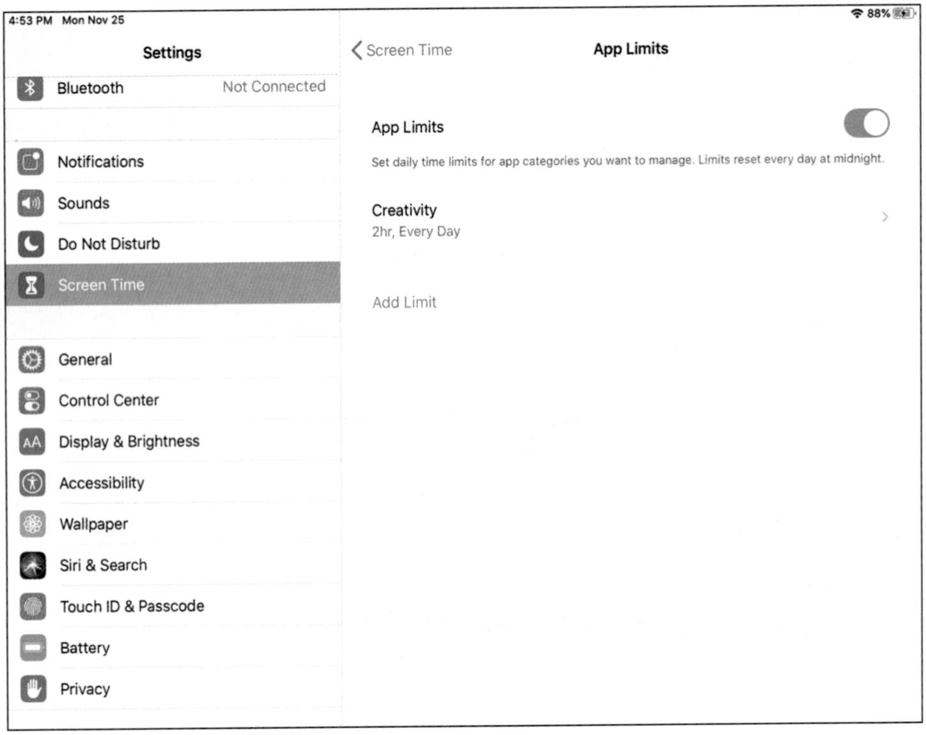

FIGURE 4-8

7. Tap the Add Limit button on the App Limits screen to add more limits, or tap the Screen Time button at the top of the screen to exit the App Limits screen.

Your iPad will notify you when you've reached an app's limit: the screen will become gray, displaying an hourglass, and the app's icon is also grayed out on the Home screen where it resides. If you'd like more time, tap the blue Ignore Limit button in the center of the screen, and then tap One More Minute, Remind Me in 15 Minutes, or Ignore Limit For Today (see **Figure 4-9**). Tap Cancel if you'd like to adhere to the limit you've set for the app.

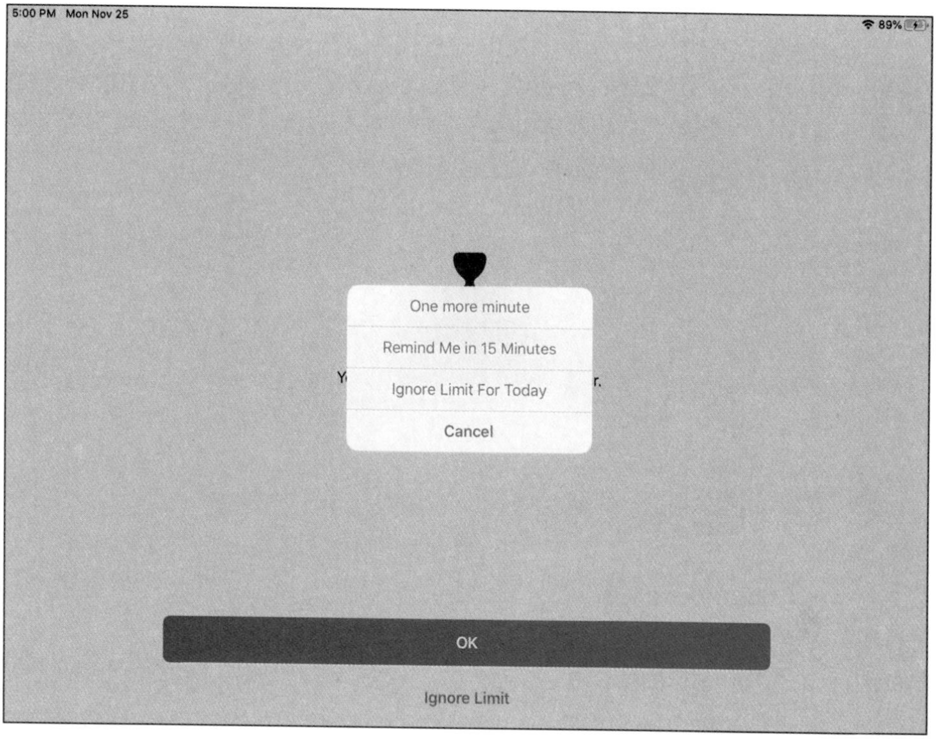

One more minute

Remind Me in 15 Minutes

Y   Ignore Limit For Today   r.

Cancel

OK

Ignore Limit

FIGURE 4-9

TIP

If you enabled a passcode for Screen Time, you must enter it before overriding the app's time limit.

Set Content and Privacy Restrictions

Screen Time helps you prevent access to content that you don't want to be accessed on your iPad, and you can also use it to set privacy limits. Content to be restricted could be apps, websites, media (movies, music, etc.), books, and more.

WARNING

If you're going to restrict content and set privacy restrictions, it's advisable to enable the Screen Time passcode. That way, only someone knowledgable of the passcode can alter the settings you're about to make. This is highly recommended, especially if you're original intent is to provide safety for any children who may use your iPad.

To set content and privacy options:

1. Open Screen Time options in the Settings app.

2. Tap Content & Privacy Restrictions and then toggle the Content & Privacy Restrictions switch to On (green), as shown in **Figure 4-10**.

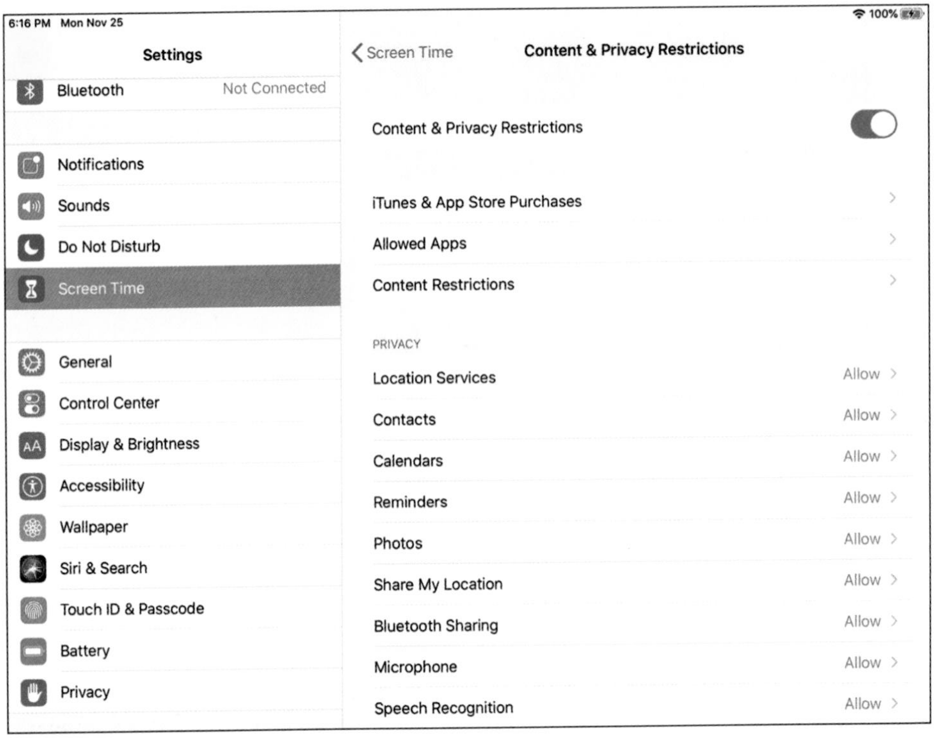

FIGURE 4-10

3. Tap iTunes & App Store Purchases to allow or block installation of apps, deletion of apps, or in-app purchases (purchases that may occur within an app, such as buying upgrades for characters in games). Also decide whether users always require a password when making purchases in the iTunes Store or App Store (I very much recommend using this option if other people use your iPad).

4. Tap the Back button in the upper part of the screen to return to the Content & Privacy Restrictions screen, and then tap Allowed Apps. This feature allows you to enable or disable apps that are created by Apple and are installed on your iPad by default. As you can see in **Figure 4-11**, all of them are enabled to start. If you'd like to disable any of them, simply tap the switch to turn it Off (white). This will completely remove the app from the Home Screen; re-enabling the app will place it back on the Home Screen.

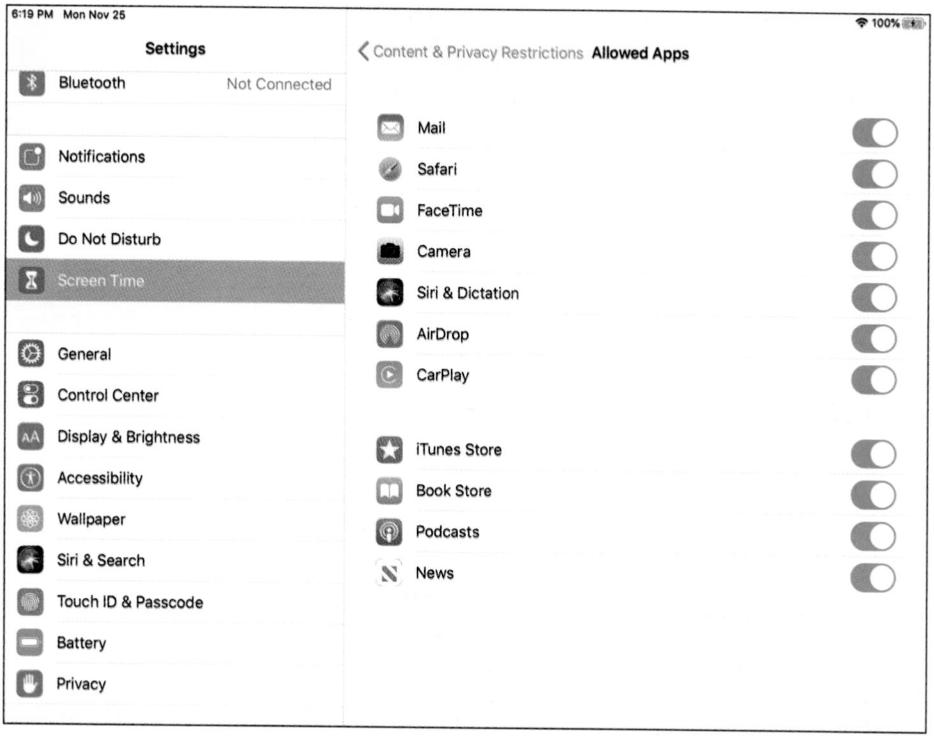

FIGURE 4-11

5. Tap the Content & Restrictions button in the upper part of the screen to return to the Content & Privacy Restrictions screen, and then tap Content Restrictions.

6. In the Allowed Store Content section, you can make restrictions based on certain criteria. For example, you can limit which movies are available for purchase or rent in the iTunes Store based on their ratings, as shown in **Figure 4-12**. Tap the Content Restrictions button in the upper part of the screen to return to the previous screen.

FIGURE 4-12

7. The Web Content section lets you restrict access to websites. From there you're able to allow unrestricted access to the web, limit access to adult websites, and further limit access to only a list of specific websites that you can customize (shown in **Figure 4-13**). You may remove sites from the list by dragging their names to the left and tapping the red Delete button that appears. You may add websites to the list by tapping the blue Add Website button at the bottom of the list. Tap the Content Restrictions button in the upper part of the screen to return to the previous screen.

8. Options in the Siri and Game Center sections let you prevent access to untoward content or language, as well as disabling multiplayer games, adding friends to games, and turning off the ability to record your iPad's screen. Tap the Content Restrictions button in the upper part of the screen to return to the previous screen from either of these sections.

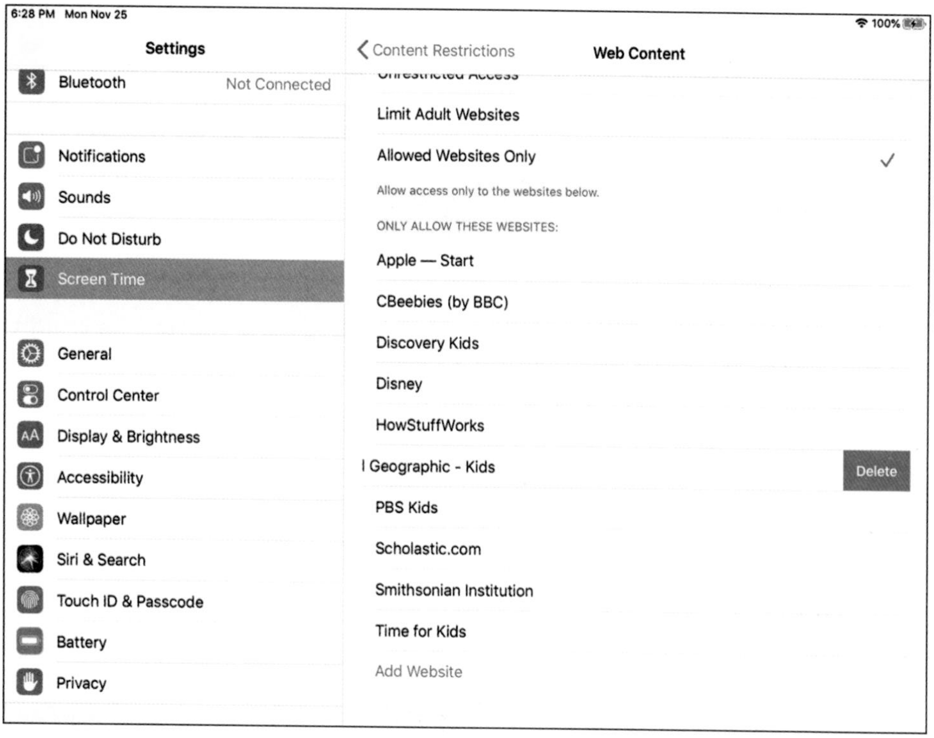

Settings   ‹ Content Restrictions   **Web Content**

✻ Bluetooth Not Connected	Unrestricted Access
	Limit Adult Websites
▣ Notifications	Allowed Websites Only ✓
◀)) Sounds	Allow access only to the websites below.
☾ Do Not Disturb	ONLY ALLOW THESE WEBSITES:
⧗ Screen Time	Apple — Start
	CBeebies (by BBC)
⚙ General	Discovery Kids
▣ Control Center	Disney
AA Display & Brightness	HowStuffWorks
⬤ Accessibility	I Geographic - Kids [Delete]
✽ Wallpaper	PBS Kids
▲ Siri & Search	Scholastic.com
◉ Touch ID & Passcode	Smithsonian Institution
▭ Battery	Time for Kids
✋ Privacy	Add Website

FIGURE 4-13

9. Tap the Back button in the upper part of the screen to return to the Content & Privacy Restrictions screen, and then view the items listed in the Privacy section. This area lists features and functions built-in to your iPad. Tapping one shows you which apps are accessing the feature or function, enabling you to limit access to specific apps or to turn off access to them altogether (by selecting Don't Allow Changes).

10. Finally, the Allow Changes section of the Content & Privacy Restrictions screen lets you determine whether changes may be made to such features of your iPad such as Volume Limit settings, Cellular Data options, and more.

Manage Children's Accounts

If you have children in your life that use devices linked to your Apple ID through Family Sharing (covered in Chapter 12), you can manage their activities using Screen Time.

1. Open Screen Time in the Settings app.

2. Scroll down to the Family section and tap the name of a child's account. Then tap Turn On Screen Time.

3. Tap Continue and move step by step through the process of enabling Screen Time for the child's account.

4. Tap the Start and End options to set times for Downtime, and then tap the Set Downtime button (shown in **Figure 4-14**), or tap Not Now to skip.

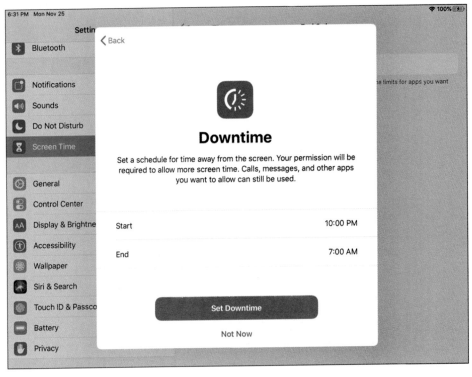

FIGURE 4-14

5. Tap the circles next to app categories, or just tap All Apps & Categories, to set App Limits for the child's account. Tap Set next to Time Amount to set a time limit, and then tap the Set App Limit button at the bottom of the screen. Of course, you can also tap Not Now to skip.

6. In the Content & Privacy screen, tap the Continue button, shown in **Figure 4-15**.

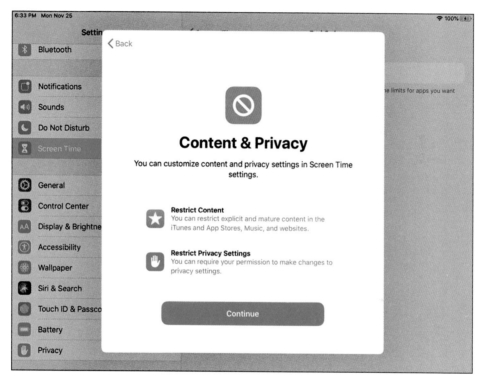

FIGURE 4-15

7. Set a Screen Time Passcode to prevent changes from being made to the settings for this account, if prompted.

WARNING

Don't forget the Screen Time Passcodes you use for Screen Time accounts! Write them down somewhere safe if you need help remembering.

8. Screen Time is now activated for the child's account. You may make changes to the account's Screen Time settings at any time.

2

Beginning to Use Your iPad

IN THIS CHAPTER

» Use Magnifier

» Set brightness and wallpapers

» Set up and use VoiceOver

» Set up subtitles, captioning, and other hearing settings

» Turn on additional physical and motor settings

» Learn with Guided Access

» Control your iPad with your voice

Chapter **5**

Making Your iPad More Accessible

iPad users are a very diverse group, and some face visual, motor, or hearing challenges. If you're one of these folks, you'll be glad to hear that Apple offers some handy accessibility features for your iPad.

To make your screen easier to read, you can use the Magnifier, adjust the brightness, or change wallpaper. You can also set up the VoiceOver feature to read onscreen elements out loud. Then you can turn a slew of features on or off, including Zoom, Invert Colors, Speak Selection, Large Type, and more.

If hearing is your challenge, you can do the obvious thing and adjust the system volume. The iPad also allows you to use mono audio (useful when you're wearing headphones) and an LED flash when an alert sounds.

Features that help you deal with physical and motor challenges include an AssistiveTouch feature if you have difficulty using the iPad touchscreen, Switch Control for working with adaptive accessories, and the Home Button and Call Audio Routing settings that allow you to adjust how quickly you have to tap the iPad screen to work with features and whether you can use a headset or speaker to answer calls.

The Guided Access feature helps if you have difficulty focusing on one task. It also provides a handy mode for showing presentations of content in settings where you don't want users to flit off to other apps, as in school or a public kiosk.

Finally, Voice Control, Numbers, and Grids are welcome additions to accessibility features in iPadOS 13.

Use Magnifier

The Magnifier feature uses your iPad's camera to help you magnify objects. Magnifier is considered an accessibility feature, but almost everyone needs a magnifier at one time or another. To access Magnifier:

1. Tap Settings ➪ Accessibility, as shown in **Figure 5-1**.

2. Tap Magnifier and then toggle the Magnifier switch to On (green).

3. Press the Home button or the top button (iPad Pro models only) three times to turn Magnifier on.

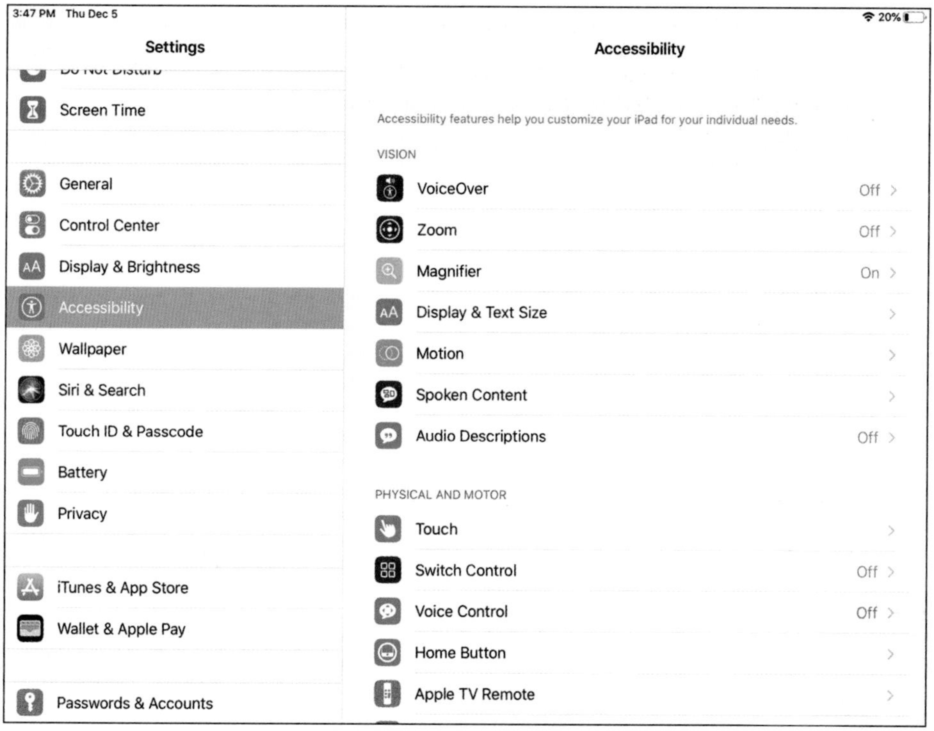

FIGURE 5-1

When Magnifier is on, you can use the back camera of your iPad just like a magnifying glass. In fact, it's like an illuminated magnifying glass. You see the magnified image on your screen. A slider lets you set the degree of magnification, as shown in **Figure 5-2**. You can also turn on a light by tapping the lightning bolt icon (if your iPad includes one) and lock the magnification level. The icon containing three circles lets you change the colors. Use the round button (like a camera shutter) to have the iPad adjust its focus for what you're pointing at.

TIP You can combine magnification with your iPad's portability so that you can reach up to (or behind) an object and magnify something that would not only be too small to see otherwise but would be out of view entirely.

Magnification slider

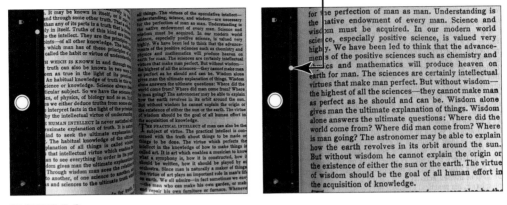

FIGURE 5-2

Set Brightness and Night Shift

Especially when using iPad as an e-reader, you may find that a slightly less bright screen reduces strain on your eyes. To manually adjust screen brightness, follow these steps:

1. Tap the Settings icon on the Home screen.

TIP

If glare from the screen is a problem for you, consider getting a screen protector. This thin film both protects your screen from damage and reduces glare. You can easily find them on Amazon, and just about any cellphone dealer or tech store carries them.

2. In Settings, go to Accessibility ⇨ Display & Text Size.

3. Tap the Auto-Brightness On/Off switch (see **Figure 5-3**) to turn off this feature (the button turns white when off).

4. Tap Display & Brightness on the left side of the screen, and then tap and drag the Brightness slider (refer to **Figure 5-4**) to the right to make the screen brighter or to the left to make it dimmer.

5. Press the Home button or swipe up on the screen (iPad Pro models only) to close Settings.

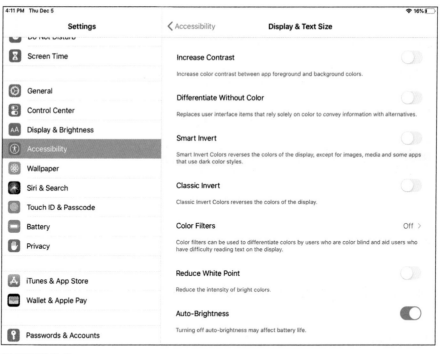

FIGURE 5-3

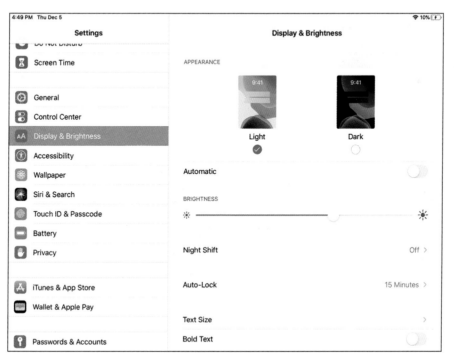

FIGURE 5-4

TIP

In the Apple Books e-reader app, you can set a sepia tone for the page. This might be easier on your eyes. See Chapter 13 for more about using Apple Books.

Night Shift is another option in Display & Brightness that you can use during hours of darkness. It changes the screen colors to reduce the amount of blue in the images on your iPad. Bright blue light seems to interfere with sleep in some people, so turning on Night Shift if you read before bed (or in bed) may help you sleep better.

Change the Wallpaper

The default iPad background image on your iPad may be pretty, but it may not be the one that works best for you. Choosing different wallpaper may help you see all the icons on your Home screen. Follow these steps:

1. Tap the Settings icon on the Home screen.

2. In Settings, tap Wallpaper.

3. In the Wallpaper settings, tap Choose a New Wallpaper.

4. Tap a wallpaper category, as shown in **Figure 5-5**, to view choices.

5. Tap a sample to select it.

TIP

If you prefer to use a picture that's on your iPad, tap an album in the lower part of the Wallpaper screen to locate a picture; tap to use it as your wallpaper.

6. In the preview that appears (see **Figure 5-6**), tap the Set button in the lower-right, then tap your choice of

   • Set Lock Screen (the screen that appears when you lock the iPad by tapping the power button)

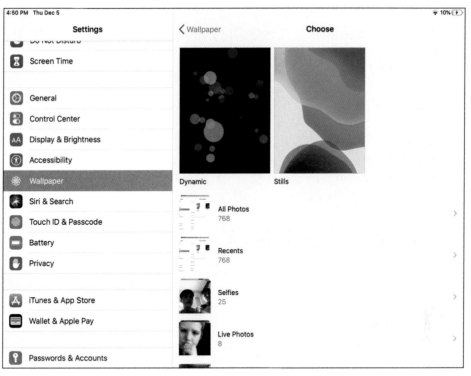

FIGURE 5-5

TECHNICAL STUFF

- Set Home Screen
- Set Both

  Some wallpaper may allow you to select either

- Still (the picture is static)
- Perspective (the picture seems to move when you move your iPad)

7. Press the Home button or swipe up from the bottom of the screen (iPad Pro models).

You return to your Home screen with the new wallpaper set as the background.

FIGURE 5-6

Set Up VoiceOver

VoiceOver reads the names of screen elements and settings to you, but it also changes the way you provide input to the iPad. In Notes, for example, you can have VoiceOver read the name of the Notes buttons to you, and when you enter notes, it reads words or characters that you've entered. It can also tell you whether such features as Auto-Correction are on.

To turn on VoiceOver, follow these steps:

1. Tap the Settings icon on the Home screen.

2. In Settings, tap Accessibility.

3. In the Accessibility pane, tap VoiceOver.

4. In the VoiceOver pane, shown in **Figure 5-7**, tap the VoiceOver On/ Off switch to turn on this feature (the button becomes green). With VoiceOver on, you must first single-tap to select an item such as a button, which causes VoiceOver to read the name of the button to you. Then you double-tap the button to activate its function.

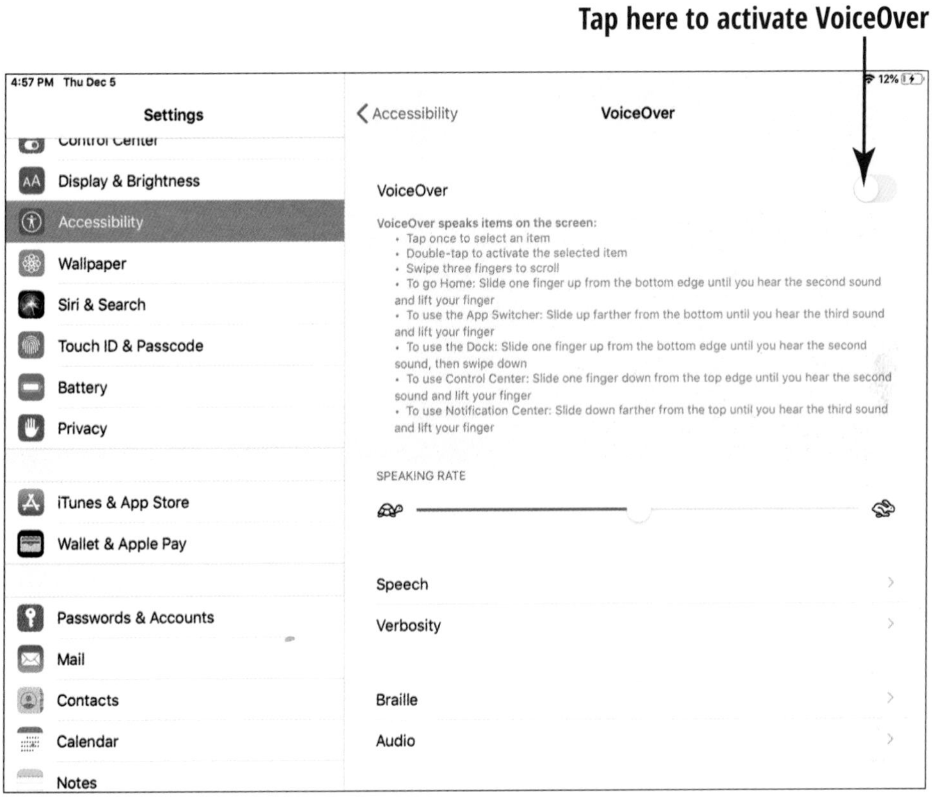

Tap here to activate VoiceOver

FIGURE 5-7

5. Tap the VoiceOver Practice button to select it and then double-tap the button to open VoiceOver Practice. (This is the new method of tapping that VoiceOver activates.) Practice using gestures (such as pinching or flicking left), and VoiceOver tells you what action each gesture initiates.

6. Tap the Done button and then double-tap the same button to return to the VoiceOver dialog box.

7. Tap the Verbosity button once and then double-tap to open its options:

- Tap the Speak Hints On/Off switch and then double-tap the switch to turn the feature on (or off). VoiceOver speaks the name of each tapped item.

- Tap once and then double-tap the VoiceOver button in the upper-left corner to go back to the VoiceOver screen.

TIP

You can change the language that VoiceOver speaks. In General settings, tap Language & Region, tap iPad Language, and then select another language. However, this action also changes the language used for labels on Home icons and various settings and fields in iPad. Be careful with this setting, lest you choose a language you don't understand by accident and have a very difficult time figuring out how to change it back.

8. If you want VoiceOver to read words or characters to you (for example, in the Notes app), scroll down, tap and double-tap Typing, and then tap and double-tap Typing Feedback.

9. In the Typing Feedback dialog box, tap and then double-tap to select the option you prefer. The Words option causes VoiceOver to read words to you, but not characters, such as the "dollar sign" ($). The Characters and Words option causes VoiceOver to read both and so on.

10. Press the Home button or swipe up from the bottom of the screen (iPad Pro models) to return to the Home screen.

The following section shows how to navigate your iPad after you've turned on VoiceOver.

TIP

You can use the Accessibility Shortcut setting to help you more quickly turn the VoiceOver, Zoom, Switch Control, Assistive-Touch, Grayscale, or Invert Colors features on and off:

1. In the Accessibility screen, tap Accessibility Shortcut (at the very bottom of the screen).

2. In the screen that appears, choose what you want three presses of the Home button to activate. Now three presses with a single finger on the Home button provide you with the option you selected wherever you go in iPad.

Use VoiceOver

After VoiceOver is turned on (see preceding section), you need to figure out how to use it. I won't kid you — using it is awkward at first, but you'll get the hang of it.

Here are the main onscreen gestures you should know how to use:

» **Tap an item to select it.** VoiceOver then speaks its name.

» **Double-tap the selected item.** This action activates the item.

» **Flick three fingers.** It takes three fingers to scroll around a page with VoiceOver turned on.

TIP

If tapping with two or three fingers seems difficult for you, try tapping with one finger from one hand and one or two from the other. When double- or triple-tapping, you have to perform these gestures as quickly as you can for them to work.

Table 5-1 provides additional gestures to help you use VoiceOver. If you want to use this feature often, I recommend the VoiceOver section of the iPad online User Guide, which goes into great detail about using VoiceOver. You'll find the User Guide at `https://support.apple.com/manuals/iPad`. When there, just click on the model of iPad or the version of iPad OS you have to read its manual. You can also get an Apple Books version of the manual through that app in the Book Store (see Chapter 13 for more information).

Check out some of the settings for VoiceOver, including a choice for Braille, Language Rotor for making language choices, the ability to navigate images, and a setting to have iPad speak notifications.

TABLE 5-1 VoiceOver Gestures

Gesture	Effect
Flick right or left	Select the next or preceding item
Tap with two fingers	Stop speaking the current item
Flick two fingers up	Read everything from the top of the screen
Flick two fingers down	Read everything from the current position
Flick three fingers up or down	Scroll one page at a time
Flick three fingers right or left	Go to the next or preceding page
Tap three fingers	Speak the scroll status (for example, line 20 of 100)
Flick four fingers up or down	Go to the first or last element on a page
Flick four fingers right or left	Go to the next or preceding section (as on a web page)

Make Additional Vision Settings

Several Vision features are simple on/off settings that you can turn on or off after you tap Settings ⇨ Accessibility:

» **Zoom:** The Zoom feature enlarges the contents displayed on the iPad screen when you double-tap the screen with three fingers. The Zoom feature works almost everywhere in iPad: in Photos, on web pages, on your Home screens, in your Mail, in Music, and in Videos. Give it a try!

» **Magnifier:** Enable Magnifier to use your iPad's built-in camera as a magnifying glass. Just triple-click the Home button to activate it (after you've turned the feature on, of course).

» **Display Accommodations:** Includes such features as

• Color Filters (aids in case of color blindness)

• Reduce White Point (helps reduce the intensity of bright colors)

- Invert Colors (which reverses colors on your screen so that white backgrounds are black and black text is white). Classic Invert will invert all colors, while Smart Invert will not invert colors for items like images, multimedia, and some apps that may use darker color styles.

  The Invert Colors feature works well in some places and not so well in others. For example, in the Photos application, pictures appear almost as photo negatives (which is a really cool trick to try). Your Home screen image will likewise look a bit strange. And don't even think of playing a video with this feature turned on! However, if you need help reading text, White on Black can be useful in several apps.

» **Spoken Content:** Options here include the ability to have your iPad speak items you've selected or hear the content of an entire screen, highlight content as it's spoken, and more.

» **Larger Text (under Accessibility ⇨ Display & Text Size):** If having larger text in such apps as Contacts, Mail, and Notes would be helpful to you, you can turn on the Larger Text feature and choose the text size that works best for you.

» **Bold Text (under Accessibility ⇨ Display & Text Size):** Turning on this setting restarts your iPad (after asking you for permission to do so) and then causes text in various apps and in Settings to be bold.

» **Button Shapes (under Accessibility ⇨ Display & Text Size):** This setting applies shapes to buttons so that they're more easily distinguishable. For an example, check out the Accessibilty button near the top of the screen after you enable Button Shapes by toggling its switch to On. Turn it back off and notice the difference (shown in **Figure 5-8**).

» **Reduce Transparency (under Accessibility ⇨ Display & Text Size):** This setting helps increase legibility of text by reducing the blurs and transparency effects that make up a good deal of the iPad user interface.

» **Increase Contrast (under Accessibility ⇨ Display & Text Size):** Use this setting to set up backgrounds in some areas of iPad and apps with greater contrast, which should improve visibility.

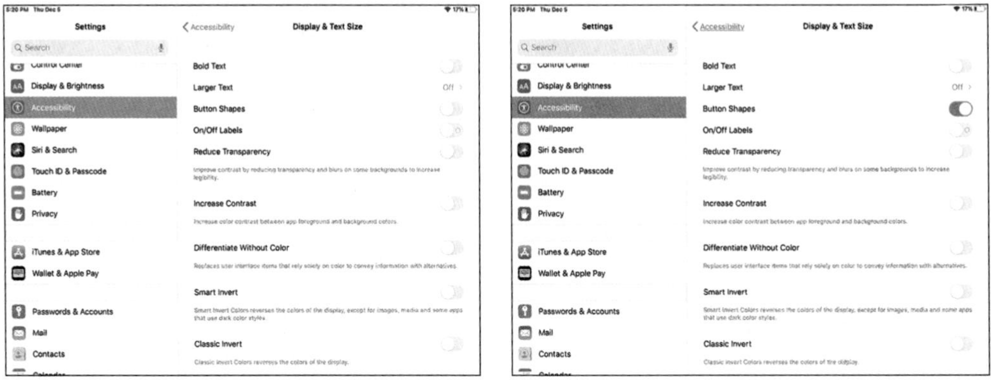

FIGURE 5-8

>> **Reduce Motion (under Accessibility ⇨ Motion):** Tap this accessibility feature and then tap the On/Off setting to turn off the parallax effect, which causes the background of your Home screens to appear to float as you move the iPad around.

>> **On/Off Labels (under Accessibility ⇨ Display & Text Size):** If you have trouble making out colors and therefore find it hard to tell when an On/Off setting is On (green) or Off (white), use this setting to add a circle to the right of a setting when it's off and a white vertical line to a setting when it's on.

Use iPad with Hearing Aids

If you have Bluetooth enabled or use another style of hearing aid, your iPad may be able to detect it and work with its settings to improve sound. Follow these steps to connect your hearing aid to your iPad.

1. Tap Settings on the Home screen.

2. Tap Accessibility, scroll down to the Hearing section, and tap Hearing Devices. On the next screen, shown in **Figure 5-9**, your iPad searches for MFi (Made for iPhone) hearing aid devices.

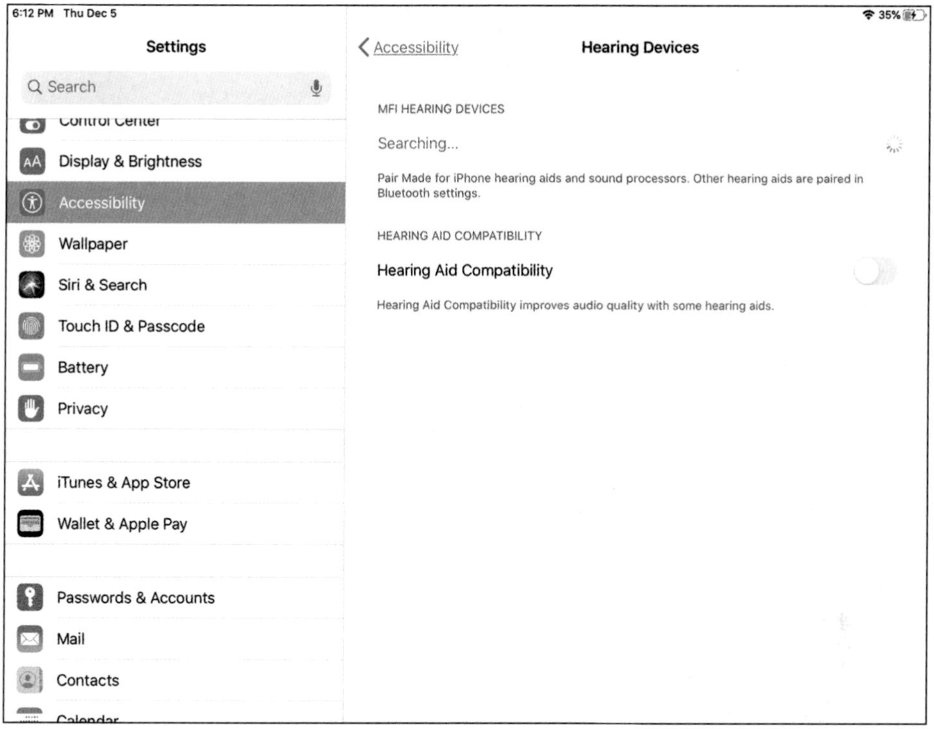

![Screenshot of iPad Settings showing the Hearing Devices screen. The left panel shows Settings menu items: Control Center, Display & Brightness, Accessibility (highlighted), Wallpaper, Siri & Search, Touch ID & Passcode, Battery, Privacy, iTunes & App Store, Wallet & Apple Pay, Passwords & Accounts, Mail, Contacts, Calendar. The right panel shows Hearing Devices with MFI Hearing Devices "Searching..." and Hearing Aid Compatibility toggle.]

FIGURE 5-9

TIP

If you have a non-MFi hearing aid, add your hearing aid in Bluetooth settings. To do so, go to Settings ⇨ Bluetooth, make sure the Bluetooth toggle switch is On (green), and select your hearing aid in the list of devices.

3. When your device appears, tap it.

TIP

Using the stereo effect in headphones or a headset breaks up sounds so that you hear a portion in one ear and a portion in the other ear. The purpose is to simulate the way your ears process sounds. If there is only one channel of sound, that sound is sent to both ears. However, if you're hard of hearing or deaf in one ear, you're hearing only a portion of the sound in your hearing ear, which can be frustrating. If you have such hearing challenges and want to use iPad with a headset connected, you should turn on Mono Audio (go to Settings ⇨ Accessibility ⇨ Audio & Visual). When it's turned on, all sound is combined and distributed to both ears. You can use the slider below Mono Audio to direct more sound to the ear you hear best with.

Adjust the Volume

Though individual apps (such as Music and TV) have their own volume settings, you can set your iPad system volume for your ringer and alerts as well to help you better hear what's going on. Follow these steps:

1. Tap Settings on the Home screen and then tap Sounds.

TIP

In the Sounds settings, you can turn on or off the sounds that iPad makes when certain events occur (such as receiving new Mail or Calendar alerts). These sounds are turned on by default.

2. In the Sounds settings that appear (see **Figure 5-10**), tap and drag the Ringer and Alerts slider to adjust the volume of these audible attention grabbers:

3. Press the Home button to return to the Home screen.

Settings	Sounds
6:35 PM Thu Dec 5	📶 40%
Q Search 🎤	RINGER AND ALERTS
	◀ ━━━━━━━━━━━━ 🔊
📱 Notifications	Change with Buttons 🔘
🔊 Sounds	The volume of the ringer and alerts can be adjusted using the volume buttons.
🌙 Do Not Disturb	SOUNDS
⏳ Screen Time	Ringtone Opening ›
	Text Tone Note ›
⚙️ General	New Mail None ›
🎛 Control Center	Sent Mail Swoosh ›
AA Display & Brightness	Calendar Alerts Chord ›
♿ Accessibility	Reminder Alerts Chord ›
🖼 Wallpaper	AirDrop Pulse ›
Siri & Search	
Touch ID & Passcode	Keyboard Clicks 🔘
🔋 Battery	Lock Sound 🔘
✋ Privacy	

FIGURE 5-10

Set Up Subtitles and Captioning

Closed captioning and subtitles help folks with hearing challenges enjoy entertainment and educational content. Follow these steps:

1. Tap Settings on the Home screen, and then tap Accessibility.

2. Scroll down to the Hearing section and tap Subtitles & Captioning.

3. On the following screen, tap the On/Off switch to turn on Closed Captions + SDH (Subtitles for the Deaf and Hard of Hearing).

   You can also tap Style and choose a text style for the captions, as shown in **Figure 5-11**. A neat video helps show you what your style will look like when the feature is in use.

4. Press the Home button or swipe up from the bottom of the screen (iPad Pro models) to return to the Home screen.

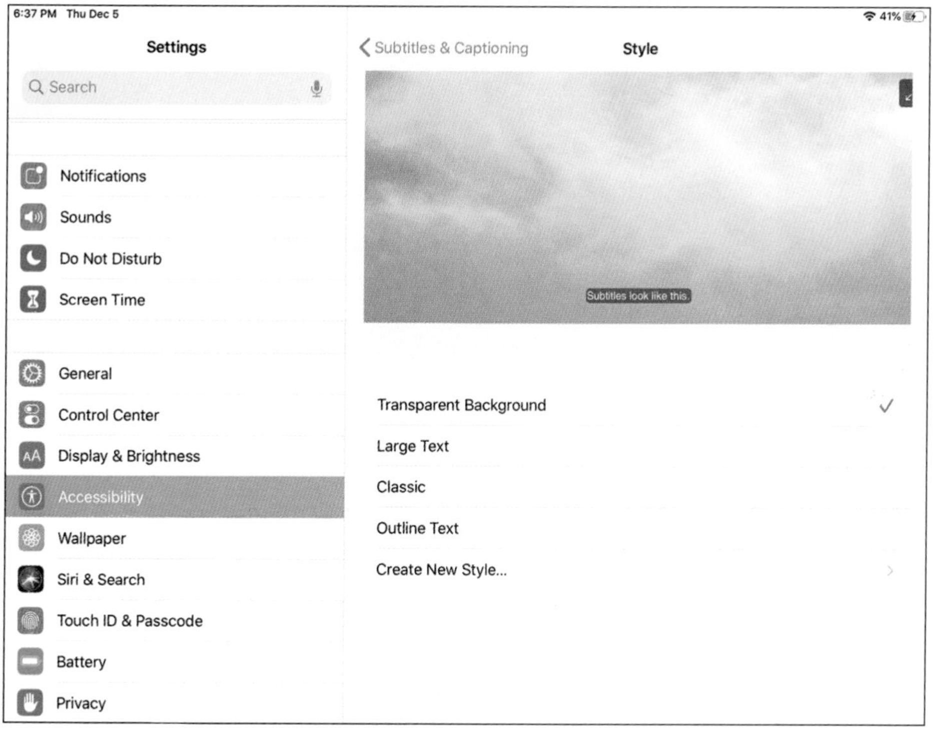

FIGURE 5-11

Turn On and Work with AssistiveTouch

If you have difficulty using buttons, the AssistiveTouch Control Panel aids input using the touchscreen.

1. To turn on AssistiveTouch, tap Settings on the Home screen and then tap Accessibility.

2. In the Accessibility pane, scroll down and tap Touch, then tap AssistiveTouch. In the pane that appears, tap the On/Off switch for AssistiveTouch to turn it on (see **Figure 5-12**). A gray square (called the AssistiveTouch Control Panel) then appears on the right side of the screen; you'll see it on your iPad's screen, but it doesn't display in screenshots, such as Figure 5-12. This square now appears in the same location in whatever apps you display on your iPad, though you can move it around with your finger.

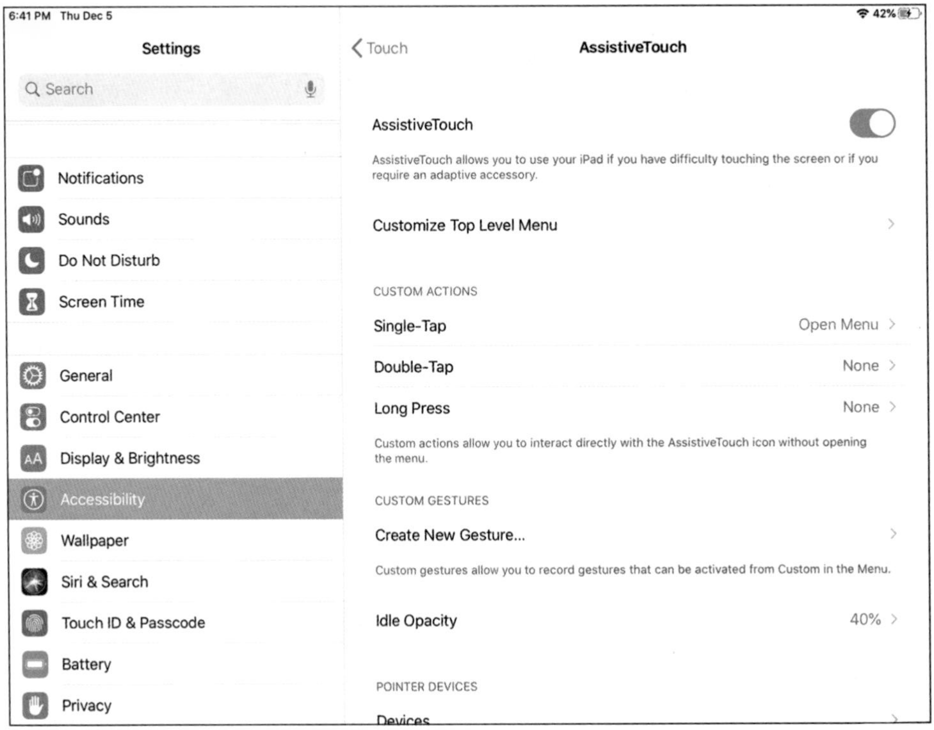

FIGURE 5-12

3. Tap the AssistiveTouch Control Panel to display options, as shown in **Figure 5-13**. The panel includes Notifications and Control Center options.

FIGURE 5-13

4. You can tap Custom or Device on the panel to see additional choices, tap Siri to activate the personal assistant feature, tap Notifications or Control Center to display those panels, or press Home to go directly to the Home screen. After you choose an option, pressing the Home button or swiping up from the bottom of the screen (iPad Pro models) takes you back to the Home screen.

Table 5-2 shows the major options available in the AssistiveTouch Control panel and their purpose.

TABLE 5-2   **AssistiveTouch Controls**

Control	Purpose
Siri	Activates the Siri feature, which allows you to speak questions and make requests of your iPad
Custom	Displays a set of gestures with only the Pinch gesture preset; you can tap any of the other blank squares to add your own favorite gestures
Device	You can rotate the screen, lock the screen, lock rotation of the screen, turn the volume up or down, or shake iPad to undo an action using the presets in this option
Home	Sends you to the Home screen
Control Center	Open the Control Center common commands
Notifications	Open Notifications with reminders, Calendar appointments, and so on

Turn On Additional Physical and Motor Settings

Use these On/Off settings in the Accessibility settings to help you deal with how fast you tap and how you answer incoming calls:

» **Home Button (non-iPad Pro models only):** Sometimes if you have dexterity challenges, it's hard to double-press or triple-press the Home button fast enough to make an effect. Choose the Slow or Slowest option when you tap this setting to allow you a bit more time to make that second or third tap. Also, the Rest Finger to Open feature at the bottom of the screen is helpful by allowing you to simply rest your finger on the Home button to open your iPad using Touch ID (if enabled), as opposed to needing to press the Home button.

» **Call Audio Routing (under Accessibility ⇨ Touch):** If you prefer to use your speaker phone to receive incoming calls, or you typically use a Bluetooth headset with your iPad that allows you to tap a button to receive a call, tap this option and then choose Bluetooth Headset or Speaker. Speakers and headsets can both provide a better hearing experience for many.

TIP

If you have certain adaptive accessories that allow you to control devices with head gestures, you can use them to control your iPad, highlighting features in sequence and then selecting one. Use the Switch Control feature in the Accessibility settings to turn this mode on and make settings.

Focus Learning with Guided Access

Guided Access is a feature that you can use to limit a user's access to iPad to a single app, and even limit access in that app to certain features.

1. Tap Settings and then tap Accessibility.

2. Scroll down and tap Guided Access; then, on the screen that follows, tap the Guided Access switch to turn the feature On (green).

3. Tap Passcode Settings and then tap Set Guided Access Passcode to activate a passcode so that those using an app can't return to the Home screen to access other apps. You may also activate Touch ID or Face ID (iPad Pro models only) to perform the same function.

4. In the Set Passcode dialog box that appears (see **Figure 5-14**), enter a passcode using the numeric pad. Enter the number again when prompted.

5. Press the Home button or swipe up from the bottom of the screen (iPad Pro models) to return to the Home screen, then tap an app to open it.

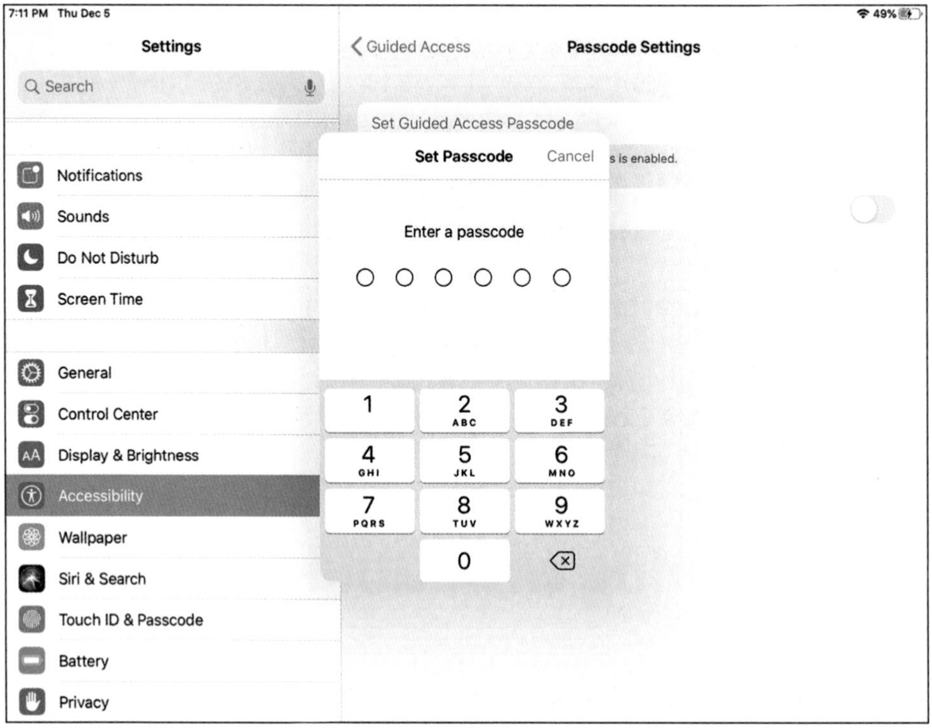

FIGURE 5-14

6. Rapidly press the Home button or top button (iPad Pro models) three times. You're presented with some Accessibility Shortcuts options on the screen; tap the Guided Access button, and then tap the Options button along the bottom of the screen to display these options in a dialog window:

- **Sleep/Wake Button:** You can put your iPad to sleep or wake it up with three presses of the Home button.

- **Volume Buttons:** You can tap Always On or Always Off. If you don't want users to be able to adjust volume using the volume toggle on the side of the iPad, for example, use this setting.

- **Motion:** Turn this setting off if you don't want users to move the iPad around — for example, to play a race car driving game.

- **Keyboards:** Use this setting to prohibit people using this app from entering text using the keyboard.

- **Touch:** If you don't want users to be able to use the touchscreen, turn this off.

- **Time Limit:** Tap this and use settings that are displayed to set a time limit for the use of the app.

7. Tap outside the dialog window to hide the options.

TIP

At this point, you can also use your finger to circle areas of the screen that you want to disable, such as a Store button in the Music app.

8. Press the Start button (upper-right corner) and then press the Home button or top button (iPad Pro models) three times. Enter your passcode, if you set one, and tap End.

9. Tap the Home button or swipe up from the bottom of the screen (iPad Pro models) again to return to the Home screen.

Control Your iPad with Voice Control

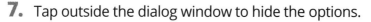

iPadOS 13 introduces an exciting accessibility innovation: the ability to control your iPad using your voice! As part of Voice Control, you can also use numbers and grid overlays to command your iPad to perform tasks. This feature is a real game–changer for a lot of folks.

1. Tap Settings and then tap Accessibility.

2. Scroll down and tap Voice Control. Then on the screen that follows (see **Figure 5-15**), tap Set Up Voice Control to begin.

TIP

You can easily tell when Voice Control is on, as there will be a blue circle containing a microphone in the upper-left corner of your iPad's screen.

3. Read through the information screens, tapping Continue to advance through them. Afterwards, you'll see the Voice Control toggle switch is set to On (green).

TIP

Pay particular attention to the What can I say? screen. It tells you in simple terms the commands you can use to get started with Voice Control, such as "Go home" and "Show grid."

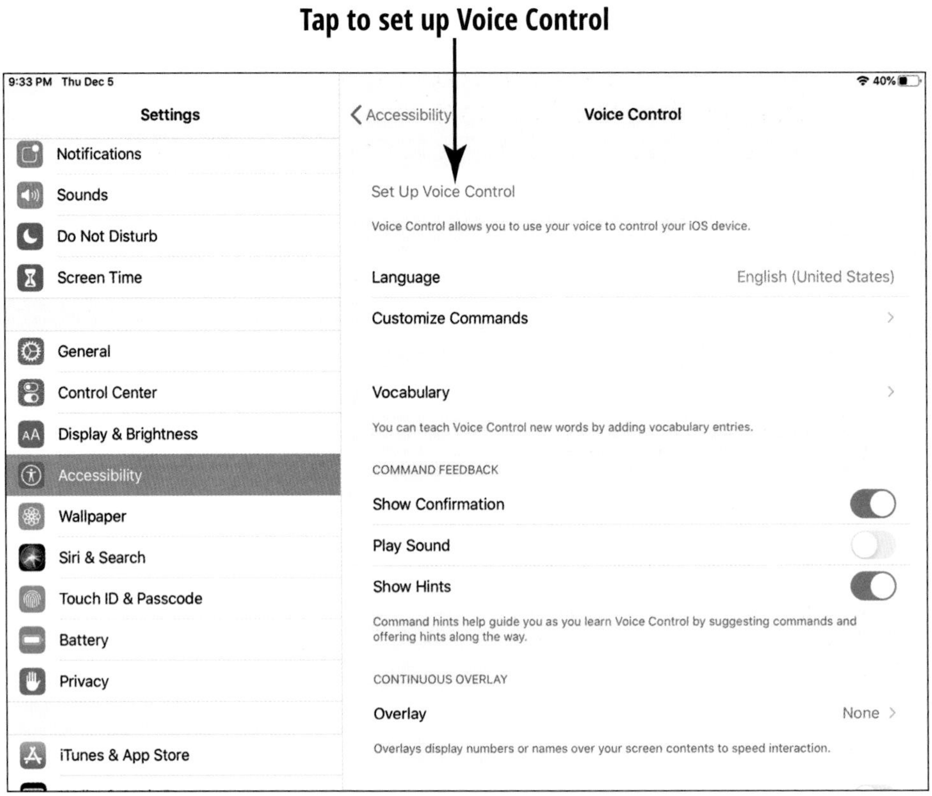

Tap to set up Voice Control

FIGURE 5-15

4. Tap Customize Commands to see what commands are built in to Voice Control (shown in **Figure 5-16**), enable or disable commands, and even create your own custom commands. I suggest taking your time in this section of the Voice Control options, as you'll be surprised at just what all you can do out of the gate with this amazing tool. Tap the Voice Control button in the upper-middle of the screen to return to the main Voice Control options.

5. You may need or want to use words that Voice Control doesn't know or understand, so Apple's given you the ability to add words. This is particularly useful with dictation. In the Voice Control options, tap

Vocabulary and then tap the + in the upper-right to add your own words. Type the word or phrase you'd like to add in the Add New Entry window and then tap the Save button. Tap Voice Control in the upper-left to return to the main Voice Control screen.

9:38 PM Thu Dec 5		🌙 📶 39% 🔋
Settings	‹ Voice Control **Customize Commands**	
📱 Notifications	🔍 Search	🎤
🔊 Sounds		
🌙 Do Not Disturb	Create New Command...	›
⏳ Screen Time		
	Basic Navigation	›
⚙️ General	Overlays	›
🎛 Control Center	Basic Gestures	›
AA Display & Brightness	Advanced Gestures	›
♿ Accessibility	Dictation	›
🌼 Wallpaper	Text Navigation	›
🔍 Siri & Search	Text Selection	›
👆 Touch ID & Passcode	Text Editing	›
🔋 Battery	Text Deletion	›
✋ Privacy	Device	›
	Accessibility	›
🅐 iTunes & App Store		

FIGURE 5-16

6. Overlays are a fantastic accessibility addition to iPadOS 13. If you use them, clickable items on the screen are labeled with numbers, names, or a numbered grid. Whenever you want to click an item, simply execute a command such as "tap three" to "tap" the item with your voice. Each of the three overlays are displayed in **Figure 5-17**.

TIP

The number and name labels will fade to a light gray so you can more clearly see the screen when not actively using the feature, but will darken again when you do use it.

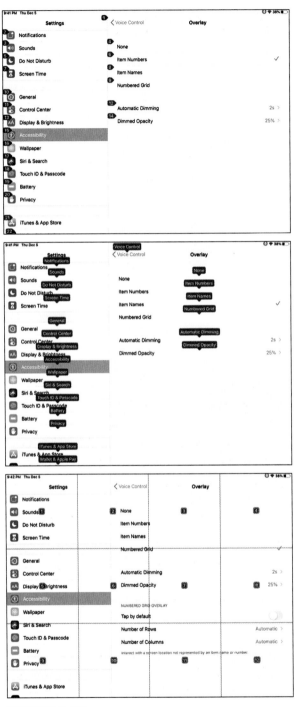

FIGURE 5-17

Chapter **6**

Conversing with Siri

One of the most popular features on your iPad is Siri, a personal assistant feature that responds to the commands you speak to your iPad. With Siri, you can ask for nearby restaurants, and a list appears. You can dictate your email messages rather than type them. You can open apps with a voice command or open the App Store. Placing a FaceTime call to your mother is as simple as saying, "Call Mom." Want to know the capital of Rhode Island? Just ask. Siri checks several online sources to answer questions ranging from the result of a mathematical equation to the next scheduled flight to Rome (Italy or Georgia). You can have Siri search photos and videos and locate what you need by date, location, or album name. Ask Siri to remind you about an app you're working in, such as Safari, Mail, or Notes, at a later time so that you can pick up where you left off.

You can also have Siri perform tasks, such as returning calls and controlling Music. Siri can play music at your request and identify tagged songs (songs that contain embedded information that identifies them by categories such as artist or genre of music) for you. You can also hail a ride with Uber or Lyft, watch live TV just by saying "Watch ESPN" (or, say, another app you might use, such as CBS), find tagged photos, make payments with some third-party apps, and more.

With iPadOS 13, Siri can offer you curated suggestions for Safari, Maps, and Podcasts. Siri also features new voice technology that allows it to sound more natural and smooth, particularly when speaking long phrases.

Activate Siri

When you first turn on your iPad, Apple walks you through the process of registering and setting it up onscreen. Tap Get Started to begin making settings for your location, using iCloud, and so on, and at one point, you will see the option to activate Siri. As you begin to use your device, iPad reminds you about using Siri by displaying a message.

TIP If you buy a car with the Car Play feature, you can interact with your car using your voice and Siri.

TIP Siri is available on the iPad only when you have Internet access, but remember that cellular data charges may apply when Siri checks online sources. In addition, Apple warns that available features may vary by area.

If you didn't activate Siri during the registration process, you can use Settings to turn Siri on by following these steps:

1. Tap the Settings icon on the Home screen.

2. Tap Siri & Search (see **Figure 6-1**).

3. In the Siri & Search dialog box on the right, toggle the On/Off switch to On (green) to activate any or all of the following features:

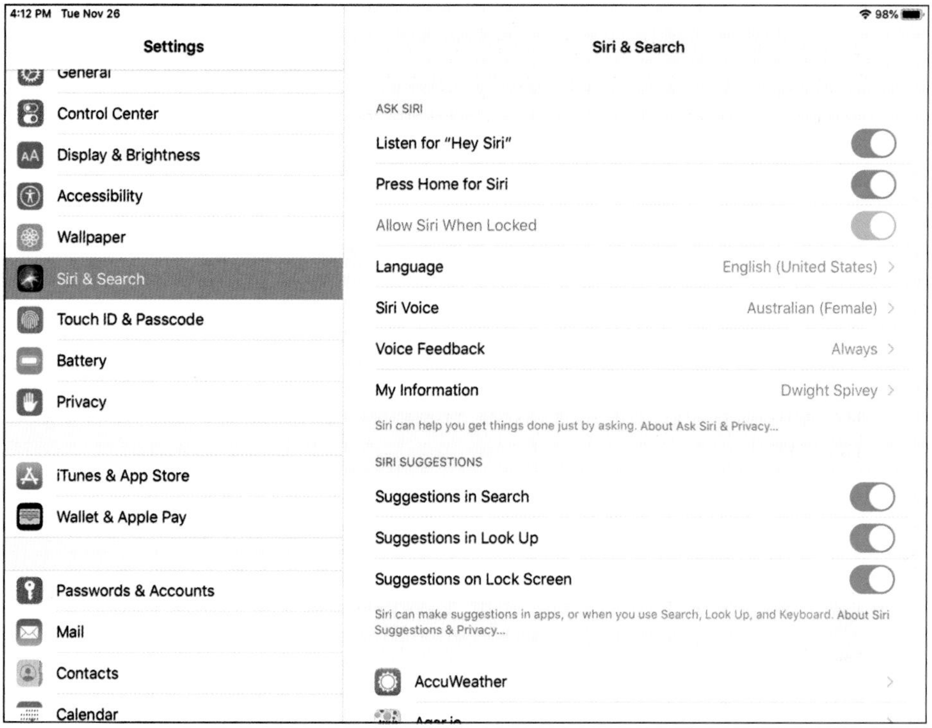

FIGURE 6-1

- If you want to be able to activate Siri for hands-free use, toggle the Listen for "Hey Siri" switch to turn on the feature. When you first enable "Hey Siri," you'll be promted to set up the feature. Just walk through the steps to enable it and continue.

  With this feature enabled, just say "Hey, Siri," and Siri opens up, ready for a command. In addition, with streaming voice recognition, Siri displays in text what it's hearing as you speak, so you can verify that it has understood you correctly. This streaming feature makes the whole process of interacting with Siri faster.

  Some iPad models must be plugged into a power source to use the "Hey Siri" feature and others don't. Visit `https://support.apple.com/en-us/HT209014` to find out if your model supports using "Hey Siri" without needing to be plugged in.

- Press Home for Siri requires you to press the Home button to activate Siri. Alternatively, iPad Pro users will see Press Top Button for Siri, requiring the press of the Top button to activate Siri.

- Allow Siri When Locked allows you to use Siri even when the iPad is locked.

4. If you want to change the language Siri uses, tap Language and choose a different language in the list that appears.

5. To change the nationality or gender of Siri's voice from American to British or Australian (for example), or from female to male, tap Siri Voice and make your selections.

6. Let Siri know about your contact information by tapping My Information and selecting yourself from your Contacts.

TIP

If you want Siri to verbally respond to your requests only when the iPad isn't in your hands, tap Voice Feedback and choose Hands-Free Only. Here's how this setting works and why you may want to use it: In general, if you're holding your iPad, you can read responses on the screen, so you might choose not to have your device talk to you out loud. But if you're cooking dinner while helping your spouse make travel plans and want to speak requests for destinations and hear the answers rather than have to read them, Hands-Free Only is a useful setting.

Understand All That Siri Can Do

Siri allows you to interact by voice with many apps on your iPad.

REMEMBER

No matter what kind of action you want to perform, first press and hold the Home button until Siri opens.

You can pose questions or ask to do something like make a FaceTime call or add an appointment to your calendar, for example. Siri can also search the Internet or use an informational service called Wolfram|Alpha to provide information on just about any topic.

TIP

To see examples of what Siri can do for you, engage Siri but don't say anything. In a few seconds, Siri will display a list like the one in **Figure 6-2**.

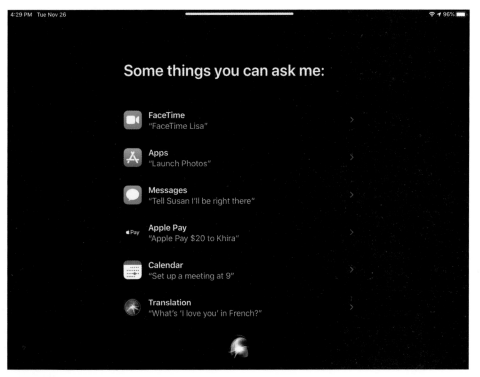

Some things you can ask me:

FaceTime
"FaceTime Lisa"   >

Apps
"Launch Photos"   >

Messages
"Tell Susan I'll be right there"   >

Apple Pay
"Apple Pay $20 to Khira"   >

Calendar
"Set up a meeting at 9"   >

Translation
"What's 'I love you' in French?"   >

FIGURE 6-2

Siri also checks with Wikipedia and Twitter to get you the information you ask for. In addition, you can use Siri to tell iPad to return a call, play your voice mail, open and search the App Store, control Music playback, dictate test messages, and much more.

With iPadOS 13, Siri learns your daily habits and will offer suggestions throughout the day when appropriate. For example, say you usually stop by the local coffee shop around the same time each morning and use the shops app to order a drink from your iPad. Siri will pick up on this activity and eventually begin asking if you'd like to order a drink when you're within proximity of the coffee shop.

Siri knows what app you're using, though you don't have to have that app open to make a request involving it. However, if you are in the Messages app, you can make a statement like "Tell Susan I'll be late," and Siri knows that you want to send a message. You can also ask Siri to remind you about what you're working on, and Siri notes what you're working on, in which app, and reminds you about it at a later time you specify.

TIP

If you want to dictate text in an app like Notes, use the Dictation key on the onscreen keyboard to do so. See the section "Use Dictation," later in this chapter, for more about this feature.

Siri requires no preset structure for your questions; you can phrase things in several ways. For example, you might say, "Where am I?" to see a map of your current location, or you could say, "What is my current location?" or "What address is this?" and get the same results.

If you ask a question about, say, the weather, Siri responds to you both verbally and with text information (see **Figure 6-3**) or by opening a form, as with email, or by providing a graphic display for some items, such as maps. When a result appears, you can tap it to make a choice or open a related app.

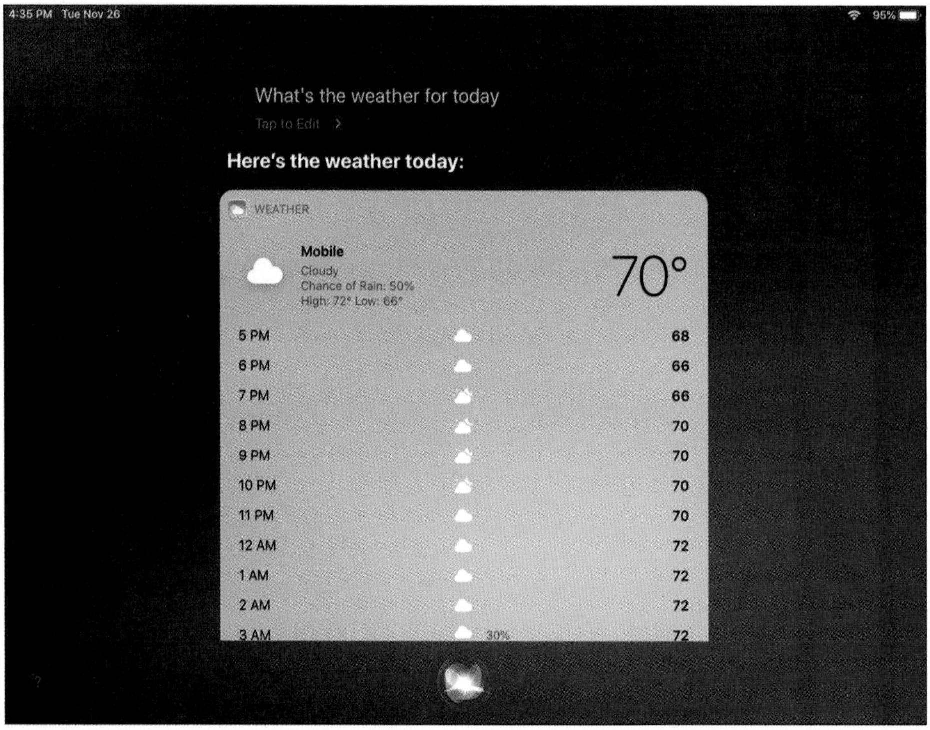

4:35 PM Tue Nov 26   95%

What's the weather for today
Tap to Edit >

Here's the weather today:

WEATHER		
Mobile Cloudy Chance of Rain: 50% High: 72° Low: 66°		70°
5 PM		68
6 PM		66
7 PM		66
8 PM		70
9 PM		70
10 PM		70
11 PM		70
12 AM		72
1 AM		72
2 AM		72
3 AM	30%	72

FIGURE 6-3

Siri works with FaceTime, the App Store, Music, Messages, Reminders, Calendar, Maps, Mail, Weather, Stocks, Clock, Contacts, Notes, social media apps (such as Twitter), and Safari (see **Figure 6-4**). In the following sections, I provide a quick guide to some of the most useful ways you can use Siri.

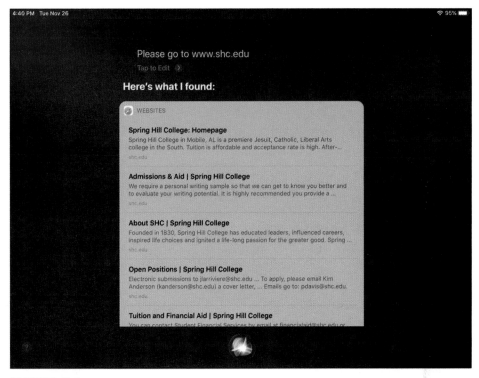

FIGURE 6-4

TIP

Siri now supports many different languages, so you can finally show off those language lessons you took in high school. Some languages supported include Chinese, Dutch, English, French, German, Italian, Spanish, Arabic, Danish, Finnish, Hebrew, Japanese, Korean, and more!

Get Suggestions

Siri anticipates your needs by making suggestions when you swipe from left to right on the Home screen and tap within the Search field at the top of the screen. Siri will list contacts you've communicated with recently, apps you've used, and nearby businesses, such as restaurants, gas stations, or coffee spots. If you tap on an app in the suggestions, it will open displaying the last viewed or listened to item.

Additionally, Siri lists news stories that may be of interest to you based on items you've viewed before.

Call Contacts via FaceTime

First, make sure that the person you want to call is entered in your Contacts app and include that person's phone number in his record. If you want to call somebody by stating your relationship to her, such as "Call sister," be sure to enter that relationship in the Add Related Name field in her contact record. Also make sure that the settings for Siri (refer to Figure 6-1) include your own contact name in the My Information field. (See Chapter 8 for more about creating contact records.)

To call contacts via FaceTime, follow these steps:

1. Press and hold the Home button (or say "Hey, Siri," if you're using that feature) until Siri appears.

2. Speak a command, such as "Make a FaceTime call to Cindy," or say "FaceTime Mom."

3. If you have two contacts who might match a spoken name, Siri responds with a list of possible matches (see **Figure 6-5**). Tap one in the list or state the correct contact's name to proceed.

4. The call is placed. To end the call before it completes, press the Home button and then tap End.

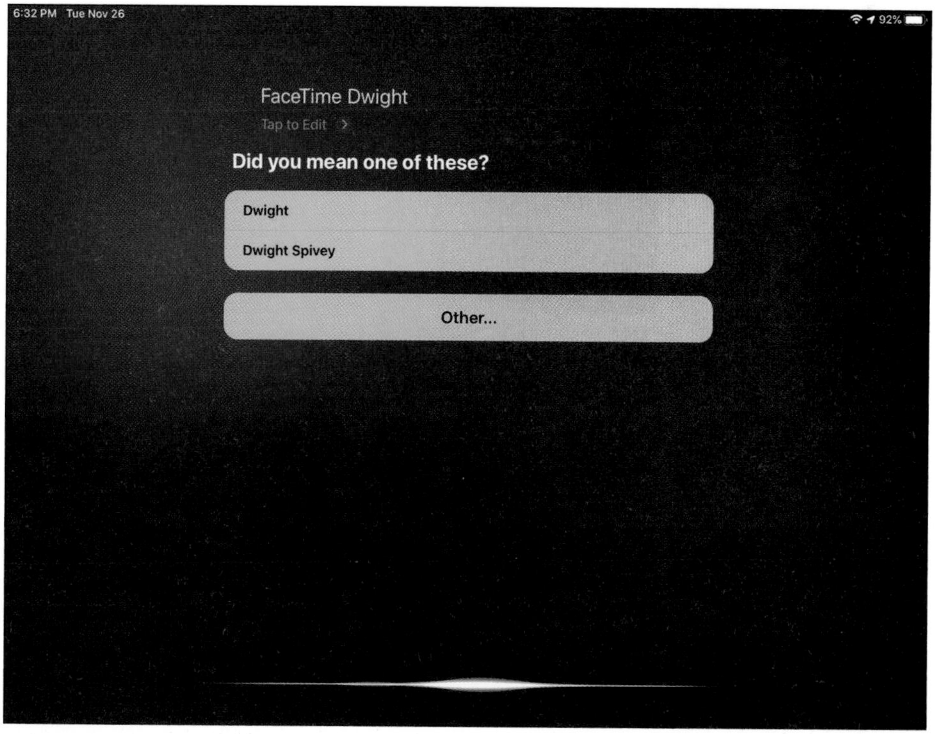

FIGURE 6-5

To cancel any spoken request, you have three options: Say "Cancel," tap the Siri button on the Siri screen (looks like swirling bands of light), or press the Home button. If you're using a headset or Bluetooth device, tap the End button on the device.

TIP

Create Reminders and Alerts

You can also use Siri with the Reminders app:

1. To create a reminder or alert, press and hold the Home button or Top button (iPhone Pro models) and then speak a command, such as "Remind me to call Dad on Thursday at 10 a.m." or "Wake me up tomorrow at 6:15 a.m."

2. A preview of the reminder or alert is displayed (see **Figure 6-6**). Tell Siri to Cancel or Remove if you change your mind.

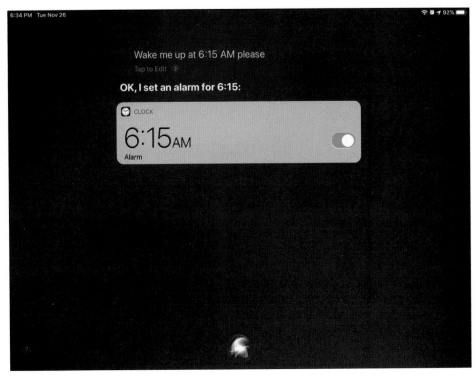

FIGURE 6-6

3. If you want a reminder ahead of the event that you created, activate Siri and speak a command, such as "Remind me tonight about the play on Thursday at 8 p.m." A second reminder is created, which you can confirm or cancel if you change your mind.

Add Tasks to Your Calendar

You can also set up events on your Calendar using Siri:

1. Press and hold the Home button and then speak a phrase, such as "Set up meeting at 3 p.m. tomorrow."

2. Siri sets up the appointment (see **Figure 6-7**) and asks you to let it know if you want to make changes.

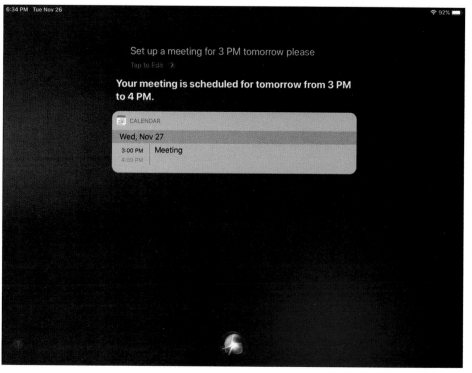

FIGURE 6-7

Play Music

You can use Siri to play music from the Music app:

1. Press and hold the Home button until Siri appears.

2. To play music, speak a command, such as "Play music" or "Play Jazz radio station" to play a specific song, album, or radio station, as seen in **Figure 6-8**.

You can use the integration of iPad with Shazam, a music identifier app (you'll need to download it from the App Store), to identify tagged music.

1. When you're near an audio source playing music, press and hold the Home button or Top button (iPad Pro) to activate Siri.

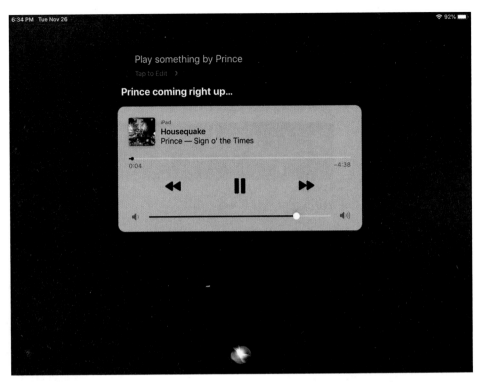

FIGURE 6-8

2. Ask Siri a question, such as "What music is playing?" or "What's this song?"

3. Siri listens for a bit. If Siri recognizes the song, it shows you the song name, artist, any other available information, and the ability to purchase the music in the iTunes Store.

TIP

If you're listening to music or a podcast with earphones plugged in and stop midstream, the next time you plug in earphones, Siri recognizes that you may want to continue with the same item.

Get Directions

You can use the Maps app and Siri to find your current location, get directions, find nearby businesses (such as restaurants or a bank), or get a map of another location. Be sure to turn on Location Services to allow Siri to know your current location (go to Settings and tap Privacy⇨Location Services; make sure Location Services is on and that Siri & Dictation is turned on further down in these settings).

Here are some of the commands that you can try to get directions or a list of nearby businesses:

» **"Where am I?"** Displays a map of your current location.
» **"Where is Spring Hill College?"** Displays a map of that city, as shown in **Figure 6-9**.

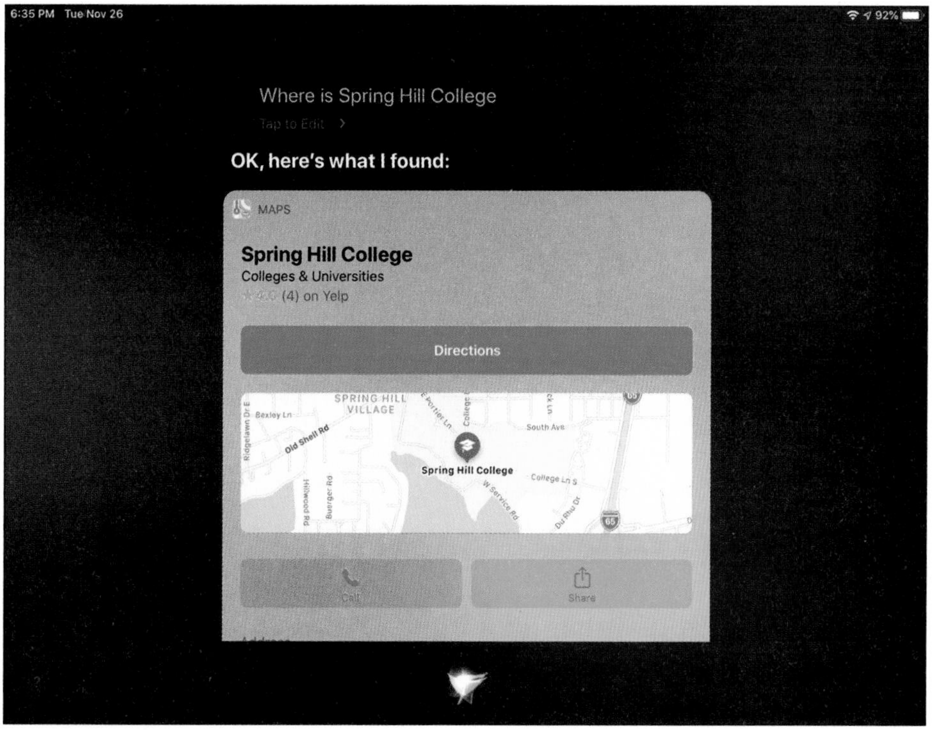

FIGURE 6-9

» **"Find pizza restaurants."** Displays a list of restaurants near your current location; tap one to display a map of its location.

» **"Find Bank of America."** Displays a map with the location of the indicated business (or in some cases, several nearby locations, such as a bank branch and all ATMs).

» **"Get directions to the Empire State Building."** Loads a map with a route drawn and provides a narration of directions to the site from your current location.

TIP

After a location is displayed on a map, tap the Information button on the location's label to view its address, phone number, and website address, if available.

Ask for Facts

Siri uses online sources including Wikipedia to look up facts in response to questions, such as "What is the capital of Kansas?", "What is the square root of 2,300?", or "How large is Mars?" Just press and hold the Home button and ask your question; Siri consults its resources and returns a set of relevant facts.

You can also get information about other things, such as the weather, stocks, or the time. Just say a phrase like one of these to get what you need:

Search the Web

Although Siri can use its resources to respond to specific requests such as "Who is the Queen of England?", more general requests for information will cause Siri to search further on the web. Siri can also search Twitter for comments related to your search.

For example, if you speak a phrase, such as "Find a website about birds" or "Find information about the World Series," Siri can respond in a couple of ways. The app can simply display a list of search results by using the default search engine specified in your settings for Safari or by suggesting, "If you like, I can search the web for such and such." In the first instance, just tap a result to go to that website. In the second instance, you can confirm that you want to search the web or cancel.

Send Email, Messages, or Tweets

You can create an email or an instant message using Siri and existing contacts. For example, if you say "Email John Michael Bassett," a form opens that is already addressed to that stored contact. Siri asks for a subject and then a message. Speak your message contents and then say "Send" to speed your message on its way.

Siri also works with messaging apps, such as Messages. If you have the Messages app open and you say "Tell Victoria I'll call soon," Siri creates a message for you to approve and send.

Use Dictation

Text entry isn't Siri's strong point. Instead, you can use the Dictation key that appears with a microphone symbol on the onscreen keyboard (see **Figure 6-10**) to speak text rather than type it. This feature is called Dictation.

To use dictation:

1. Go to any app where you enter text, such as Notes or Mail, and tap in the document or form. The onscreen keyboard appears.

2. Tap the Dictation key on the keyboard and speak your text.

3. To end the dictation, tap Done.

When you finish speaking text, you can use the keyboard to make edits to the text Siri entered, although as voice recognition programs go, Dictation is pretty darn accurate. If a word sports a blue underline, which means there may be an error, you can tap to select and make edits to it.

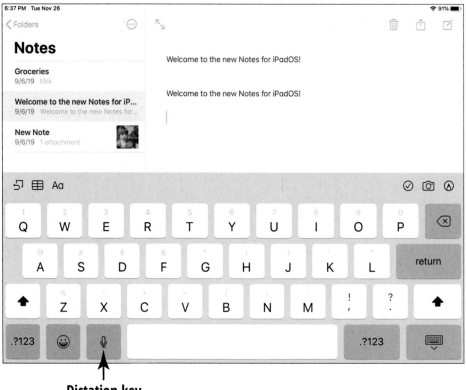

Dictation key

FIGURE 6-10

Translate Words and Phrases

One of Siri's coolest features is the ability to translate English into multiple languages (including Mandarin, French, German, Italian, Spanish, and more), with support for over 40 language pairs, according to Apple. That's great if you're on a road trip and don't speak the local language.

TECHNICAL STUFF

Apple is continually expanding this feature, and its potential is very exciting.

1. Activate Siri.

2. Say "translate" followed by your phrase and the language of your choice, as illustrated in **Figure 6-11**.

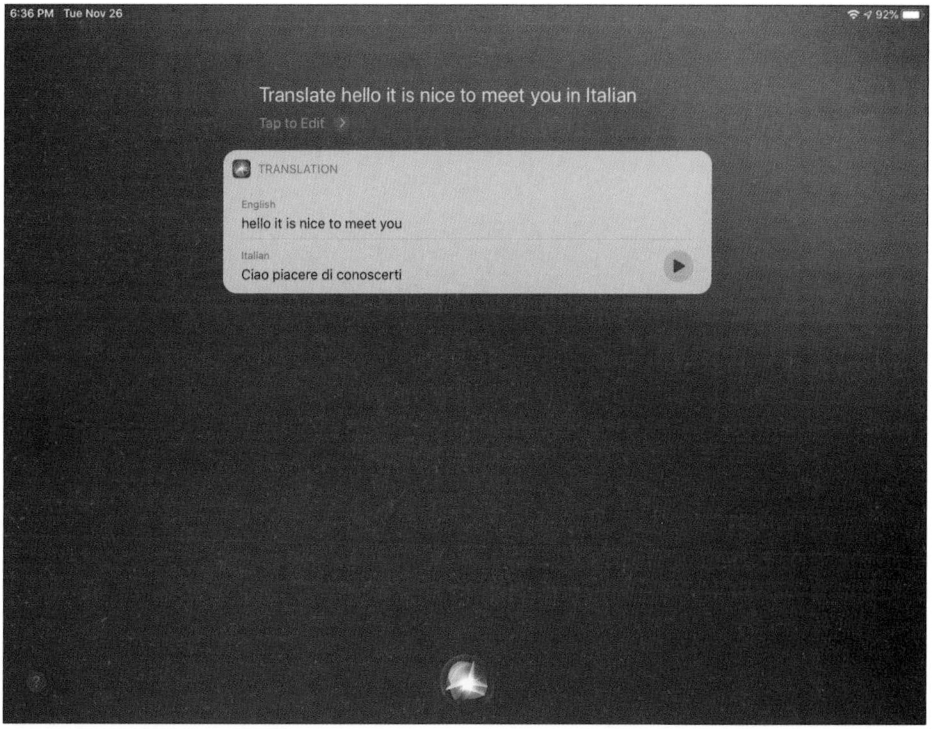

FIGURE 6-11

3. Siri displays the translation on your screen and speaks it while also providing a phonetic translation to help with pronunciation.

Tap the Play button to the left of the translation to hear Siri speak it again.

TIP

Type Your Commands or Questions

Type to Siri is another great feature of Siri. It allows you to type commands or inquiries instead of verbalizing them.

This feature is great if you have difficulty speaking or if you're in a situation where you're not able to speak.

TIP

To enable this feature:

1. Go to Settings ⇨ Accessibility.
2. Tap Siri and then toggle the switch for Type to Siri to On (green).
3. Now, when you activate Siri, a keyboard appears for you to enter your commands or questions (see **Figure 6-12**).

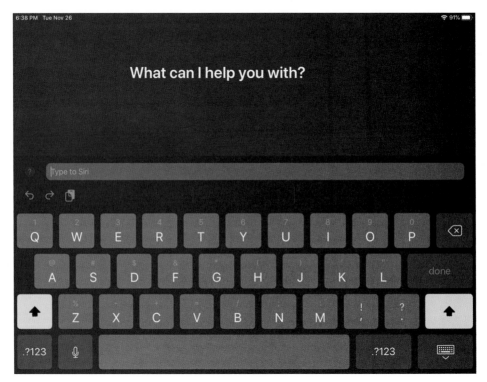

FIGURE 6-12

Chapter **7**

Expanding Your iPad Horizons with Apps

S ome apps (short for *applications*), such as News and Music, come preinstalled on your iPad with iPadOS. But you can choose from a world of other apps out there for your iPad — some for free (such as USA Today) and some for a price (typically, ranging from 99 cents to about $10, though some can top out at much steeper prices).

Apps range from games to financial tools (such as loan calculators) to apps that help you when you're planning an exercise regimen or taking a trip. Still more apps are developed for use by private entities, such as hospitals and government agencies.

In this chapter, I suggest some apps that you may want to check out, explain how to use the App Store feature of your iPad to find, purchase, and download apps, and detail how to organize your apps. We'll also find out a bit about having fun with games on your iPad.

Search the App Store

Access the App Store by tapping the App Store icon on the Home screen. You can start by exploring the Today tab (which features special apps and articles), by Categories, or by the Top Charts (see the buttons along the bottom of the screen). Or you can tap Search and find apps on your own. Tap an app to see more information about it.

If you've got the time, you can find lots of happy surprises by simply browsing the App Store, but if you' re in a hurry or already know what you're looking for, a search is the best way to go.

To search the App Store:

1. Tap the App Store icon on the Home screen; by default, the first time you use App Store, it will open to the Today tab, as shown in **Figure 7-1.**

2. At this point, you have several options for finding apps:

   - Scroll downward to view various featured apps and articles, such as The Daily List and Our Favorites.

     Tap a category to see more apps in it.

   - Tap the Apps tab at the bottom of the screen to browse by the type of app you're looking for or search by categories (tap the See All button in the Top Categories section), such as Lifestyle or Medical, as shown in **Figure 7-2.**

   - Tap the Games tab at the bottom of the screen to see the newest releases and bestselling games. Explore by paid apps, free apps, by categories, and even by special subjects such as The Most Beautiful Games and What We're Playing Today.

FIGURE 7-1

- Tap the Search button at the bottom of the screen, then tap in the
  Search field, enter a search term, and tap the result you want to
  view.

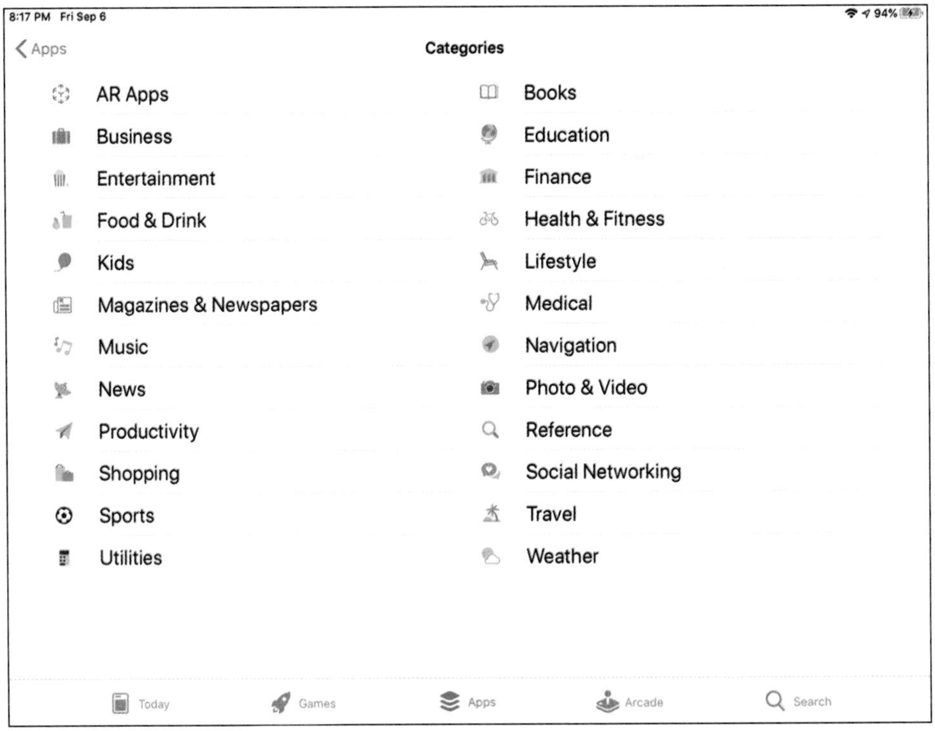

< Apps   **Categories**

⚙	AR Apps	📖	Books
🏛	Business	🎓	Education
🎬	Entertainment	🏦	Finance
🍴	Food & Drink	🚴	Health & Fitness
💬	Kids	🛋	Lifestyle
📰	Magazines & Newspapers	⚕	Medical
🎵	Music	🧭	Navigation
🐾	News	📷	Photo & Video
✈	Productivity	🔍	Reference
🛍	Shopping	💬	Social Networking
⚽	Sports	🏖	Travel
⚙	Utilities	🌤	Weather

📱 Today   🚀 Games   📚 Apps   🎮 Arcade   🔍 Search

FIGURE 7-2

Get Applications from the App Store

Buying or getting free apps requires that you have an iTunes account, which I covered in Chapter 3. After you have an account, you can use the saved payment information there to buy apps or download free apps with a few simple steps:

1. With the App Store open, tap the Apps tab and then tap the See All button (blue text to the right) in the Top Free Apps section, as shown in **Figure 7-3.**

2. Tap the Get button for an app that appeals to you or, if you'd like more information, simply tap the app's icon. If you already have the app and an update is available for it, the button will be labeled

Update. If you've previously downloaded the app, but it's no longer on you iPad, the icon looks like a cloud with a downward arrow; tap to download it again.

See All button

FIGURE 7-3

To get a paid app, you tap the same button, which is then labeled with a price.

TIP If you've opened an iCloud account, you can set it up so that anything you purchase on your iPad is automatically pushed to other Apple iPadOS or iOS devices (such as an iPhone or another iPad) and your iTunes library, and vice versa. See Chapter 3 for more about iCloud.

3. A sheet opens on-screen listing the app and the iTunes account being used to get/purchase the app. Tap Enter Password at the bottom of the sheet, tap the Password field, and then enter the password. Alternatively, you may simply only need to use Touch ID or Face ID (whichever your iPad model supports) to approve the download/purchase. The Get button changes to the Installing button, which looks like a circle; the thick blue line on the circle represents the progress of the installation.

4. The app downloads, and you can find it on one of the Home screens. If you purchase an app that isn't free, your credit card or gift card balance is charged at this point for the purchase price.

Organize Your Applications on Home Screens

By default, the first Home screen contains preinstalled apps, and the second contains a few more preinstalled apps. Once those initial screens are fully populated with app icons, other screens are created to contain any further apps you download or sync to your iPad. At the bottom of any iPad Home screen (just above the Dock), dots indicate the number of Home screens you've filled with apps; a solid white dot specifies which Home screen you're on now, as shown in **Figure 7-4**.

1. Press the Home button to open the last displayed Home screen.

2. Flick your finger from right to left to move to the next Home screen. To move back, flick from left to right.

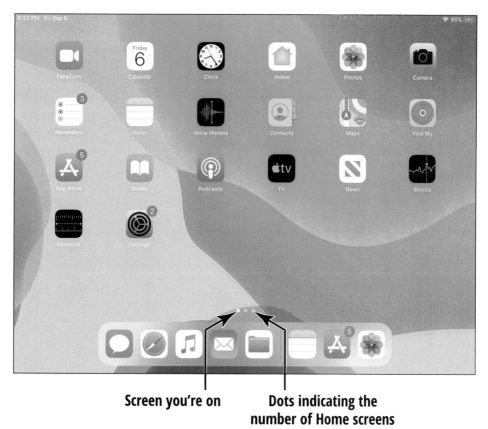

Screen you're on   **Dots indicating the number of Home screens**

FIGURE 7-4

3. To reorganize apps on a Home screen, press and hold any app on that page to open a contextual menu; tap Rearrange Apps, as shown in **Figure 7-5**. Alternatively, press and hold the app icon just a bit longer to skip the menu, if you prefer.

4. The app icons begin to jiggle (see **Figure 7-6**), and many (not all) apps will sport a Delete button (a gray circle with a black X on it).

Tap here to rearrange apps

FIGURE 7-5

5. Press, hold, and drag an app icon to another location on the screen to move it.

TIP

To move an app from one page to another, while the apps are jiggling, you can press, hold, and drag an app to the left or right to move it to the next Home screen. You can also manage which app resides on which Home screen and change the order of the Home screens from iTunes when you've connected your iPad to iTunes on your computer via a cable or wireless sync.

6. Press the Home button (or swipe up from the bottom if you have an iPad Pro) to stop all those icons from jiggling!

A Delete button

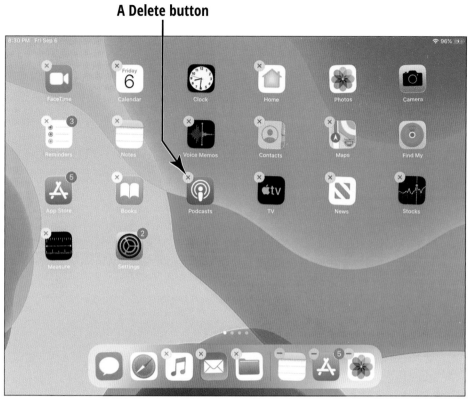

FIGURE 7-6

Organize Apps in Folders

iPad lets you organize apps in folders so that you can find them more easily. The process is simple:

1. Press and hold an app until all apps start jiggling.

2. Drag one app on top of another app.

   The two apps appear in a box with a placeholder name in a box above them (see **Figure 7-7**).

3. To change the name, tap in the field at the end of the placeholder name, and the keyboard appears.

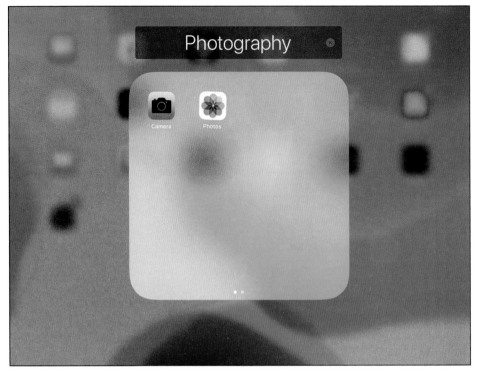

FIGURE 7-7

4. Tap the Delete key to delete the placeholder name and type one of your own.

5. Tap Done and then tap anywhere outside the box to close it.

6. Press the Home button to stop the icons from dancing around. You see your folder on the Home screen where you began this process.

TIP

Here's a neat trick that allows you to move multiple apps together at the same time:

1. Press and hold the first app you'd like to move until the apps are jiggling.

2. Move the app just a bit so that it's no longer in its original place.

3. With your free hand, tap the other app(s) you'd like to move along with the first app. As you tap additional apps, their icons "move under" or "attach themselves" to the first app.

4. Once you've selected all your apps, move them to their new location; they'll all move together in a little app caravan.

Delete Apps You No Longer Need

When you no longer need an app you've installed, it's time to get rid of it. You can also remove most of the preinstalled apps that are native to iPadOS. If you use iCloud to push content across all Apple iPadOS or iOS devices, deleting an app on your iPad won't affect that app on other devices.

1. Display the Home screen that contains the app you want to delete.
2. Press and hold the app until all apps begin to jiggle.
3. Tap the Delete button for the app you want to delete. A confirmation like the one shown in **Figure 7-8** appears.
4. Tap Delete to proceed with the deletion.

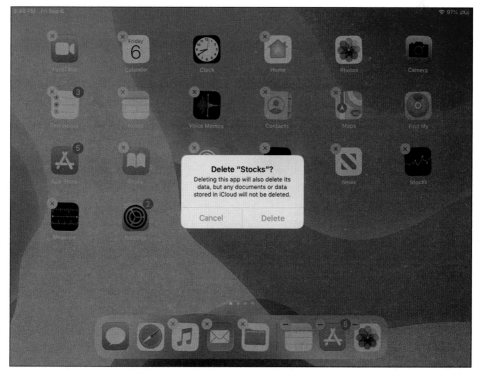

FIGURE 7-8

Update Apps

App developers update their apps all the time, so you might want to check for those updates. The App Store icon on the Home screen displays the number of available updates in a red circle. To update apps, follow these steps:

1. Tap the App Store icon on the Home screen.

2. Tap the Account button (an icon in the upper-right on the Apps screen, similar to the one shown in **Figure 7-9**); it will display a red badge with a number in it if updates are available.

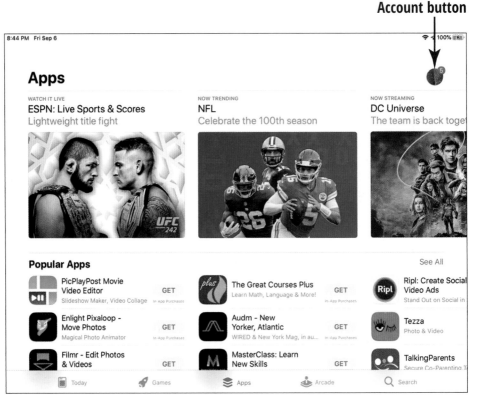

FIGURE 7-9

3. In the Account window that opens, scroll down to the Available Updates section and tap the Update button (see **Figure 7-10** for examples) for any item you want to update. Note that if you have Family Sharing turned on, there will be a folder titled Family Purchases that you can tap to display apps that are shared across your family's devices. To update all at once, tap the blue Update All button to the left.

4. You may be asked to confirm that you want to update, or to enter your Apple ID; after you do, tap OK to proceed. You may also be asked to confirm that you are over a certain age or agree to terms and conditions. If so, scroll down the terms dialog box and, at the bottom, tap Agree. The download progress is displayed.

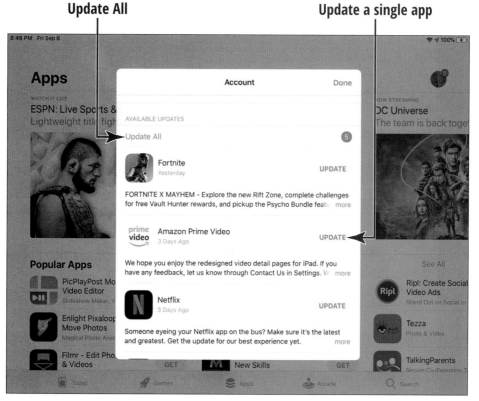

FIGURE 7-10

Purchase and Download Games

Time to get your game on!

The iPad is super for playing games, with its bright screen, portable size, and ability to rotate the screen as you play and track your motions. You can download game apps from the App Store and play them on your device.

1. Open the App Store.

2. Tap the Games button at the bottom of the screen to view the Games screen.

3. Navigating the Games screen is simple:

   • Swipe from right to left to see featured apps in such categories as "What We're Playing Today" and "Editors' Choice."

   • Swipe down to find the Top Paid and Free games or to shop by categories (tap See All to view all of the available categories).

4. Explore the list of games in the type you selected until you find something you like; tap the game to see its information screen.

5. To buy a game, tap the button labeled with either the word Get or the price (such as $2.99).

6. When the dialog box opens appears at the bottom of the screen, tap Purchase (if it's a Paid game) or Install (if it's a Free game), type your password in the Password field on the next screen, and then tap Sign In to download the game. Alternatively, use Touch ID or Face ID (for iPad models that support them) if it's enabled for iTunes and App Store purchases. The dialog box will display "Pay with Touch ID," or you'll be prompted to double-click the Side button to initiate Face ID authentication (iPad models without Home buttons only).

WARNING

I would warn against using Touch ID or Face ID for iTunes and App Store purchases. I know it's simpler than entering a password, but it can also make it easier for others to make purchases. In case you're wondering how that could be so, my children have actually tried holding my iPad in front of my face while I was asleep in a clandestine attempt at purchasing the latest game craze with Face ID. Imagine your grandkids trying to do the same and I believe you'll see where I'm coming from.

7. The game downloads. Tap the Open button to go to the downloaded game or find the games icon on your Home screen and tap to open it.

8. Have fun!

Chapter **8**

Managing Contacts

The Contacts app is the iPad equivalent of the dog-eared address book that used to sit by your phone. This app is simple to set up and use, and it has some powerful features beyond simply storing names, addresses, and phone numbers.

For example, you can pinpoint a contact's address in iPad's Maps app. You can use your contacts to address email and Facebook messages and Twitter tweets quickly. If you store a contact record that includes a website, you can use a link in Contacts to view that website instantly. In addition, of course, you can easily search for a contact by a variety of criteria, including how people are related to you, such as family or mutual friends, or by groups you create.

In this chapter, you discover the various features of Contacts, including how to save yourself time spent entering contact information by syncing contacts with such services as iCloud.

To add a contact to Contacts:

1. Tap the Contacts icon on the Home screen. An alphabetical list of contacts appears, like the one shown in **Figure 8-1**.

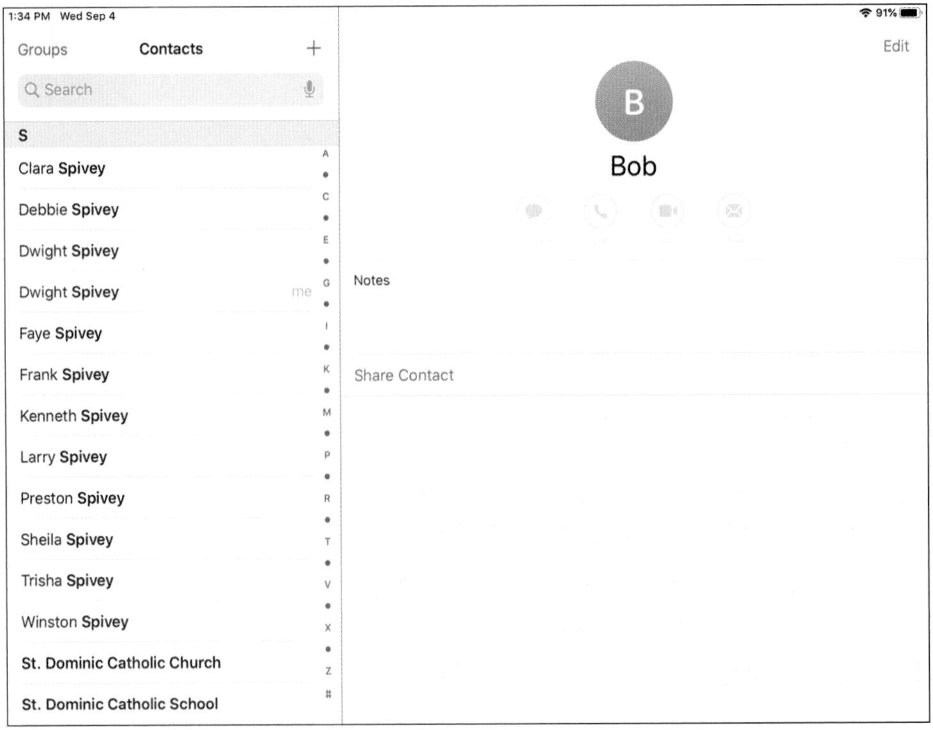

FIGURE 8-1

2. Tap the Add button, the button with the small plus sign (+) on it in the upper-right corner of the Contacts list. A blank New Contact page opens (see **Figure 8-2**). Tap in any field, and the onscreen keyboard displays.

FIGURE 8-2

TECHNICAL
STUFF

3. Enter any contact information you want.

Only one of the First name, Last name, or Company fields is required, but do feel free to add as much information as you like.

4. To scroll down the contact's page and see more fields, flick up on the screen with your finger.

5. If you want to add information (such as a mailing or street address), you can tap the relevant Add field, which opens additional entry fields.

6. To add an information field, such as Nickname or Job Title, tap the blue Add Field button at the bottom of the page. In the Add Field dialog box that appears (see **Figure 8-3**), choose a field to add.

You may have to flick up or down the screen with your finger to view all the fields.

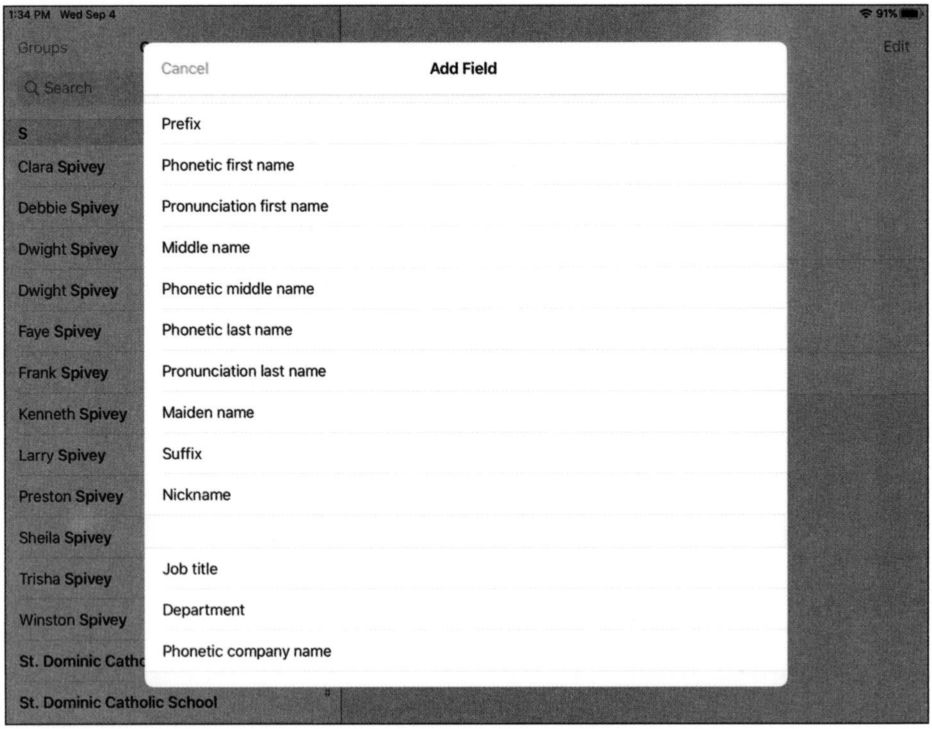

FIGURE 8-3

TIP

If your contact has a name that's difficult for you to pronounce, consider adding the Phonetic First Name or Phonetic Last Name field, or both, to that person's record (refer to Step 6).

7. Tap the Done button in the upper-right corner when you finish making entries. The new contact appears in your address book. Tap it to see details (see **Figure 8-4**).

TIP

You can choose a distinct ringtone or text tone for a new contact. Just tap the Ringtone or Text Tone field in the New Contact form or when editing a contact to see a list of options. When that person calls either on the phone or via FaceTime or texts you via SMS, MMS, or iMessage, you will recognize them from the tone that plays.

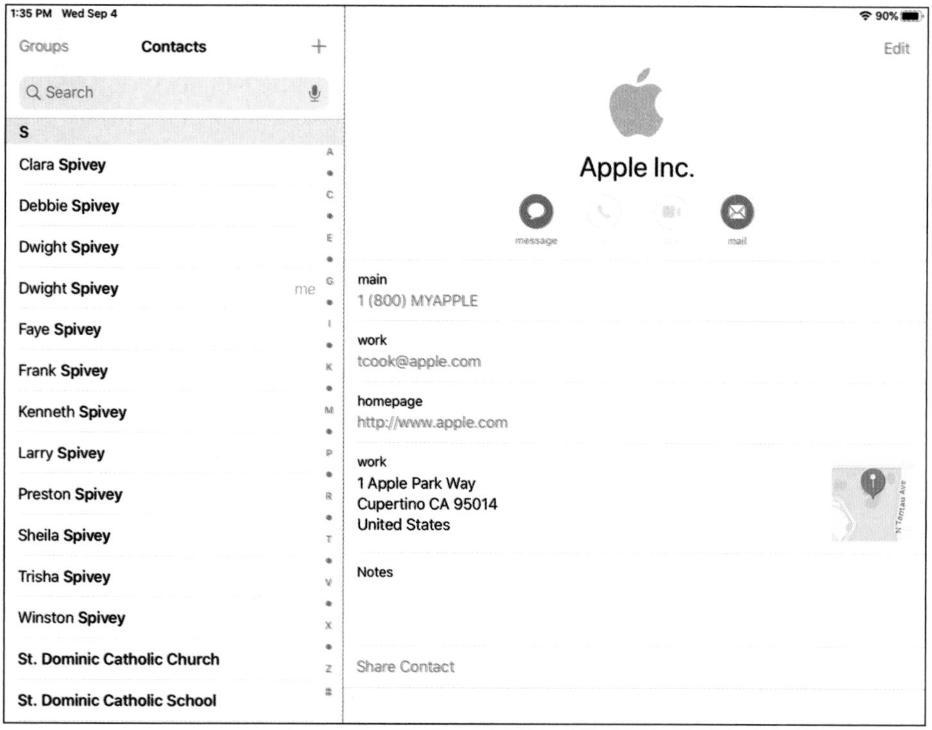

FIGURE 8-4

Sync Contacts with iCloud

You can use your iCloud account to sync contacts from your iPad to iCloud to back them up. These also become available to your email account, if you set one up.

TIP Mac users can also use iTunes or Finder (if your Mac is running macOS Catalina) to sync contacts among all your Apple devices; Windows PC users also use iTunes. See Chapter 3 for more about adjusting iTunes settings.

To sync contacts with iCloud:

1. On the Home screen, tap Settings, tap the name of your Apple ID account (at the top of the screen), and then tap iCloud.

2. In the iCloud settings shown in **Figure 8-5**, make sure that the On/Off switch for Contacts is set to On (green) in order to sync contacts.

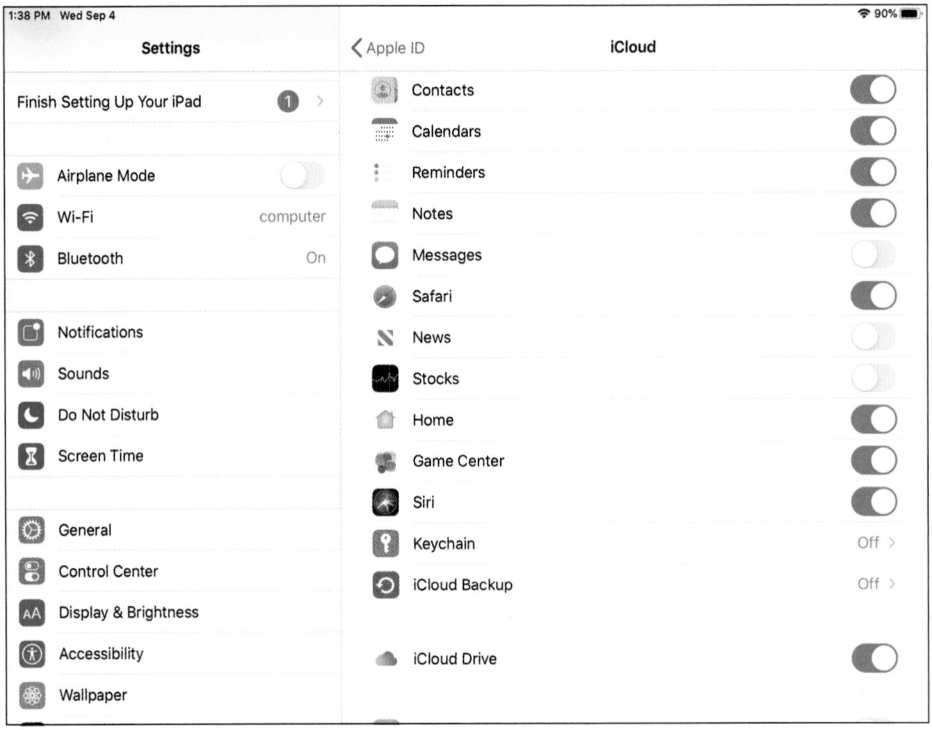

FIGURE 8-5

3. To choose which email account to sync with, tap Passwords & Accounts in the Settings list on the left and in the Accounts section, tap the email account you want to use (it will usually be listed as iCloud).

4. In the following screen (see **Figure 8-6**), toggle the Contacts switch to On to merge contacts from that account via iCloud.

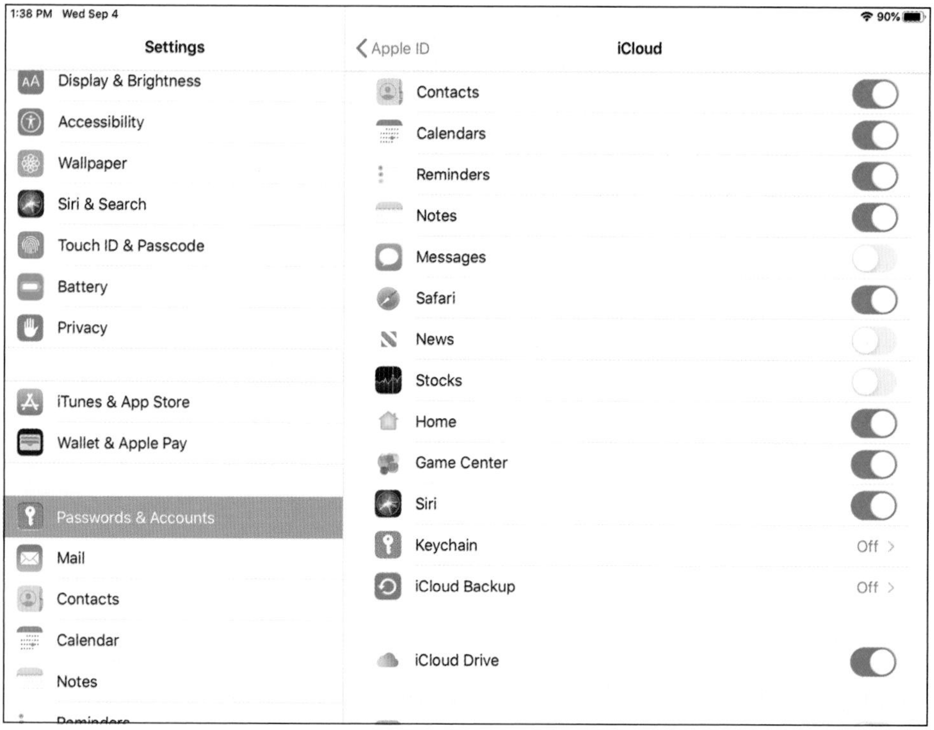

FIGURE 8-6

Assign a Photo to a Contact

To assign a photo to a contact:

1. With Contacts open, tap a contact to whose record you want to add a photo.

2. Tap the Edit button.

3. On the Info page that appears (see **Figure 8-7**), tap Add Photo.

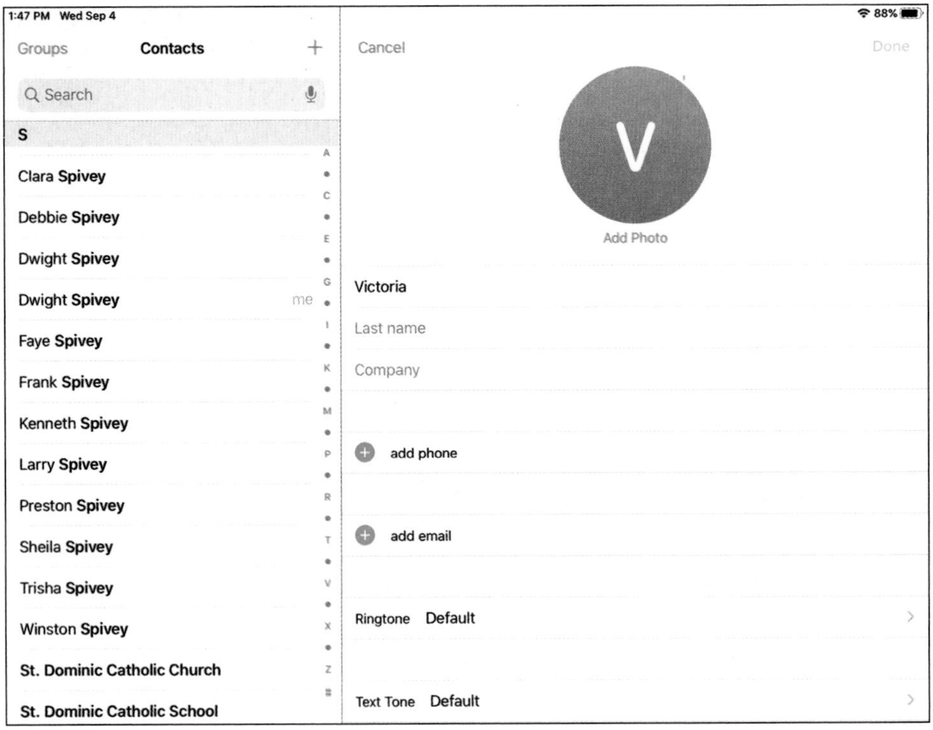

FIGURE 8-7

TIP

TIP

4. In the menu that appears, tap a suggested photo or All Photos to choose an existing photo.

You could also tap the Camera icon to take that contact's photo on the spot.

5. In the Photos dialog box that appears, choose a source for your photo (such as Favorites, Camera Roll, or other album).

6. In the photo album that appears, tap a photo to select it. The Move and Scale dialog box, shown in **Figure 8-8**, appears.

Center the photo the way you want it by dragging it with your finger.

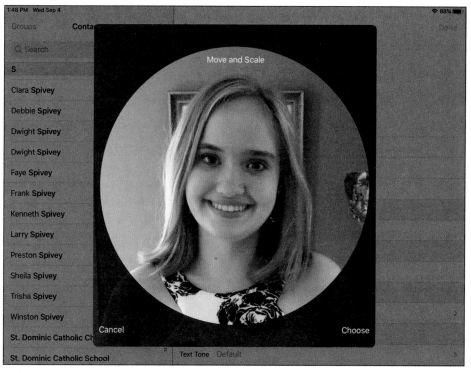

FIGURE 8-8

7. Tap the Choose button to use the photo for this contact. If prompted, you may also select a filter to use with the photo.

8. Tap Done in the upper-right corner to save changes to the contact. The photo appears on the contact's Info page (see **Figure 8-9**).

While in the Photos dialog box, in Step 6, you can modify the photo before saving it to the contact information. You can unpinch your fingers on the iPad screen to expand the photo and move it around the space to focus on a particular section. Then tap the Choose button to use the modified version.

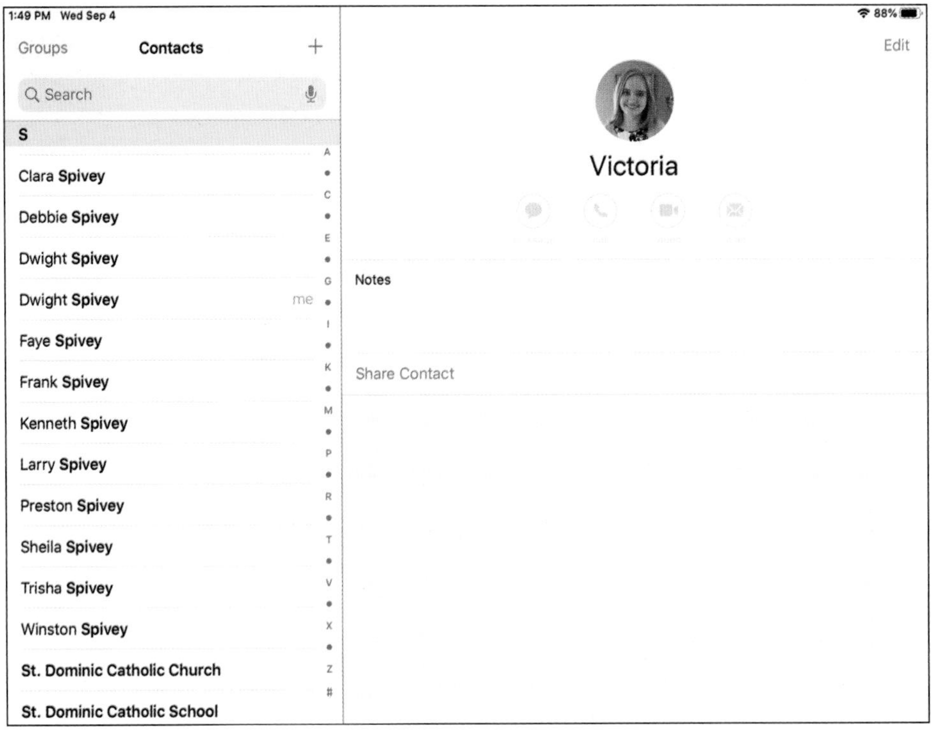

Groups **Contacts** +   Edit

Q Search 🎤

S

Clara **Spivey**

Debbie **Spivey**

Dwight **Spivey**

Dwight **Spivey**   me

Faye **Spivey**

Frank **Spivey**

Kenneth **Spivey**

Larry **Spivey**

Preston **Spivey**

Sheila **Spivey**

Trisha **Spivey**

Winston **Spivey**

St. Dominic Catholic Church

St. Dominic Catholic School

Victoria

Notes

Share Contact

FIGURE 8-9

Add Social Media Information

iPad users can add social media information to their Contacts so that
they can quickly tweet (send a short message to) others using Twitter,
comment to a contact on Facebook, and more. Social media platforms
available in Contacts are Twitter, Facebook, Flickr, LinkedIn, Myspace,
and Sina Weibo.

To add social media information to contacts:

1. Open the Contacts app.

2. Tap the Edit button in the upper-right corner of the screen.

3. Scroll down and tap Add Social Profile.

TIP

You may add multiple social profiles if you like.

4. Twitter is the default service that pops up, but you can easily change it to a different service by tapping "Twitter" and selecting from the list of services, shown in **Figure 8-10**. Tap Done after you've selected the service you'd like to use.

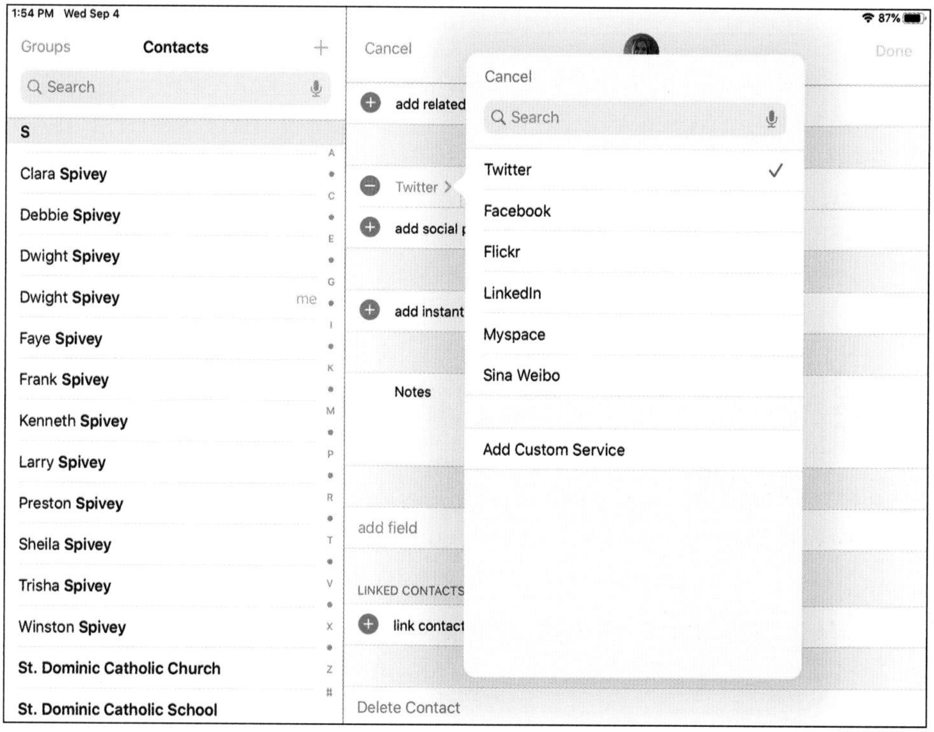

FIGURE 8-10

5. Enter the information for the social profile as needed.

6. Tap Done, and the information is saved. The social profile account is now displayed when you select the contact, and you can send tweets, Facebook messages, or what-have-you by simply tapping the username, tapping the service you want to use to contact the person, and then tapping the appropriate command (such as Facebook posting).

Assign a Relationship Label to a Contact

You can quickly designate relationships in a contact record if those people are saved to Contacts. One great use for this feature is using Siri to simply say "FaceTime daughter" to FaceTime someone who is designated in your contact information as your daughter.

TIP

There's a setting for Linked Contacts in the Contacts app when you're editing a contact's record. Using this setting isn't like adding a relation; rather, if you have records for the same person that have been imported into Contacts from different sources, such as Google or Twitter, you can link them to show only a single contact.

To assign a relation to a contact:

1. Tap a contact and then tap Edit.

2. Scroll down the record and tap Add Related Name. The field labeled Mother (see **Figure 8-11**) now appears. If the contact you're looking for is indeed your mother, leave it as is; otherwise, tap Mother and select the appropriate relationship from the list provided.

3. Tap the blue Information button (looks like a circle with an "i") in Related Name field, and your Contacts list appears. Tap the related person's name, and it appears in the field.

4. Tap Add Related Name and continue to add additional names as needed.

5. Tap Done to complete the edits.

TIP

After you add relations to a contact record, when you select the person in the Contacts main screen, all the related people for that contact are listed there.

FIGURE 8-11

Delete a Contact

When it's time to remove a name or two from your Contacts, it's easy to do:

1. With Contacts open, tap the contact you want to delete.

2. On the Information page (refer to **Figure 8-4**), tap the Edit button.

3. On the Info page that displays, drag your finger upward to scroll down and then tap the Delete Contact button at the bottom.

4. The confirmation dialog box, shown in **Figure 8-12**, appears; tap the Delete Contact button to confirm the deletion.

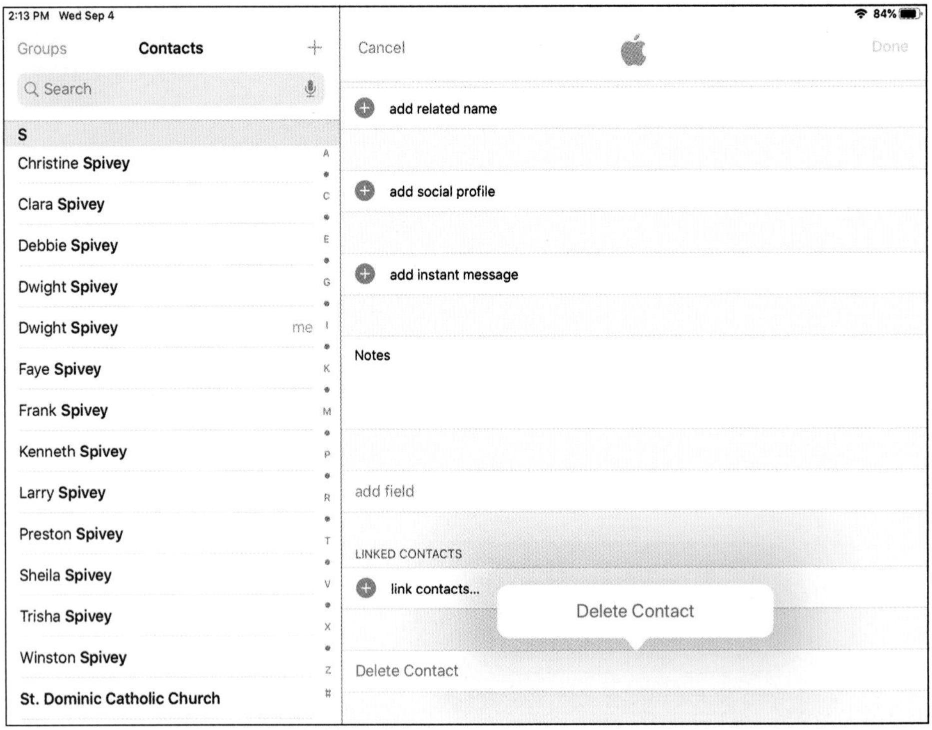

Groups **Contacts** +	Cancel Done

Q Search

S

Christine **Spivey**

Clara **Spivey**

Debbie **Spivey**

Dwight **Spivey**

Dwight **Spivey**   me

Faye **Spivey**

Frank **Spivey**

Kenneth **Spivey**

Larry **Spivey**

Preston **Spivey**

Sheila **Spivey**

Trisha **Spivey**

Winston **Spivey**

St. Dominic Catholic Church

⊕ add related name

⊕ add social profile

⊕ add instant message

Notes

add field

LINKED CONTACTS

⊕ link contacts...

Delete Contact

Delete Contact

FIGURE 8-12

TIP

During this process, if you change your mind before you tap Delete, tap anywhere on the screen outside of the confirmation dialog box, and then tap the Cancel button in Step 4. Be careful: After you tap Delete, there's no going back! Your contact is deleted from your iPad and also any other device that syncs to your iPad via iCloud, Google, or other means.

Chapter 9

Getting Social with Your iPad

FaceTime is an excellent video-calling app that lets you call people who have FaceTime on their devices using either a phone number or an email address. You and your friend, colleague, or family member can see each other as you talk, which makes for a much more personal calling experience.

iMessage is a feature available through the preinstalled Messages app for instant messaging (IM). IM involves sending a text message to somebody's iPad, iPod touch, Mac running macOS 10.8 or later, or iPhone (using the person's phone number or email address to carry on an instant conversation). You can even send audio and video via Messages.

Social media apps keep you in close digital contact with friends, family, and the rest of the world, and have become as important a digital staple as email, if not more so for some folks. Facebook, Twitter, and Instagram are some of the most popular social media apps.

In this chapter, I introduce you to FaceTime and the Messages app and review their simple controls. You also take a look at finding, installing, and customizing Facebook, Twitter, and Instagram. In no time, you'll be socializing with all and sundry.

Understand Who Can Use FaceTime

Here's a quick rundown of the device and information you need for using FaceTime's various features:

» You can use FaceTime to call people over a Wi-Fi connection who have an iPhone 4 or later, an iPad 2 or a third-generation iPad or later, all iPad mini and iPad Pro models, a fourth-generation iPod touch or later, or a Mac (running macOS 10.6.6 or later). If you want to connect over a cellular connection, you're limited to iPhone 4s or later and iPad third generation or later (as long as the iPad supports cellular data).

» You can use a phone number to connect with anybody with either an iOS device or a Mac and an iCloud account.

» The person you're contacting must have allowed FaceTime to be used in Settings.

FaceTime works with the iPad's built-in cameras so that you can call other folks who have a device that supports FaceTime. You can use FaceTime to chat while sharing video images with another person. This preinstalled app is useful for seniors who want to keep up with distant family members and friends and see (as well as hear) the latest and greatest news.

You can make and receive calls with FaceTime using a phone number or an email account and make calls to those with an iCloud account. When connected, you can show the person on the other end what's going on around you. Just remember that you can't adjust audio volume from within the app or record a video call. Nevertheless, on the positive side, even though its features are limited, this app is straightforward to use.

You can use your Apple ID and iCloud account to access FaceTime, so it works pretty much right away. See Chapter 3 for more about getting an Apple ID.

Make a FaceTime Call with Wi-Fi or Cellular

If you know that the person you're calling has FaceTime available on his device, adding that person to your iPad's Contacts is a good idea so you can initiate FaceTime calls from within Contacts if you like or from the Contacts list you can access through the FaceTime app.

When you call somebody using an email address, the person must be signed in to his Apple iCloud account and have verified that the address can be used for FaceTime calls.

To make a FaceTime call:

1. Tap the FaceTime icon to launch the app.

   If you've made or received FaceTime calls already, you will see a list of recent calls in the FaceTime menu on the left side of the screen. You can simply tap one of those to initiate a new call, or continue to learn how to start a new call from scratch.

2. Tap the + in the upper-right corner of the FaceTime menu to open the New FaceTime screen. Tap the To field to enter or find a contact in your Contacts list (as shown in **Figure 9-1**).

FIGURE 9-1

3. Tap one of the green buttons to choose a Video or Audio call at the top of the screen. Video includes your voice and image; Audio includes only your voice.

TIP

You'll see a Video button if that contact's device supports FaceTime video and an Audio button if the contact's device supports FaceTime audio. (If you haven't saved this person in your contacts and you know the phone number to call or email, you can just enter that information in the Enter Name, Email, or Number field.)

4. When the person accepts the call, you see a large screen that displays the recipient's image and a small screen referred to as a Picture in Picture (PiP) containing your image superimposed (see **Figure 9-2**). You can tap and drag your PiP to another location on the screen, if you prefer.

FIGURE 9-2

Accept and End a FaceTime Call

If you're on the receiving end of a FaceTime call, accepting the call is about as easy as it gets. To accept and end a FaceTime call, follow these steps:

1. When the call comes in, tap the Accept button to take the call (see **Figure 9-3**).

   To reject the call, tap the Decline button.

2. Chat away with your friend, swapping video images. To end the call, tap the End button (the red button in **Figure 9-2**) in the call controls window.

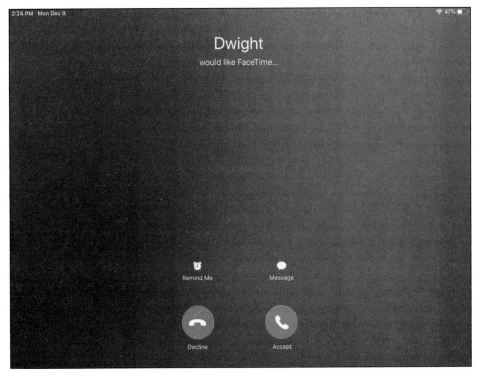

FIGURE 9-3

TIP

To mute sound during a call, tap the Mute button in the call controls window, which looks like a microphone with a line through it (refer to Figure 9-2). Tap the button again to unmute your iPad.

FaceTime in iPadOS 13 allows group calls for up to 32 people! You can have a family reunion without leaving your front porch. To add more folks to a current call:

1. Swipe up on the call controls window to expand it (see **Figure 9-4**).

2. Tap the Add Person button.

3. Tap the To field, enter or find a contact, tap a contact to add them to the To field, and finally, tap the green Add Person to FaceTime button to place them in the call.

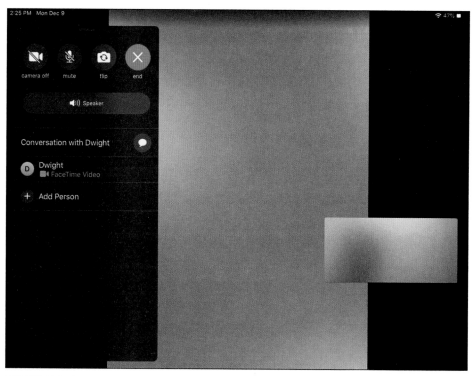

FIGURE 9-4

Switch Views

When you're on a FaceTime call, you might want to use iPad's built-in, rear-facing camera to show the person you're talking to what's going on around you.

1. Tap the Flip button (see Figure 9-2 or Figure 9-4) in the call controls window to switch from the front-facing camera that's displaying your image to the back-facing camera that captures whatever you're looking at.

2. Tap the Switch Camera button again to switch back to the front camera displaying your image.

Set Up an iMessage Account

iMessage is a feature available through the preinstalled Messages app that allows you to send and receive instant messages (IMs) to others using an Apple iOS device, iPadOS device, or suitably configured Macs. iMessage is a way of sending instant messages through a Wi-Fi network, but you can send messages through your cellular connection without having iMessage activated, assuming your iPad supports cellular data.

TECHNICAL
STUFF

Instant messaging differs from email or tweeting in an important way. Whereas you might email somebody and wait for days or weeks before that person responds, or you might post a tweet that could sit there awhile before anybody views it, with instant messaging, communication happens almost immediately. You send an IM, and it appears on somebody's Apple device right away.

Assuming that the person wants to participate in a live conversation, the chat begins immediately, allowing a back-and-forth dialogue in real time.

To set up an iMessage account:

1. To set up Messages, tap Settings on the Home screen.

2. Tap Messages. The settings shown in **Figure 9-5** appear.

3. If iMessage isn't set to On (refer to Figure 9-5), tap the On/Off switch to toggle it On (green).

TIP

Be sure that the phone number and/or email account associated with your iPad under the Send & Receive setting is correct. (It should be set up automatically based on your iCloud settings.) If it isn't, tap the Send & Receive field, add an email or phone, and then tap Messages to return to the previous screen.

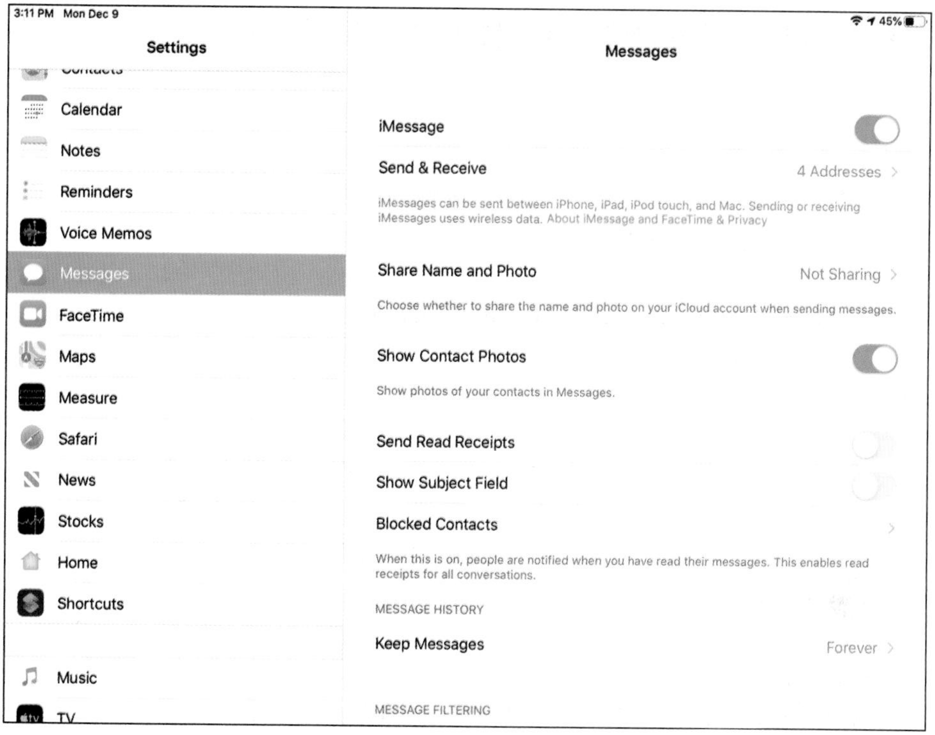

Settings

Messages

Contacts

Calendar

Notes

Reminders

Voice Memos

Messages

FaceTime

Maps

Measure

Safari

News

Stocks

Home

Shortcuts

Music

TV

iMessage
◉

Send & Receive
4 Addresses ›

iMessages can be sent between iPhone, iPad, iPod touch, and Mac. Sending or receiving iMessages uses wireless data. About iMessage and FaceTime & Privacy

Share Name and Photo
Not Sharing ›

Choose whether to share the name and photo on your iCloud account when sending messages.

Show Contact Photos
◉

Show photos of your contacts in Messages.

Send Read Receipts
◯

Show Subject Field
◯

Blocked Contacts
›

When this is on, people are notified when you have read their messages. This enables read receipts for all conversations.

MESSAGE HISTORY

Keep Messages
Forever ›

MESSAGE FILTERING

FIGURE 9-5

4. To allow a notice to be sent to the sender when you've read a message, tap the On/Off switch for Send Read Receipts. You can also choose to show a subject field in your messages.

5. Press the Home button or swipe up from the bottom of the screen (iPad Pro models only) to leave Settings.

TIP

To enable or disable email accounts used by Messages, tap Send & Receive and then tap an email address to enable (check mark appears to the left) or disable it (no check mark appears to the left).

Use Messages to Address, Create, and Send Messages

After you set your iMessage account, you're ready to use Messages.

1. From the Home screen, tap the Messages button.

2. Tap the New Message button (blue circle containing a pen-and-paper icon) in the top-right corner of the Messages list (on the left of the screen) to begin a conversation.

3. In the form that appears (see **Figure 9-6**), you can address a message in a few ways:

   - Begin to type a name in the To field, and a list of matching contacts appears.

   - Tap the Dictation key (looks like a microphone) on the onscreen keyboard and speak the address.

   - Tap the plus (+) button on the right side of the To field, and the Contacts list is displayed.

4. Tap a contact on the list you chose from in Step 3. If the contact has both an email address and a phone number stored, the Info dialog box appears, allowing you to tap one or the other, which addresses the message.

5. To create a message, simply tap in the message field (near the bottom of the screen if the onscreen keyboard is collapsed), shown in **Figure 9-6**, and type your message.

6. To send the message, tap the Send button (the round blue button with the white arrow in Figure 9-6). When your recipient (or recipients) responds, you'll see the conversation displayed on the screen. Tap in the message field again to respond to the last comment.

TIP

You can address a message to more than one person by simply choosing more recipients in Step 2 of the preceding list.

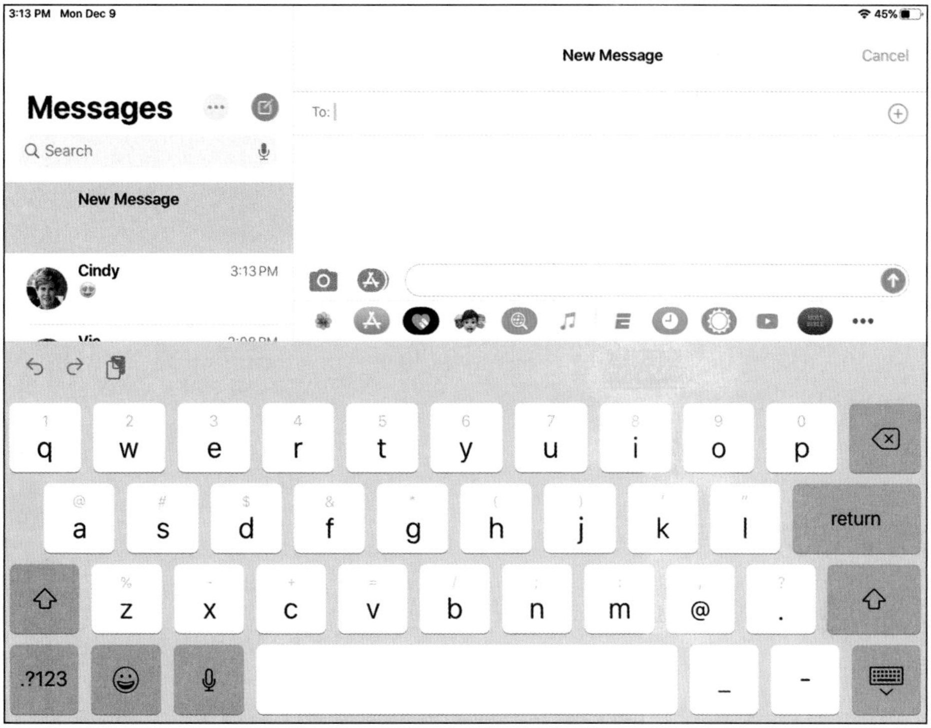

FIGURE 9-6

Read Messages

When you receive a message, it's as easy to read as email — easier, to be honest!

1. Tap Messages on the Home screen.

2. When the app opens, you see a list of text conversations you've engaged in.

3. Tap a conversation to see the message string, including all attachments, as shown in **Figure 9-7**.

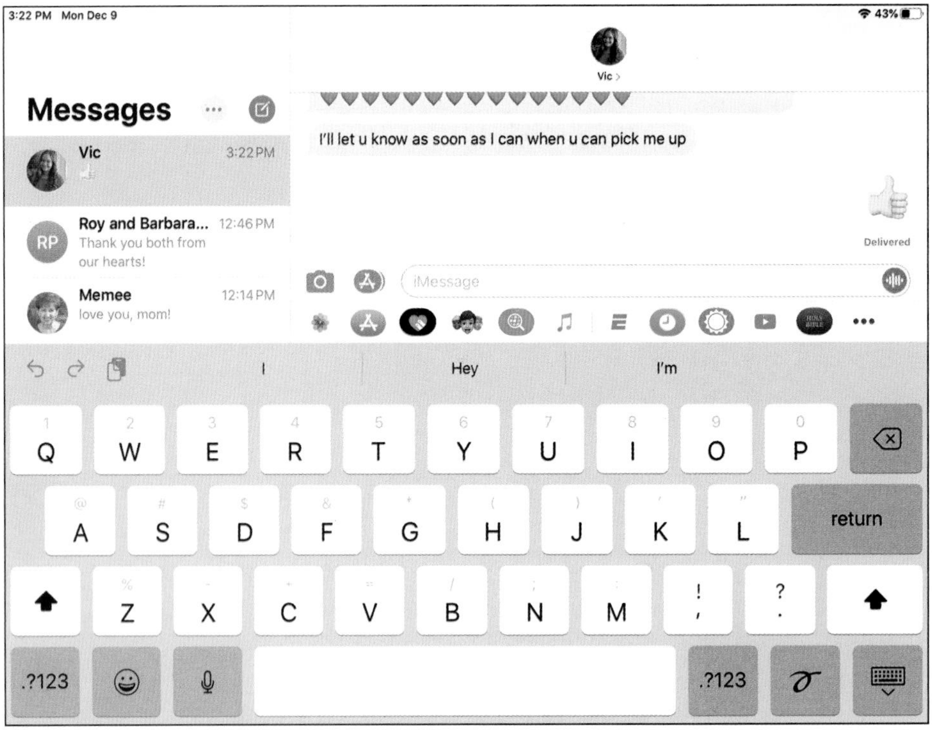

FIGURE 9-7

Clear a Conversation

When you're done chatting, you might want to delete a conversation to remove the clutter before you start a new chat.

1. With Messages open and your conversations displayed, swipe to the left on the message you want to delete.

2. Tap the Delete button next to the conversation you want to get rid of (see **Figure 9-8**).

Tap the Hide Alerts button to keep from being alerted to new messages in the conversation. Swipe again and tap the Show Alerts button to reactivate alerts for the conversation.

TIP

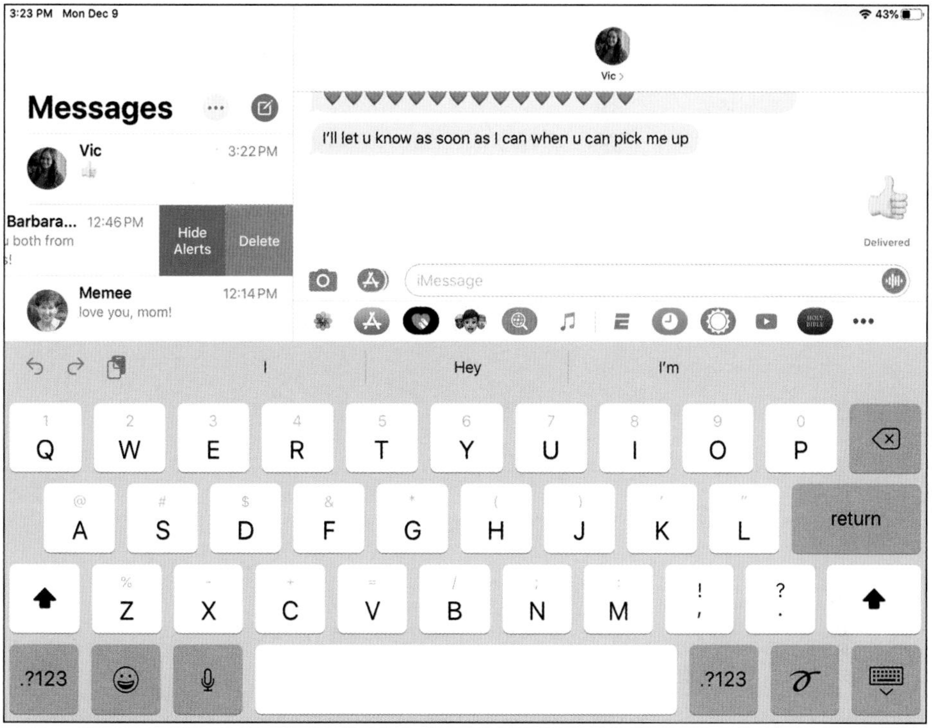

FIGURE 9-8

Send Emojis in Place of Text

Emojis are small pictures that can help convey a feeling or idea — for example, smiley faces and sad faces to show emotions, thumbs-up to convey approval, and the like.

To send an emoji in place of text:

1. From within a conversation, tap the Emoji key on the onscreen keyboard. If you can't see the keyboard, tap in the Message field to display it.

2. When the emojis appear (see **Figure 9-9**), swipe left and right to find the right emoji for the moment and tap to select it. You can add as many as you like to the conversation.

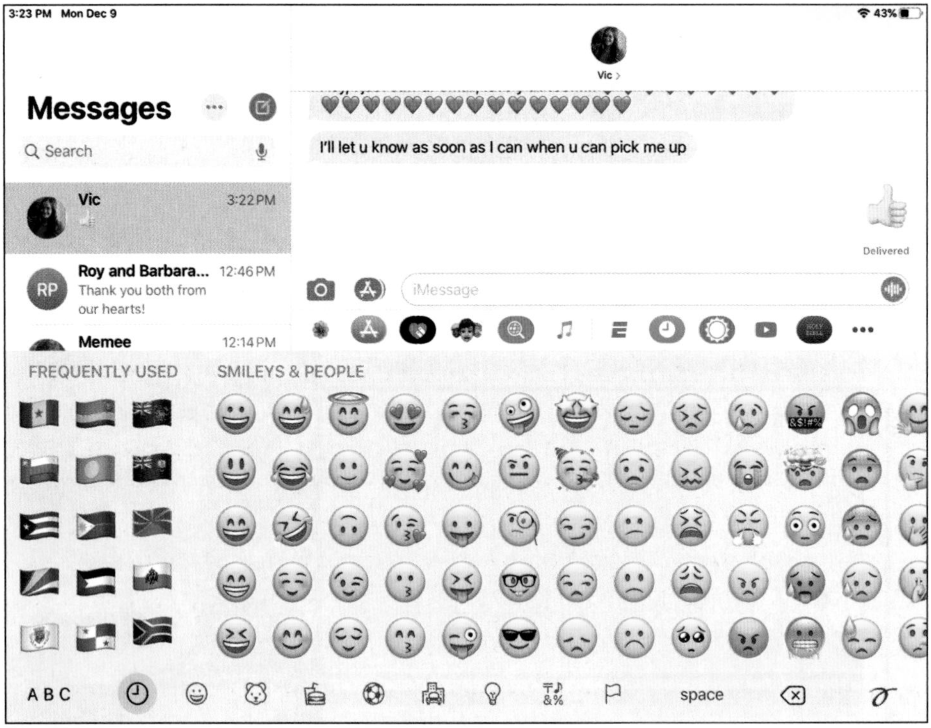

FIGURE 9-9

Use the App Drawer

The App Drawer allows you to add items that spice up your messages with information from other apps that are installed on your iPad, as well as drawings and other images from the web.

To use the App Drawer:

1. Tap the App Drawer icon (looks like an A) to the left of the iMessage field in your conversation. The App Drawer will display at the bottom of the screen.

2. Tap an item in the App Drawer to see what it offers your messaging.

The App Drawer is populated by

» **The App Store:** Tap the App Store all the way to the left of the App Drawer to find tons of stickers, games, and apps for your messages.

» **Digital Touch:** Allows you to send special effects in Messages. These can range from sending your heartbeat to sketching a quick picture to sending a kiss.

» **Other apps you have installed may also appear if they have the ability to add functions and information to your messages.** For example, send the latest scores using ESPN (as I'm doing in **Figure 9-10**) or let your friend know what the weather's like nearby using icons from the AccuWeather app. Another example could be using Fandango's app to send movie information.

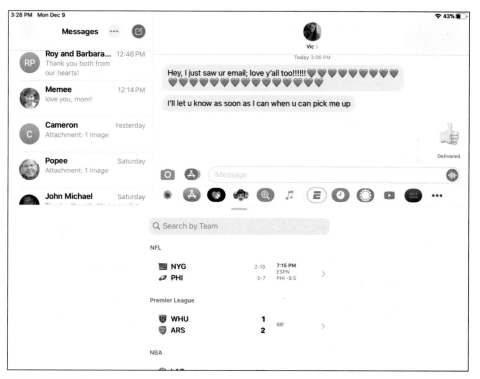

FIGURE 9-10

Digital Touch is one of the most personal ways to send special effects to others, so take a closer look at it:

1. To send a Digital Touch in a message, open a conversation and tap the Digital Touch button (black oval containing a red heart), shown in **Figure 9-11**.

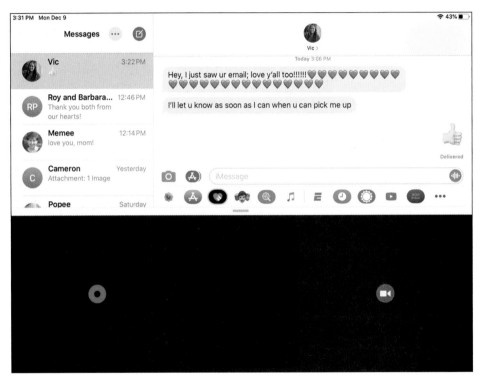

FIGURE 9-11

2. In the Digital Touch window, tap the gray expansion handle (shown in Figure 9-11 in the very middle of the screen immediately under the message field) to open the full window. Tap the Information button in the lower right (a gray circle with a white letter *i*), and you see a list of the gestures and what they do.

3. Perform a gesture in the Digital Touch window, and it will go to your recipient. If you've created a drawing, tap the blue Send button (seen in **Figure 9-12**) to send it.

FIGURE 9-12

Send and Receive Audio

When you're creating a message, you can also create an audio message:

1. With Messages open, tap the New Message button.

2. Enter an addressee's name in the To field.

3. Tap and hold the Audio button (the microphone symbol to the right of the screen in the message field).

4. Speak your message or record a sound or music near you as you continue to hold down the Audio button.

5. Release the Audio button when you're finished recording.

6. Tap the Send button (an upward-pointing arrow at the top of the recording circle). The message appears as an audio track in the recipient's Messages inbox (see **Figure 9-13**). To play the track, the recipient just taps the Play button.

FIGURE 9-13

Send a Photo or Video

When you're creating a message, you can also send a picture or create a short video message:

1. With Messages open, tap the New Message button.

2. Tap the Camera button to open the Camera app, then take a picture.

3. Once the picture is taken, you'll be able to work with it before sending it along to your recipient. In the tools that appear (shown in **Figure 9-14**), you can

- Tap Retake in the upper-left corner to take a different picture.
- Tap Edit (icon of circle containing three lines) to edit the picture.
- Tap Markup (the marker tip icon) to add notes or other text to your picture.
- Tap Effects (the star icon) to add effects to your picture.
- Tap Done to place the picture in your message but not send it yet.
- Tap the Send button (the blue circle containing the white arrow in the lower-right) to send the picture immediately.

FIGURE 9-14

Send a Map of Your Location

When responding to a message, you can also send a map showing your current location.

1. Tap a message, tap the picture of the recipient in the upper-center of the screen, then tap the Info button underneath (see **Figure 9-15**).

FIGURE 9-15

2. Tap Send My Current Location (see **Figure 9-16**) and a map will be inserted as a message attachment.

TIP

You can also share your location in the middle of a conversation rather than send a map attachment with your message. In the screen shown in Figure 9-16, tap Share My Location and then tap Share for One Hour, Share Until End of Day, or Share Indefinitely. A map showing your location appears above your conversation until you stop sharing.

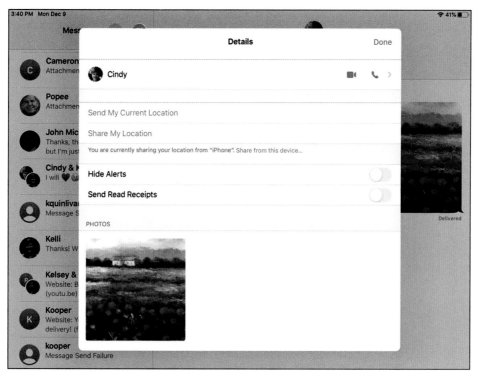

FIGURE 9-16

Understand Group Messaging

If you want to start a conversation with a group of people, you can use group messaging. Group messaging is great for keeping several people in the conversational loop.

Group messaging functionality, includes the following features:

» When you participate in a group message, you see all participants in the Info for the message (see **Figure 9-17**). You can drop people whom you don't want to include any longer and leave the conversation yourself when you want to by simply tapping Info, then tapping Leave This Conversation.

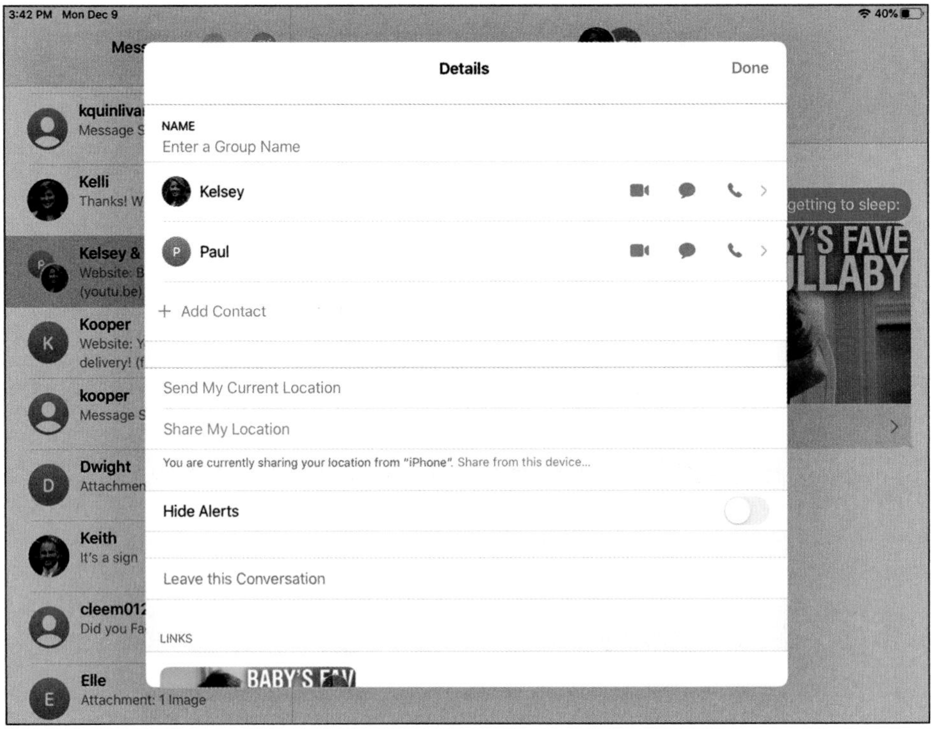

FIGURE 9-17

>> When you turn on Hide Alerts in the Details in a message (see Figure 9-17), you won't get notifications of messages from this group, but you can still read the group's messages at a later time (this also works for individuals).

Taking you further into the workings of group messages is beyond the scope of this book, but if you're intrigued, go to `https://support.apple.com/en-us/HT202724` for more information.

Activate the Hide Alerts Feature

If you don't want to get notifications of new messages from an individual or group for a while, you can use the Hide Alerts feature:

1. With a message open, tap Details.

2. Tap the Hide Alerts switch to turn the feature on (refer to Figure 9-17.

3. Later, return to Details and tap the Hide Alerts switch again to turn the feature off.

Find and Install Social Media Apps

To begin using social media apps, you first need to find and install them on your iPad. I focus on Facebook, Twitter, and Instagram in this chapter because they're currently three of the most popular social media apps, and frankly, I don't have the space here to discuss more.

To find and install the apps using the App Store, follow these steps:

1. Open the App Store.

2. Tap the Search tab at the bottom of the screen.

3. Tap the Search field and enter either Facebook, Twitter, Instagram, or any other social media app you might be interested in.

4. To download and install the app, tap the button labeled Get or the price (such as $2.99).

TECHNICAL STUFF

If you've had the app installed before but have since deleted it, you will instead see a cloud with a downward-pointing arrow (as shown in **Figure 9-18**). Tap that to begin the download.

5. When the dialog box appears at the bottom of the screen, tap Purchase (if it's a Paid app) or Install (if it's Free), type your password in the Password field on the next screen, and then tap Sign In to download the app. Alternatively, use Touch ID if you have it enabled for iTunes and App Store purchases; the dialog box will display "Pay with Touch ID" if you do. iPad Pro model users use Face ID instead of Touch ID. When you're prompted to pay (with Face ID enabled), double-click the top button and glance at your iPhone to initiate payment.

The app will download and install on one of your Home screens.

FIGURE 9-18

Create a Facebook Account

You can create a Facebook account from within the app.

TIP

If you already have a Facebook account, you can simply use that account information to log in.

To create an account in the Facebook app, follow these steps:

1. Launch the newly downloaded Facebook app.

2. Tap the Sign Up for Facebook option near the bottom of the screen, as seen in **Figure 9-19** (you almost need binoculars to see it).

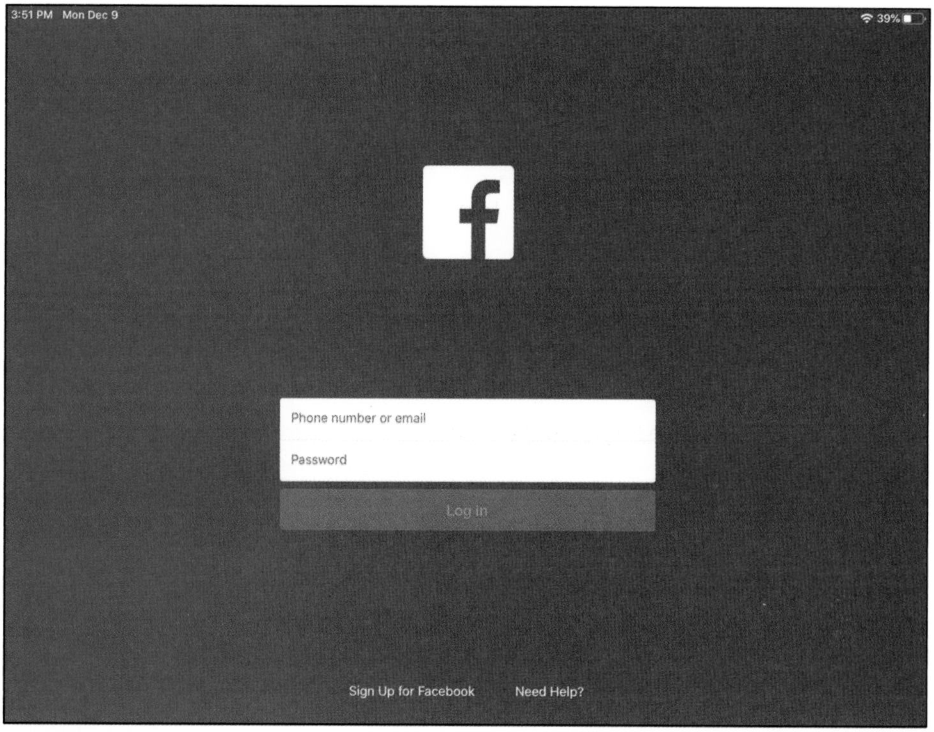

FIGURE 9-19

3. Tap Get Started and walk through the steps to complete the registration of your account.

4. When finished, you'll be logged into your account in the Facebook app.

You may also create a Facebook account by visiting its website at www.facebook.com.

TIP

Create a Twitter Account

To create an account in the Twitter app, follow these steps:

1. Open the Twitter app by tapping its icon.

2. Tap the blue Create account button in the middle of the screen, as illustrated in **Figure 9-20.**

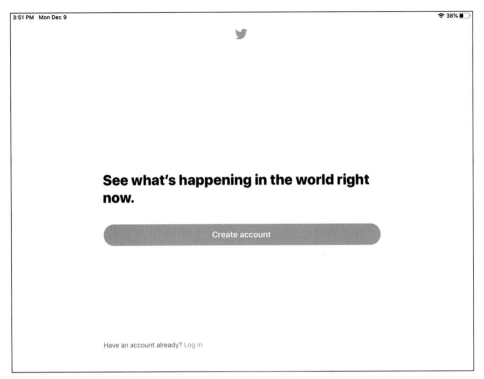

FIGURE 9-20

TIP

If you already have a Twitter account, tap the tiny Log In button at the very bottom of the screen to log in.

3. The app will ask you some questions to help you create your account.

4. When you're done, the app will log you into your new account.

TIP

Just like Facebook, you can create an account on the Twitter website at `www.twitter.com`.

Create an Instagram Account

To create an account in the Instagram app:

1. Open the Instagram app by tapping its icon.

2. Tap the blue Create New Account button in the middle of the screen, as shown in **Figure 9-21,** to walk through the steps of creating a new Instagram account.

TIP

If you already have an Instagram account, tap the really small Log In button to access it.

3. The app will ask you several questions to help you create your account.

4. When completed, the app will log you into your new account.

TIP

You can also create an account on the Instagram website at www. instagram.com.

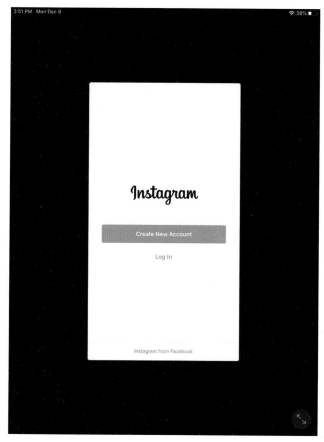

FIGURE 9-21

Chapter **10**

Browsing with Safari

Getting on the Internet with your iPad is easy, by using its Wi-Fi or cellular capabilities. After you're online, the built-in browser (software that helps you navigate the Internet's contents), Safari, is your ticket to a wide world of information, entertainment, education, and more. Safari will look familiar to you if you've used a web browser on a PC or Mac computer, though the way you move around by using the iPad touchscreen may be new to you. If you've never used Safari, this chapter takes you by the hand and shows you all the basics of making Safari work for you.

In this chapter, you see how to go online with your iPad, navigate among web pages, and use iCloud tabs to share your browsing experience between devices. Along the way, you see how to place a bookmark for a favorite site or place a web clip on your Home screen. You can also view your browsing history, save online images to your Photo Library, post photos to sites from within Safari, or email or tweet a link to a friend. You also explore Safari's Reader and Reading List features and learn how to keep yourself safer while online by using private browsing. Finally, you review the simple steps involved in printing what you find online.

Connect to the Internet

How you connect to the Internet depends on which types of connections are available:

» You can connect to the Internet via a Wi-Fi network. You can set up this type of network in your own home using your computer and some equipment from your Internet provider. You can also connect over public Wi-Fi networks, referred to as *hotspots*.

» You can use the paid data network provided by AT&T, Sprint, T-Mobile, Verizon, or most any other cellular provider, to connect from just about anywhere you can get coverage through a cellular network. Of course, you have to have an iPad model that supports cellular connections to hop on the Internet this way.

To enable cellular data (if your iPad supports it), tap Settings and then tap Cellular. Toggle the switch (just tap it) to turn on the Cellular Data setting.

To connect to a Wi-Fi network, you have to complete a few steps:

1. Tap Settings on the Home screen and then tap Wi-Fi.
2. Be sure that Wi-Fi is set to On (green) and choose a network to connect to by tapping it.

TECHNICAL STUFF

Network names should appear automatically when you're in range of them. When you're in range of a public hotspot, if access to several nearby networks is available, you may see a message asking you to tap a network name to select it. After you select a network, you may see a message asking for your password. Ask the owner of the hotspot (for example, a hotel desk clerk or business owner) for this password or enter your own network password if you're connecting to your home network.

TIP

Free public Wi-Fi networks usually don't require passwords, or the password is posted prominently for all to see (if you can't find the password, don't be shy to ask someone).

when prompted. Once done, you're connected!
ecognize the network and connect without
the password.

public Wi-Fi, someone else could possibly
vities because these are unsecured networks.
ncial accounts, making online purchases, or
sensitive information in them, when con-
tspot.

our new best friend when it comes to surfing the
it's a good idea to learn what it offers as a web-

round in Safari:

ected to a network, tap Safari on the Dock at the
me screen. Safari opens, probably displaying the
page the first time you go online (see **Figure 10-1**).

2. Put two fingers together on the screen and spread them apart to expand the view (also known as zooming in). Place your fingers on the screen about an inch or so apart and quickly bring them together to zoom back out. You can also double-tap the screen with a single finger to restore the default view size. (If you tap a link, though, your gesture will just open that link.)

TIP

Using your fingers on the screen to enlarge or reduce the size of a web page allows you to view what's displayed at various sizes, giving you more flexibility than the double-tap method.

3. Put your finger on the screen and flick upward to scroll down on the page.

4. To return to the top of the web page, put your finger on the screen and drag downward or tap the Status bar at the very top of the screen twice.

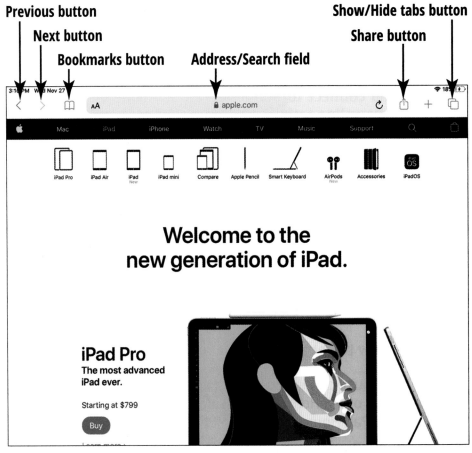

Previous button
Next button
Bookmarks button
Address/Search field
Show/Hide tabs button
Share button

FIGURE 10-1

TIP When you zoom in, you have more control by using two fingers to drag from left to right or from top to bottom on the screen. When you zoom out, one finger works fine for making these gestures.

Navigate among Web Pages

Web pages are chock full of information and gateways to other web resources. To navigate the landscape of web pages in Safari:

1. Tap in the Address field just under the Status bar. The onscreen keyboard appears (see **Figure 10-2**).

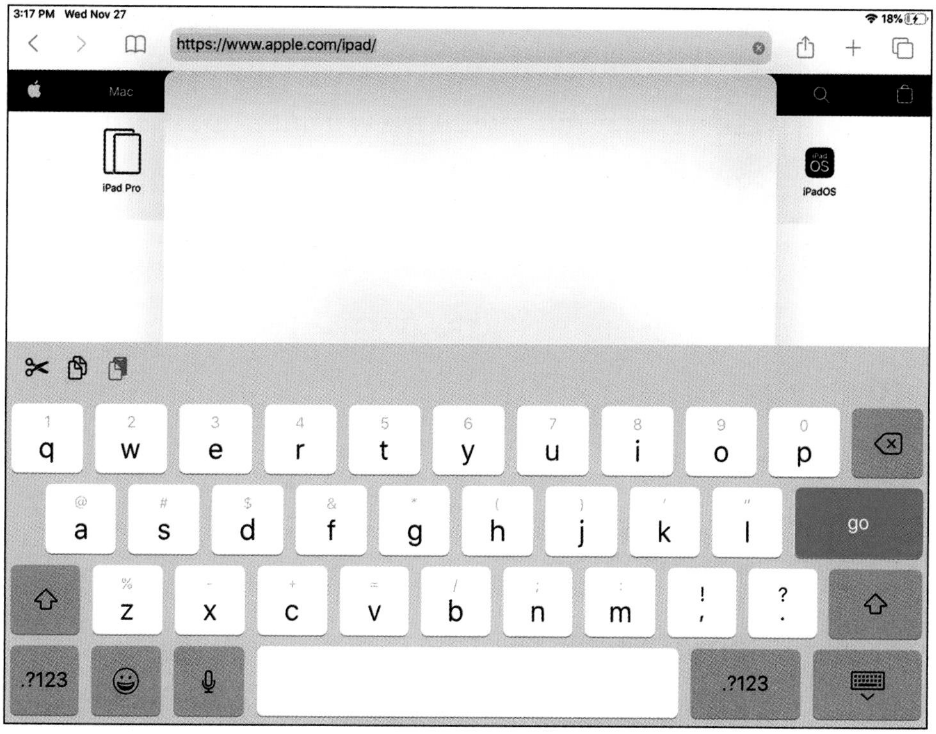

FIGURE 10-2

2. Enter a web address; for example, you can go to www.dummies.com.

3. Tap the Go key on the keyboard (refer to Figure 10-2). The website appears.

- If a page doesn't display properly, tap the Reload button at the right end of the Address field.

- If Safari is loading a web page and you change your mind about viewing the page, you can stop loading the page. Tap Cancel (looks like an X), which appears at the right end of the Address field during this process, to stop loading the page.

4. Tap the Previous button (looks like <) in the upper-left corner to go to the last page you displayed.

5. Tap the Next button (looks like >) in the upper-left corner to go forward to the page you just backed up from.

6. To follow a link to another web page (links are typically indicated by colored text or graphics), tap the link with your finger.

TIP

To view the destination web address of the link before you tap it, just touch and hold the link; a menu appears that displays the address at the top and a preview of the site, as shown in **Figure 10-3**.

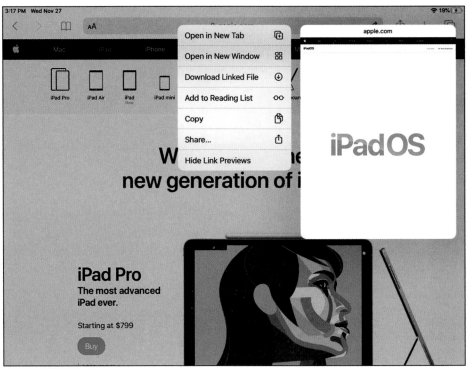

FIGURE 10-3

Use Tabbed Browsing

Tabbed browsing is a feature that allows you to have several websites open at one time so that you can move easily among those sites.

1. With Safari open and a web page already displaying, tap the Show/Hide Tabs button in the upper-right corner (refer to Figure 10-1). The new Tab view appears.

2. To add a new page (meaning that you're opening a new website), tap the New Page button (shaped like a plus [+] symbol) in the upper right of the screen (see **Figure 10-4**). A page appears with your favorite or currently open sites and an address bar.

FIGURE 10-4

TIP You can get to the same new page by simply tapping in the address bar from any site.

3. Tap in the Address field and use the onscreen keyboard to enter the web address for the website you want to open. Tap the Go key. The website opens on the page.

TIP

Repeat Steps 1 to 3 to open as many new web pages as you'd like.

4. You can now switch among open sites by tapping outside the keyboard to close it and tapping the Show/Hide Tabs button and scrolling among recent sites. Find the one you want and then tap it.

TIP

You can easily rearrange sites in the tabs window. Just touch-and-hold the tab you want to move and then drag it to the right or left in the list until it's in the spot you'd like it to be (the other sites in the window politely move to make room). To drop it in the new location, simply remove your finger from the screen.

5. To delete a tab, tap the Show/Hide Tabs button, scroll to locate the tab, and then tap the Close button in the upper-left corner of the tab (looks like an X; it may be difficult to see on some sites, but trust me, it's there).

View Browsing History

As you move around the web, your browser keeps a record of your browsing history. This record can be handy when you want to visit a site that you viewed previously but whose address you've now forgotten.

To view your browsing history:

1. With Safari open, tap the Bookmarks button.

TIP

After you master the use of the Bookmarks button options, you might prefer a shortcut to view your History list. Tap and hold the Previous button at the upper-left on any screen, and your browsing history for the current session appears. You can also tap and hold the Next button to look at sites you backtracked from.

2. On the menu shown in **Figure 10-5**, tap the History tab (looks like a clock).

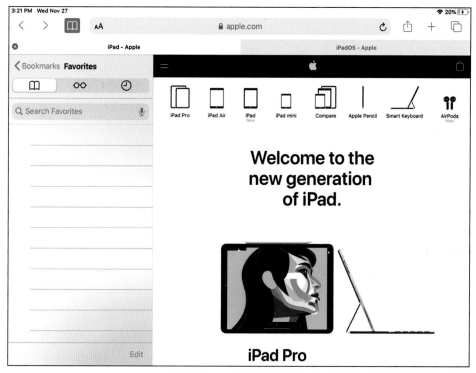

FIGURE 10-5

3. In the History list that appears (see **Figure 10-6**), tap a site to navigate to it. Tap Done to leave History and return to browsing.

TIP

To clear the history, tap the Clear button in the bottom of the History list (refer to Figure 10-6) and on the screen that appears, tap an option: The Last Hour, Today, Today and Yesterday, or All Time. This button is useful when you don't want your spouse or grandchildren to see where you've been browsing for anniversary, birthday, or holiday presents!

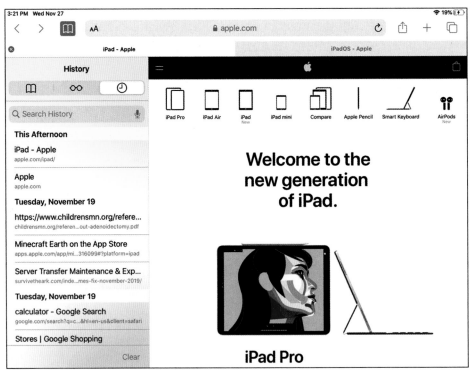

FIGURE 10-6

Search the Web

If you don't know the address of the site that you want to visit (or you want to research a topic or find other information online), get acquainted with Safari's Search feature on iPad. By default, Safari uses the Google search engine.

To search the web:

1. With Safari open, tap in the Address field (refer back to Figure 10-1). The onscreen keyboard appears.

TIP

To change your default search engine from Google to Yahoo!, Bing, or DuckDuckGo, from the Home screen, tap Settings, tap Safari, and then tap Search Engine. Tap Yahoo!, Bing, or DuckDuckGo, and your default search engine changes.

2. Enter a search term. With recent versions of Safari, the search term can be a topic or a web address because of what's called the Unified smart search field. You can tap one of the suggested sites or complete your entry and tap the Go key (see **Figure 10-7**) on your keyboard.

3. In the search results that are displayed, tap a link to visit that site.

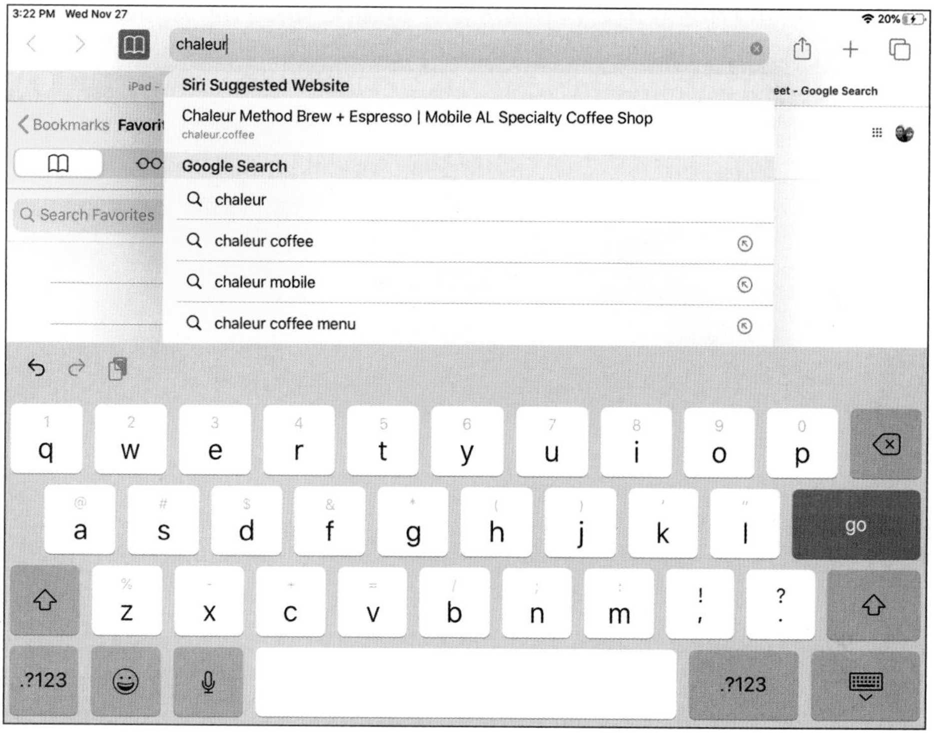

FIGURE 10-7

Add and Use Bookmarks

Bookmarks are a way to save favorite sites so that you can easily visit them again.

To add and use bookmarks:

1. With a site open that you want to bookmark, tap the Share button in the upper-right of the screen (which looks like a box with an upward-pointing arrow).

TIP

If you want to sync your bookmarks on your iPad browser, go to Settings on iPad and make sure that iCloud is set to sync with Safari.

2. On the menu that appears (see **Figure 10-8**), tap Add Bookmark. (You may need to swipe up the window to see it.)

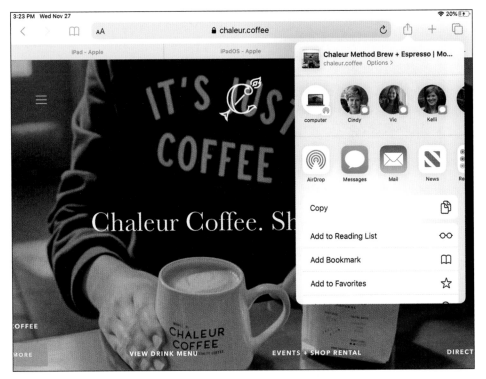

FIGURE 10-8

3. In the Add Bookmark dialog box, shown in **Figure 10-9**, edit the name of the bookmark if you want. Tap the name of the site and use the onscreen keyboard to edit its name.

4. Tap the Save button in the upper-right corner. The item is saved to your Favorites by default.

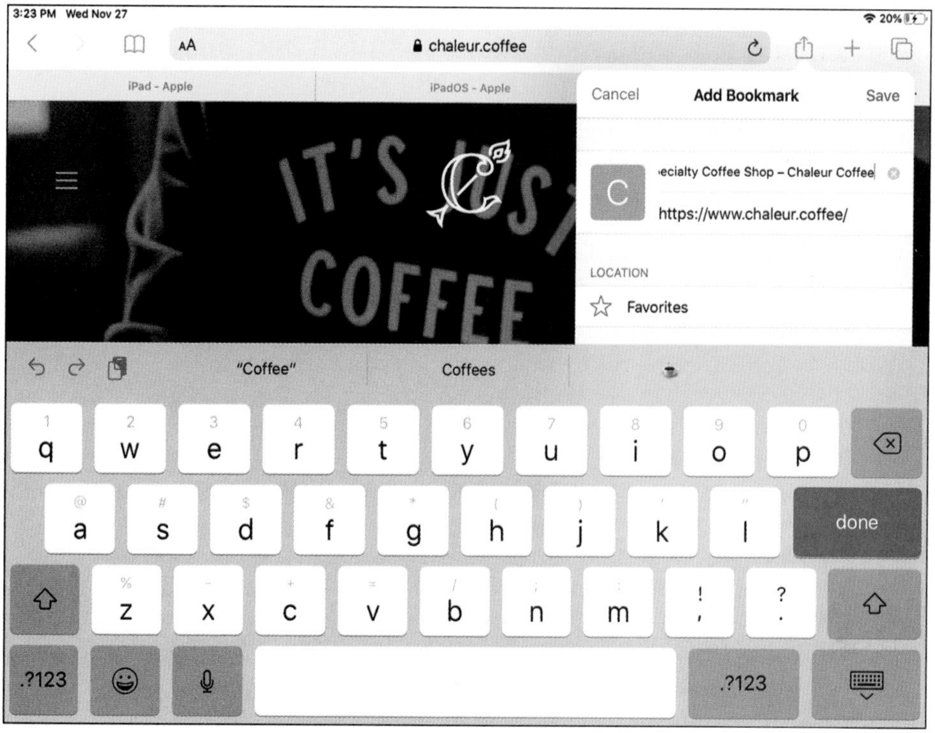

FIGURE 10-9

5. To go to the bookmark, tap the Bookmarks button.

6. On the Bookmarks menu that appears (see **Figure 10-10**), if you saved a site to a folder tap to open the folder, and then tap the bookmarked site that you want to visit.

TIP

When you tap the Bookmarks button, you can tap Edit in the lower right of the Bookmarks menu and then use the New Folder option (in the lower left) to create folders to organize your bookmarks or folders. When you next add a bookmark, you can then choose, from the dialog box that appears, any folder to which you want to add the new bookmark.

TIP

You can reorder your bookmarks quite easily. Tap the Bookmarks button, tap the Edit button (lower-right), find the bookmark you'd like to rearrange, tap and hold the three parallel lines to the right of the bookmark, and then drag it up and down the list, releasing it once you get to the place you'd like it to reside. You can also delete bookmarks from the same screen by tapping the red circle to the left of a bookmark and then tapping the red Delete button that appears to the right.

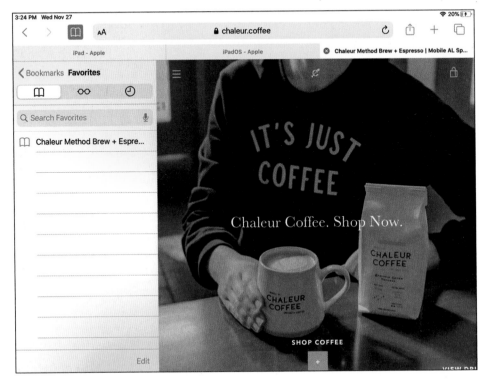

FIGURE 10-10

Save Links and Web Pages to Safari Reading List

The Safari Reading List provides a way to save content that you want to read at a later time so that you can easily call up that content again. You essentially save the content rather than a web page address, which allows you to read the content even when you're offline. You can scroll from one item to the next easily.

To save content to the Reading List, follow these steps:

1. Displaying a site that you want to add to your Reading List, tap the Share button.

2. On the menu that appears (refer to Figure 10-8), tap the Add to Reading List button. The site is added to your Reading List.

3. To view your Reading List, tap the Bookmarks button and then tap the Reading List tab (the middle tab with the eyeglasses icon near the top of the Bookmarks menu).

If you want to see both the Reading List material you've read and the material you haven't read, tap the Show Unread button in the bottom-left corner of the Reading List. To see all reading material, tap the Show All button.

TIP

4. On the Reading List that appears (see **Figure 10-11**), tap the content that you want to revisit and resume reading.

FIGURE 10-11

To delete an item, with the Reading List displaying, swipe right to left on an item; a red Delete button appears to the right. Tap this button to delete the item from the Reading List. To save an item for offline (when you're not connected to the Internet) reading,

TIP

tap the Save Offline button when you swipe. You can also swipe the item from left to right to mark it as read or unread.

Enable Private Browsing

Apple has provided some privacy settings for Safari that you should consider using.

Private Browsing automatically stops Safari from using AutoFill to save information used to complete certain entries as you type, and erases some browsing history information. This feature can keep your online activities more private. To enable Private Browsing:

1. Tap the Show/Hide Tabs button (refer to Figure 10-1).

2. Tap Private in the upper-right corner; you're now in Private Browsing Mode.

3. Tap the Private button in the upper-right corner again to disable Private Browsing.

Download Files

iPadOS 13 introduces a new Download Manager for Safari to help you efficiently download files from websites and store them to a location of your choosing. You can choose to store downloaded files on your iPhone or in iCloud.

Set the default download location for files you download in Safari. Go to Settings ⇨ Safari ⇨ Downloads and tap the location you want to use.

1. Open a site in Safari that contains a file you'd like to download.

2. Tap and hold the link for the file until the menu in **Figure 10-12** appears.

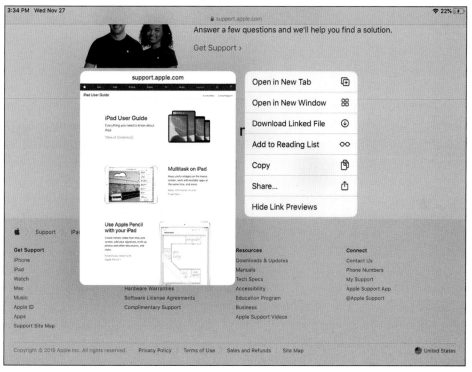

FIGURE 10-12

3. Tap the Download Linked File button to download the file to your iPhone, iCloud, or another destination.

4. The Downloads button (a circle containing a downward-pointing arrow) appears to the right of the address field at the top of the screen (see **Figure 10-13**). Tap it to see the progress of the download. If the download is finished, tap it in the Download Manager menu to open it, or tap the magnifying glass to see where the file is stored.

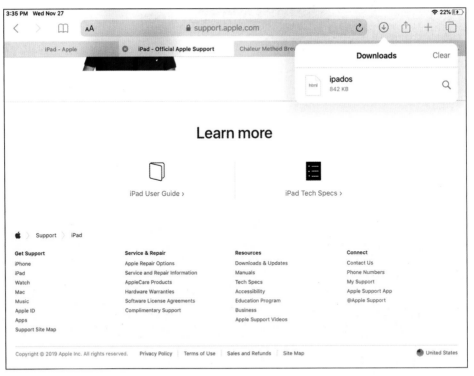

FIGURE 10-13

IN THIS CHAPTER

» **Add an email account**

» **Read, reply to, or forward email**

» **Create, format, and send emails**

» **Search email**

» **Mark or flag email**

» **Delete email**

Chapter **11**

Working with Email in Mail

Staying in touch with others by email is a great way to use your iPad. You can access an existing account using the handy Mail app supplied with your iPad or sign in to your email account using the Safari browser. In this chapter, you take a look at using Mail, which involves adding an existing email account. Then you can use Mail to write, format, retrieve, and forward messages from that account.

Mail offers the capability to mark the messages you've read, delete messages, and organize your messages in a small set of folders, as well as use a handy search feature. In this chapter, you learn all about the Mail app and its various features.

Add an Email Account

You can add one or more email accounts, including the email account associated with your iCloud account, using iPad Settings. If you have an iCloud, Microsoft Exchange (often used for business accounts), Gmail, Yahoo!, AOL, or Outlook.com (this includes Microsoft accounts from Live, Hotmail, and so on) account, iPad pretty much automates the setup.

To set up iPad to retrieve messages from your email account at one of these popular providers:

1. Tap the Settings icon on the Home screen.

2. In Settings, tap Passwords & Accounts, and the screen shown in **Figure 11-1** appears.

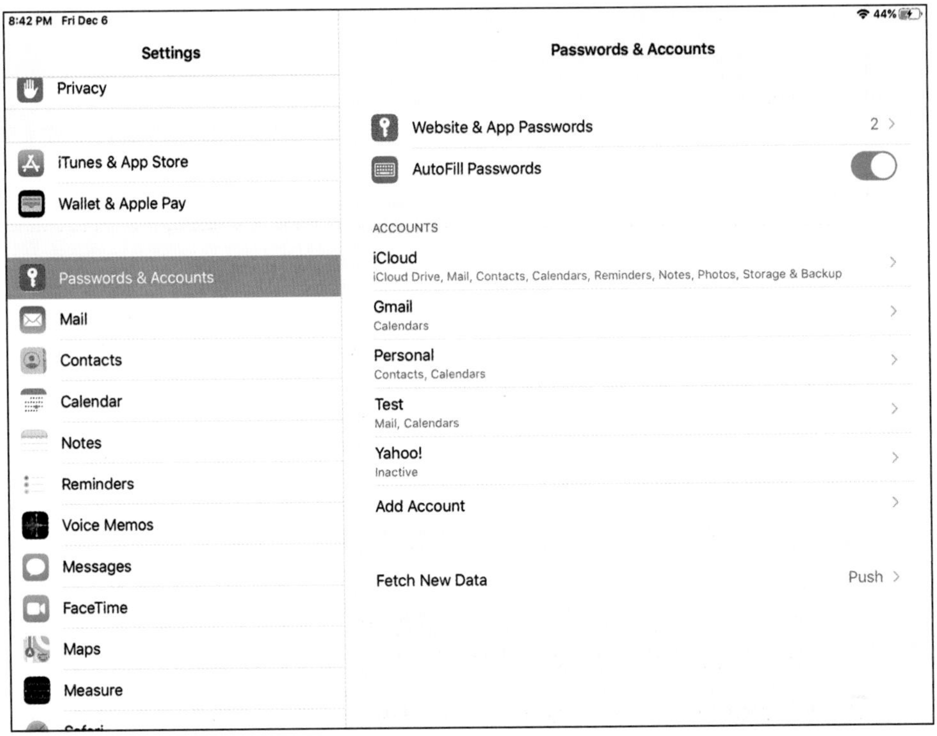

FIGURE 11-1

3. Tap Add Accounts, found at the bottom of the Accounts section. The options shown in **Figure 11-2** appear.

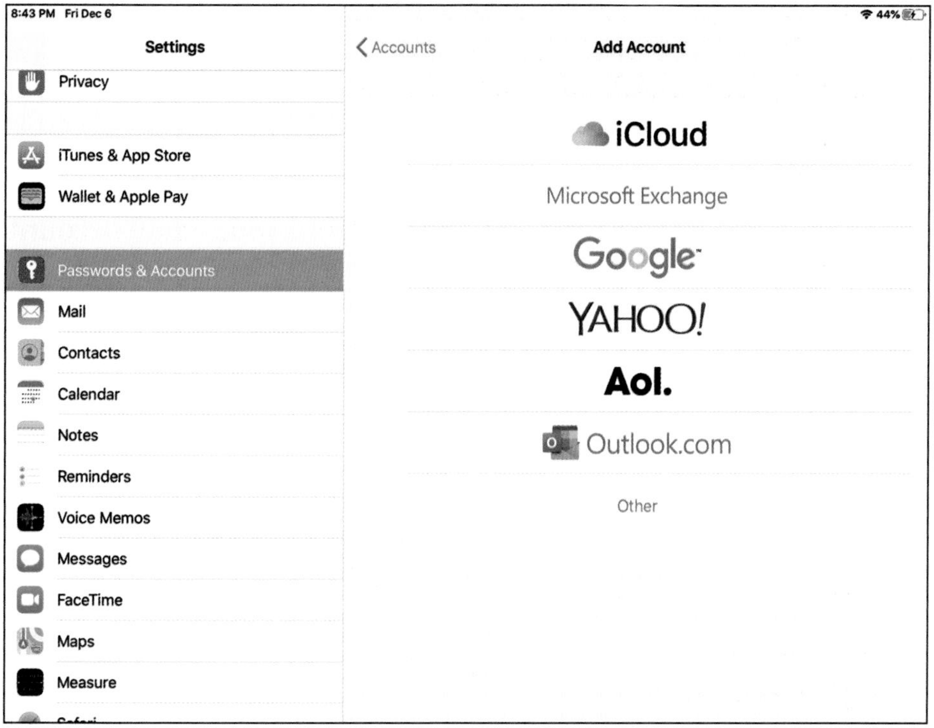

Settings   ⟨ Accounts   Add Account

Privacy

iTunes & App Store   ☁ iCloud

Wallet & Apple Pay   Microsoft Exchange

Passwords & Accounts   Google

Mail   YAHOO!

Contacts   Aol.

Calendar   o▪ Outlook.com

Notes   Other

Reminders

Voice Memos

Messages

FaceTime

Maps

Measure

FIGURE 11-2

4. Tap iCloud, Microsoft Exchange, Google, Yahoo!, AOL or Outlook.com. Enter your account information in the form that appears and follow any instructions to complete the process. (Each service is slightly different, but none are complicated.) If you have a different email service than these, skip to the next section called "Manually Set Up an Email Account."

5. After your iPad takes a moment to verify the account information, on the next screen (shown in **Figure 11-3**), you can tap any On/Off switch to have services from that account synced with your iPad.

6. When you're done, tap Save in the upper-right corner. The account is saved, and you can now open it using Mail.

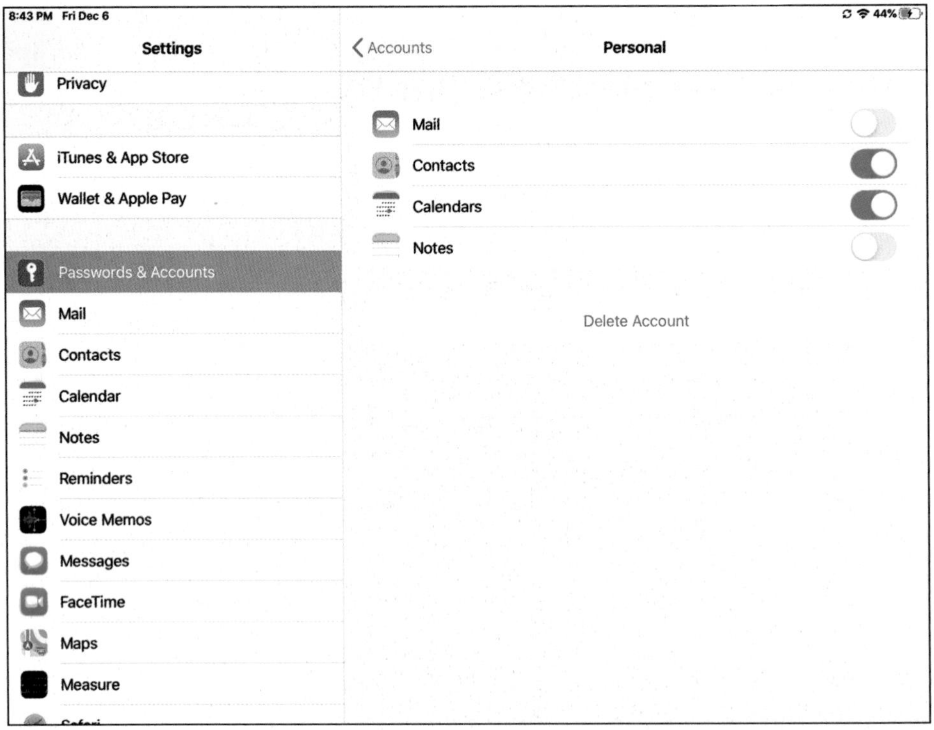

Settings

< Accounts   **Personal**

✋ Privacy

🅰 iTunes & App Store   ✉️ Mail

▦ Wallet & Apple Pay   👤 Contacts

🔑 Passwords & Accounts   📅 Calendars

✉️ Mail   📄 Notes

👤 Contacts   Delete Account

📅 Calendar

📄 Notes

⋮ Reminders

🎙 Voice Memos

💬 Messages

📷 FaceTime

🗺 Maps

⬛ Measure

FIGURE 11-3

Manually Set Up an Email Account

You can also set up most popular email accounts, such as those
available through Earthlink or a cable provider's service, by obtain-
ing the host name from the provider. To set up an existing account
with a provider other than iCloud (Apple), Microsoft Exchange, Gmail
(Google), Yahoo!, AOL, or Outlook.com, you enter the account settings yourself:

TIP

If this is the first time you're adding an account, and if you only
need to add one, just open Mail and begin from Step 3 below.

1. Tap the Settings icon on the Home screen.

2. In Settings, tap Passwords & Accounts and then tap the Add Account
   button (refer to Figure 11-1).

3. On the screen that appears (refer to Figure 11-2), tap Other.

4. On the screen shown in **Figure 11-4**, tap Add Mail Account.

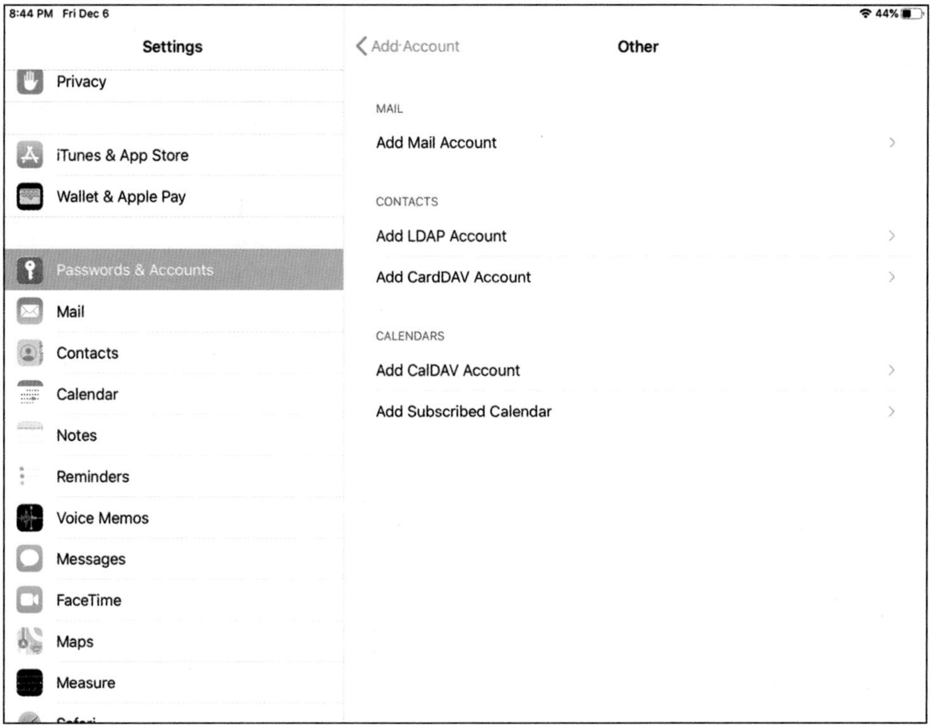

8:44 PM Fri Dec 6   🛜 44%⬛

| Settings | ‹ Add Account | Other |

| Privacy |

| | MAIL |

| iTunes & App Store | Add Mail Account | › |

| Wallet & Apple Pay | CONTACTS |

| | Add LDAP Account | › |

| Passwords & Accounts | Add CardDAV Account | › |

| Mail |

| Contacts | CALENDARS |

| Calendar | Add CalDAV Account | › |

| Notes | Add Subscribed Calendar | › |

| Reminders |

| Voice Memos |

| Messages |

| FaceTime |

| Maps |

| Measure |

FIGURE 11-4

5. In the form that appears, enter your name and an account email address, password, and description and then tap Next. iPad takes a moment to verify your account and then returns you to the Passwords & Accounts page, with your new account displayed.

TIP

Your iPad will probably add the outgoing mail server (SMTP) information for you. If it doesn't, you may have to enter it yourself. If you have a less mainstream email service, you may have to enter the mail server protocol (POP3 or IMAP — ask your provider for this information) and your password.

6. To make sure that the account is set to receive email, tap the account name. In the dialog box that appears, toggle the On/Off switch for the Mail field to On (green) and then tap the Accounts button to return to Mail settings. You can now access the account through your iPad's Mail app.

TIP

If you turn on Calendars in the Passwords & Accounts settings, any information that you've put into your calendar in that email account is brought over into the Calendar app on your iPad (discussed in more detail in Chapter 17).

Open Mail and Read Messages

To open mail and read messages:

1. Tap the Mail app icon (a blue square containing an envelope) located in the Dock on the bottom of the Home screen. A red circle on the icon, called a badge, may appear indicating the number of unread emails in your Inbox.

2. In the Mail app (see **Figure 11-5**), tap the Inbox to see your emails. If you have more than one account listed, tap the Inbox whose contents you want to display.

3. Tap a message to read it. It opens on the right side (see **Figure 11-6**).

4. If you need to scroll to see the entire message, just place your finger on the screen and flick upward to scroll down.

Email messages that you haven't read are marked with a blue circle in your Inbox. After you read a message, the blue circle disappears. You can mark a read message as unread to help remind you to read it again later. With the Inbox displayed, swipe to the right (starting your swipe just a little in from the edge of the screen) on a message and then tap Unread. If you swipe quickly to the right, you don't need to tap; it will just mark as unread automatically.

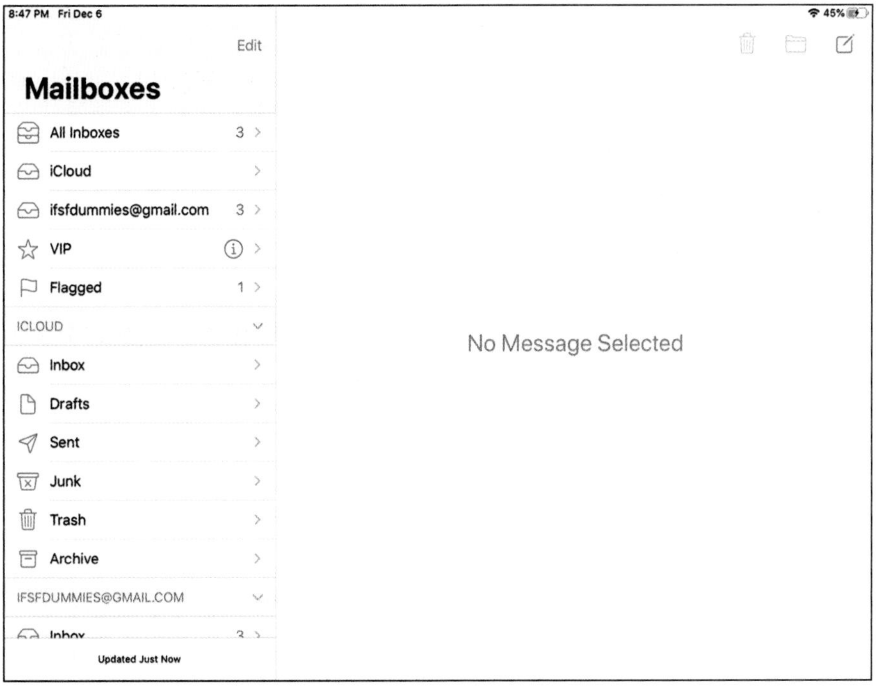

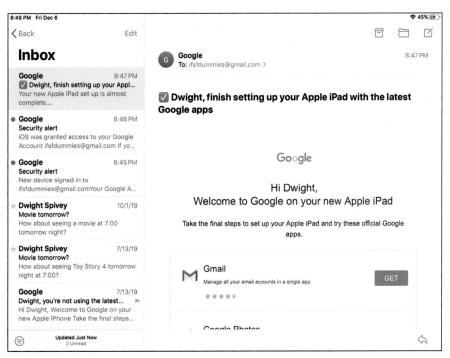

FIGURE 11-5

FIGURE 11-6

Reply To or Forward Email

To reply to or forward email:

1. With an email message open, tap the Reply/Forward button in the lower-right, which looks like a left-facing arrow (refer to Figure 11-6). Then tap Reply, Reply All (available if there are multiple recipients), or Forward in the menu that appears (see **Figure 11-7).**

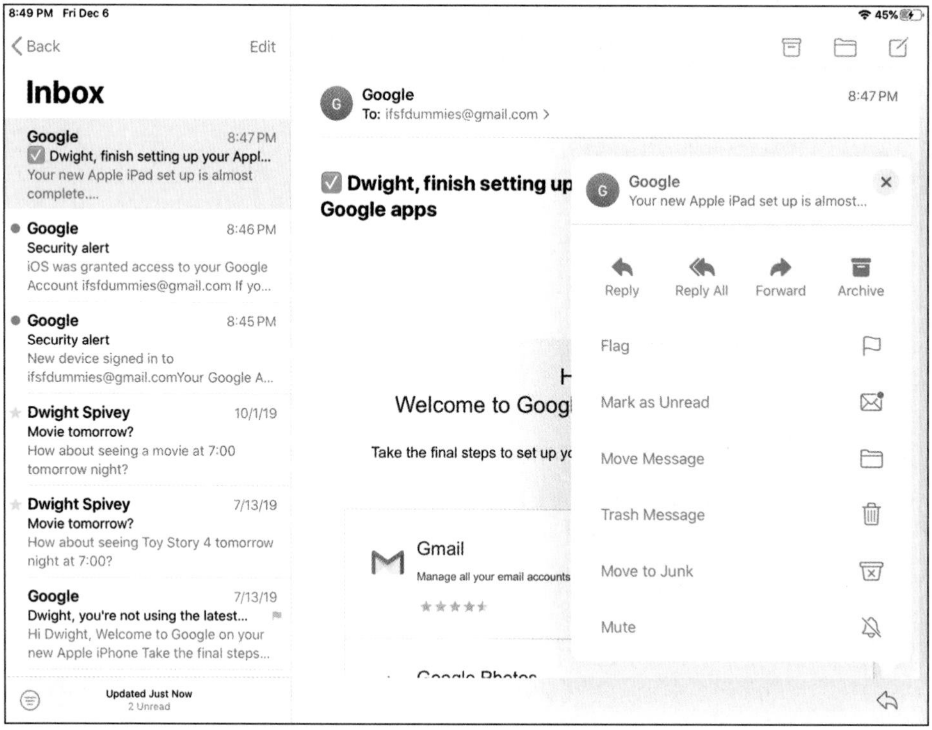

FIGURE 11-7

2. In the new email message that appears (see **Figure 11-8**), tap in the To field and enter another addressee if you like (you have to do this if you're forwarding). Next, tap in the message body and enter a message (see **Figure 11-9**).

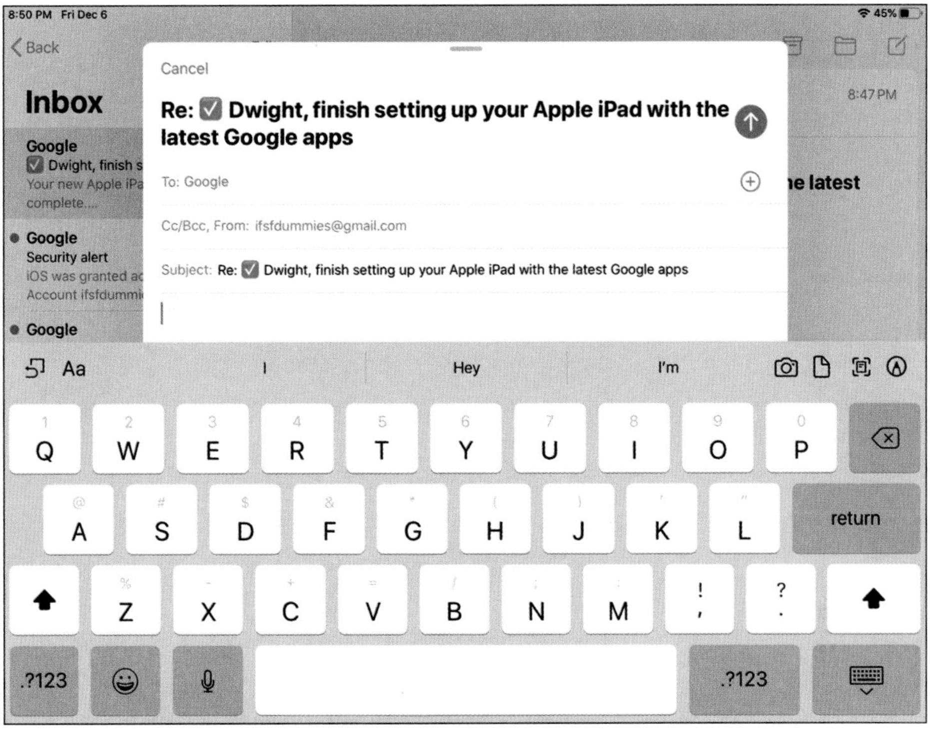

FIGURE 11-8

TIP

If you want to move an email address from the To field to the Cc or Bcc field, tap and hold the address and drag it to the other field.

3. Tap the Send button in the upper-right corner (blue circle with an upward-pointing arrow) and the email goes on its way.

TIP

If you tap Forward to send the message to somebody else and the original message had an attachment, you're offered the option of including or omitting the attachment.

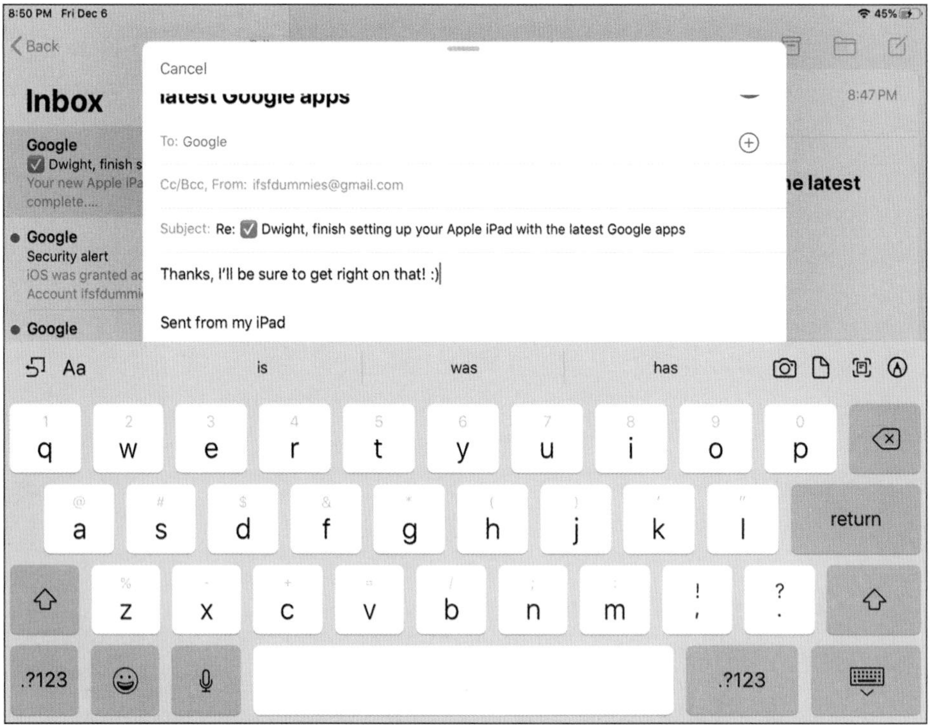

FIGURE 11-9

Create and Send a New Message

To create and send a new message:

1. With Mail open, tap the New Message button in the upper-right corner (this looks like a page with a pencil on it). A blank email appears (see **Figure 11-10**).

2. Enter a recipient's address in the To field by tapping in the field and typing the address. If you have addresses in Contacts, tap the plus sign (+) in the To field to choose an addressee from the Contacts list that appears.

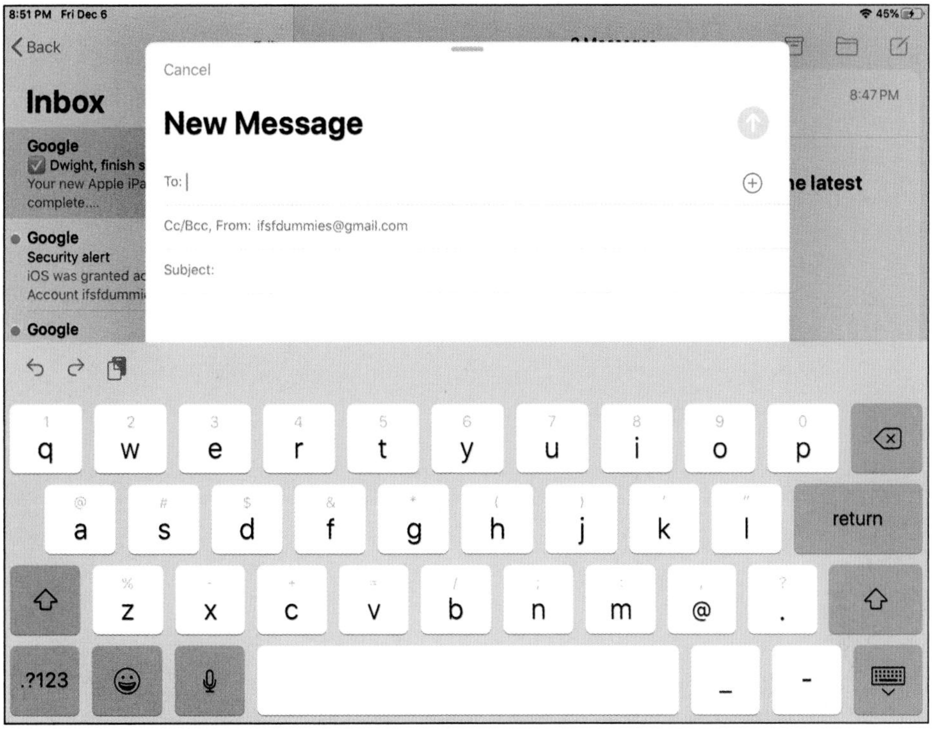

FIGURE 11-10

3. If you want to send a copy of the message to other people, tap the Cc/Bcc field. When the Cc and Bcc fields open, enter addresses in either or both. Use the Bcc field to specify recipients of blind carbon copies, which means that no other recipients are aware that that person received this reply.

4. Enter the subject of the message in the Subject field.

5. Tap in the message body and type your message.

6. If you want to check a fact or copy and paste some part of another message into your draft message, swipe down near the top of the email to display your Inbox and other folders. Locate the message, and when you're ready to return to your draft, tap the Subject of the email, which is displayed near the bottom of the screen.

7. When you've finished creating your message, tap Send.

Format Email

You can apply some basic formatting to email text. You can use bold, underline, and italic formats, and indent text using the Quote Level feature.

To format an email:

1. Press and hold the text in a message you're creating and choose Select or Select All to select a single word or all the words in the email (see **Figure 11-11**).

When you make a selection, blue handles appear that you can drag to add adjacent words to your selection. If the menu disappears after you select the text, just tap one of the selection handles, and it will reappear.

TIP

FIGURE 11-11

2. To see more tools (such as adding documents or inserting drawings), tap the arrow on the toolbar that appears to the right. To apply bold, italic, or underline formatting, tap the BIU button.

3. In the toolbar that appears (see **Figure 11-12**), tap Bold, Italic, or Underline to apply formatting.

FIGURE 11-12

4. To change the indent level, tap and hold at the beginning of a line and then tap Quote Level.

5. Tap Increase to indent the text or Decrease to move indented text farther toward the left margin.

TIP

To use the Quote Level feature, make sure that it's on. From the Home screen tap Settings, tap Mail, tap Increase Quote Level, and then toggle (tap) the Increase Quote Level On/Off switch to turn it On (green).

Mail in iPadOS 13 allows you to go beyond the basics, though. It introduces much-improved text formatting and font support, freeing you up to create some really great looking emails. However, it doesn't stop there: The new format bar (which appears above the keyboard, shown in **Figure 11-13**) allows you to easily jazz up your email with a variety of options.

FIGURE 11-13

If you see words above the keyboard and not the format bar, tap the arrow to the right of the words to bring the format bar back into view.

The new format bar enables you to format text. Just tap the Aa button to see a bevy of formatting options (shown in **Figure 11-14**) hitherto not available in Mail, such as

- » Choose Bold, Italic, Underline, and Strikethrough. (Okay, these options aren't new, but the rest are.)
- » Change the font by tapping Default Font and browsing a surprisingly extensive list of fonts to choose from.
- » Decrease or increase text size by tapping the small A or the large A, respectively.
- » Tap the color wheel to select a color for your text.
- » Insert numbered or bulletted lists.
- » Select left, center, or right justification.
- » Increase or decrease the quote level.
- » Indent or outdent paragraphs.

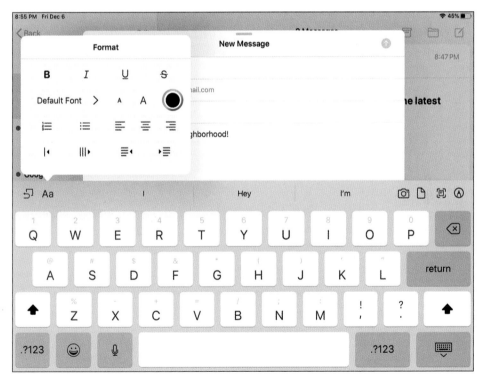

FIGURE 11-14

The format bar also offers these tools:

- » **Camera**: Tap to insert a new photo or video directly from the Camera app, or to insert one from the Photos app.

- » **Attachment**: Tap to add an attachment to the email from the Files app. (See Chapter 4 for more info about Files.)

- » **Insert Drawing**: Tap to create a new drawing and insert it into your email.

- » **Scan Document**: Tap to scan a paper document and add it to your email.

Search Email

What do you do if you want to find all messages from a certain person or containing a certain word? You can use Mail's handy Search feature to find these emails.

To search email:

1. With Mail open, tap an account to display its Inbox.

2. In the Inbox, tap in the Search field, and the onscreen keyboard appears.

TIP

You can also use the Spotlight Search feature covered in Chapter 2 to search for terms in the To, From, or Subject lines of mail messages.

3. Tap the All Mailboxes tab to view messages that contain the search term in any mailbox, or tap the Current Mailbox tab to see only matches within the current mailbox. (These options may vary slightly depending on which email service you use.)

4. Enter a search term or name, as shown in **Figure 11-15**. If multiple types of information are found, such as People or Subjects, tap the one you're looking for. Matching emails are listed in the results.

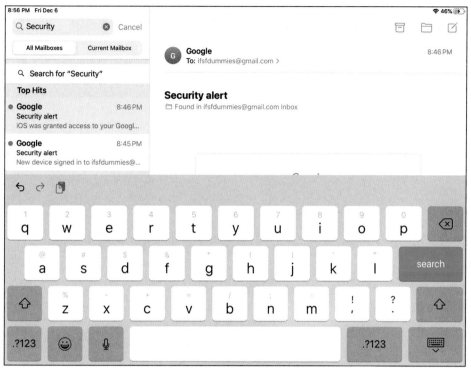

FIGURE 11-15

Mark Email as Unread or Flag for Follow-Up

You can use a simple swipe to access tools that either mark an email as unread after you've read it (placing a blue dot before the message) or flag an email (which places an orange flag to the right of it). If the email is both marked as unread and is flagged, both a blue dot and an orange flag will appear on the message. These methods help you remember to reread an email that you've already read or to follow up on a message at a later time.

To mark email as unread or to flag it for follow-up:

1. With Mail open and an Inbox displayed, swipe to the left on an email in the Inbox list to display three options: More, Flag, and Trash/Archive. Whether Trash or Archive appears is dependent on the settings for each account.

2. Tap More. On the menu shown in **Figure 11-16**, you're given several options, including Mark. Tapping Mark accesses both the Mark As Read/Unread and Flag commands. Tapping either command applies it and returns you to your Inbox.

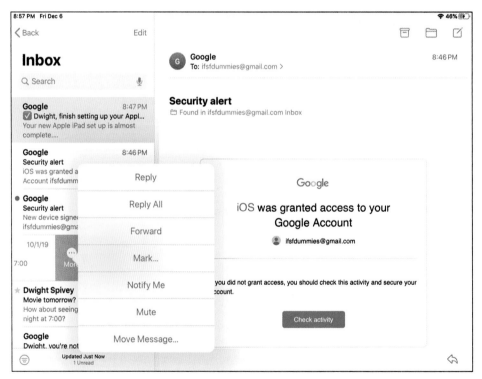

FIGURE 11-16

You can also get to the Mark As Read/Unread command by swiping to the right on a message displayed in your Inbox.

TIP

Create an Event from Email Contents

A neat feature in Mail is the ability to create a Calendar event from within an email:

1. To test this out, create an email to yourself mentioning a reservation on a specific airline on a specific date and time; you can also mention another type of reservation, such as for dinner, or mention a phone number.

2. Send the message to yourself and then open Mail.

3. In your Inbox, open the email. (The pertinent information is displayed in underlined text.)

4. Tap the underlined text, and in the menu shown in **Figure 11-17**, tap Create Event. A New Event form from Calendar appears. Enter additional information about the event and then tap Done.

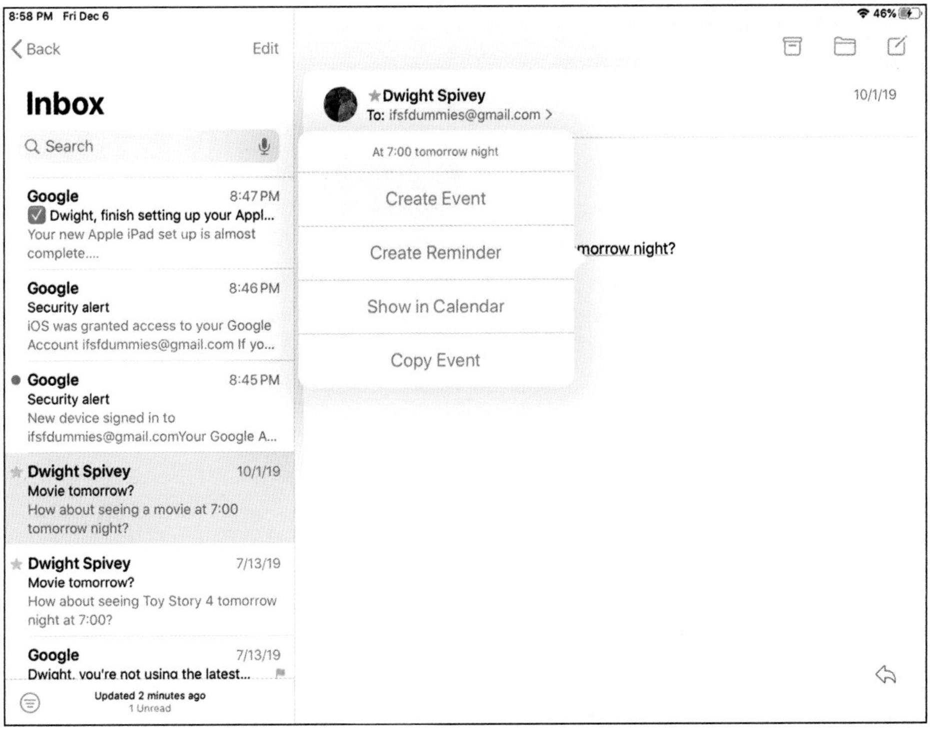

FIGURE 11-17

Delete Email

When you no longer want an email cluttering your Inbox, you can delete it.

1. With the Inbox displayed, tap the Edit button (found just to the left of center screen). Circular check buttons are displayed to the left of each message (see **Figure 11-18**).

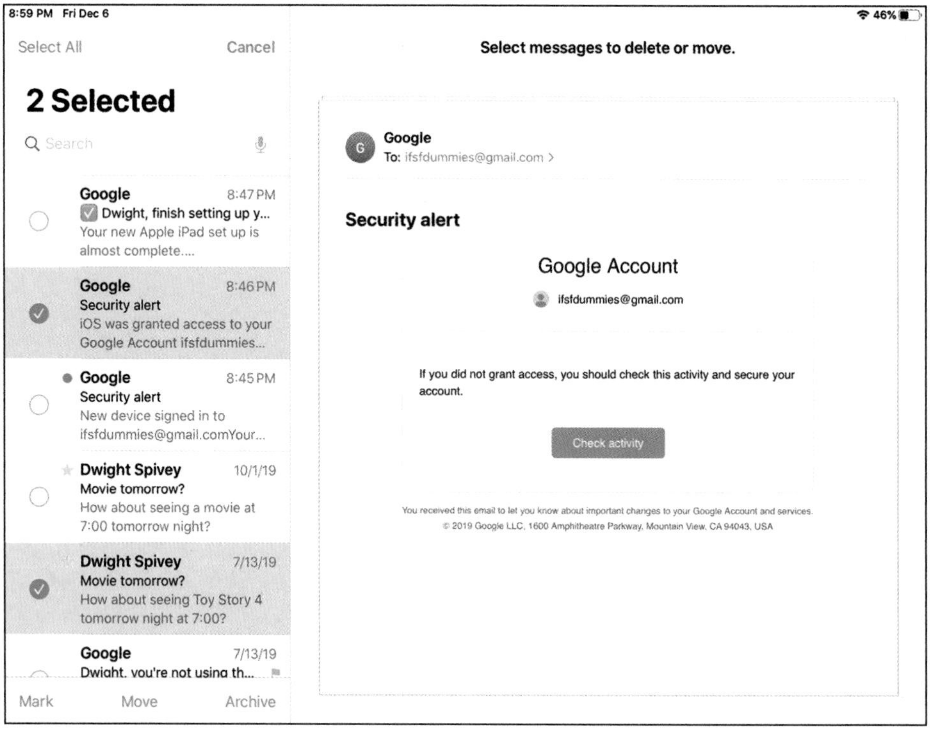

FIGURE 11-18

TIP

2. Tap the circle next to the message that you want to delete. A message marked for deletion shows a check mark in the circular check button.

You can tap multiple items if you have several emails to delete.

3. Tap the Trash or Archive button at the bottom-left corner of the Inbox dialog box. The selected messages are moved to the Trash or Archive folder.

TECHNICAL
STUFF

What's the difference between Trash and Archive? Basically, email sent to a Trash folder typically is deleted forever after a certain amount of time (usually 30 days); email sent to an Archive folder is removed from the Inbox but kept indefinitely for future use.

TIP

You can also delete an open email by tapping the Reply button in the bottom-right corner of the screen and tapping Trash/Archive Message, or swiping left on a message displayed in an Inbox and tapping the Trash or Archive button that appears.

3

Enjoying Media

Chapter **12**

Shopping the iTunes Store

The iTunes Store app that comes preinstalled on your iPad lets you easily shop for music, movies, and TV shows. As Chapter 13 explains, you can also get electronic and audiobooks via the Apple Books app.

In this chapter, you discover how to find content in the iTunes Store. You can download the content directly to your iPad or to another device and then sync it to your iPad. Finally, I cover using Apple Pay to make real-world purchases using a stored payment method.

TIP

I cover opening an iTunes account and downloading iTunes software to your computer in Chapter 3. If you need to, read Chapter 3 to see how to handle these two tasks before digging into this chapter.

Explore the iTunes Store

Visiting the iTunes Store from your iPad is easy with the built-in iTunes Store app.

If you're in search of other kinds of content, the Podcasts app and iTunes U app allow you to find and then download podcasts and online courses to your iPad.

To check out the iTunes Store, follow these steps:

1. If you aren't already signed in to iTunes, tap Settings and go to iTunes & App Store. Tap Sign In, enter your Apple ID and Password in their respective fields, and then tap Sign In.

2. Go to your Home screen and tap the iTunes Store icon (you might find it on the second Home screen).

3. Tap the Music button (if it isn't already selected) in the row of buttons at the bottom of the screen. Swipe up and down the screen, and you'll find several categories of selections, such as New Music, Pre-Orders, and Recent Releases (these category names change from time to time).

4. Flick your finger up to scroll through the featured selections or tap the See All button to see more selections in any category, as shown in **Figure 12-1.**

The navigation techniques in these steps work essentially the same in any of the content categories (the buttons at the bottom of the screen), which include Music, Movies, and TV Shows.

5. Tap the Top Charts tab at the bottom of the screen and then tap the Music tab at the top of the screen. This displays lists of bestselling songs, albums, and music videos in the iTunes Store.

A See All button

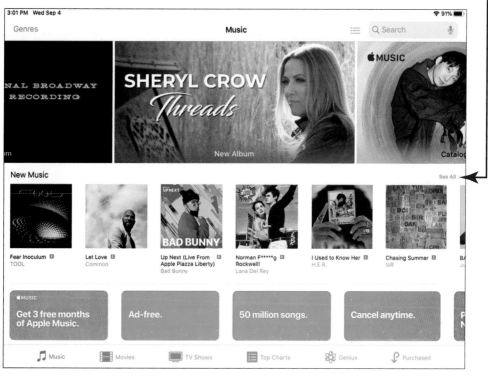

FIGURE 12-1

6. Tap any listed item to see more detail about it, as shown in
Figure 12-2, and hear a brief preview when you tap the title of
a song. Tap anywhere on the screen outside of the information
window to close it.

TIP

If you want to use the Genius playlist feature, which recommends
additional purchases based on the contents of your library in the
iTunes app on your iPad, tap the Genius button at the bottom
of the screen. If you've made enough purchases in iTunes, song
and album recommendations appear based on those purchases
as well as the content in your iTunes Match library (a fee-based
service), if you have one.

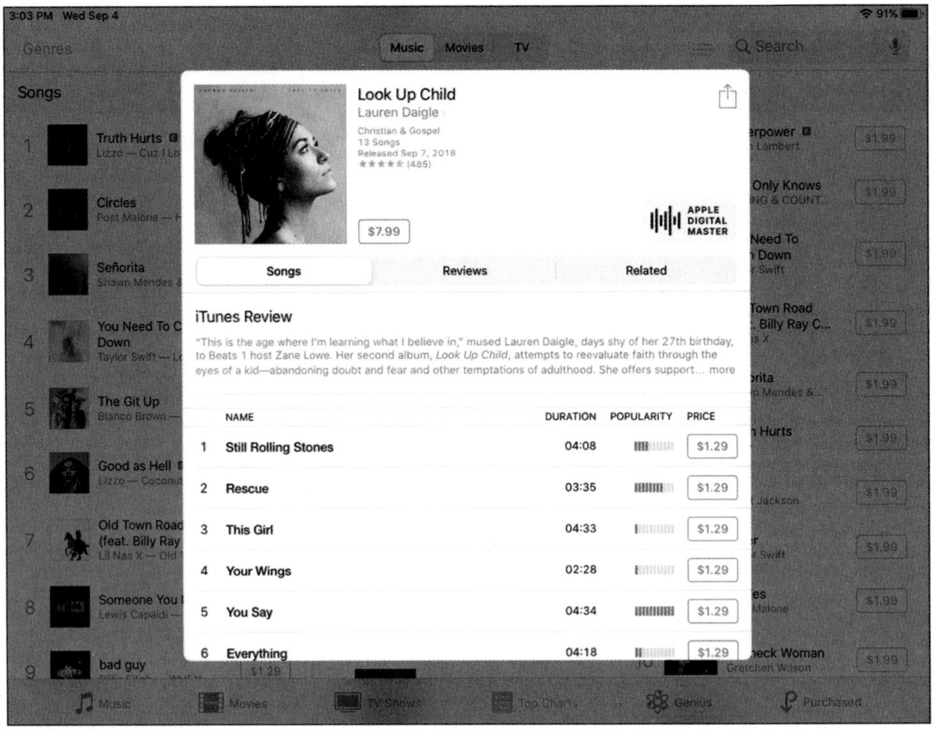

FIGURE 12-2

Find a Selection

You can look for a selection in the iTunes Store in several ways. You can use the Search feature, search by genre or category, or view artists' pages. Here's how these work:

» Tap the Search field in the upper-right corner of the screen, and the Search field shown in **Figure 12-3** appears. Tap in the field and enter a search term using the onscreen keyboard. Tap the Search button on the keyboard or, if a suggestion in the list of search results appeals to you, just tap that suggestion.

FIGURE 12-3

» Tap an item at the bottom of the screen (such as Music) and then tap the Genres button in the upper left of the screen.

A list of genres like the one shown in **Figure 12-4** appears.

» On a description page that appears when you tap a selection, you can find more offerings by the people involved with that particular work. For example, for a music selection, tap to display details about it and then tap the Reviews tab at the middle of the page to see all reviews of the album (see **Figure 12-5**). For a movie (tap Movies at the bottom of the iTunes Store Home page), tap to open details and then tap Reviews, or tap the Related tab to see more movies starring any of the lead actors.

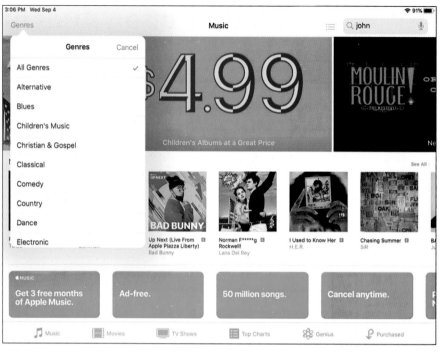

FIGURE 12-4

FIGURE 12-5

Preview Music, a Video, or an Audiobook

You might want to preview an item before you buy it. If you like it, buying and downloading are easy and quick.

To preview items in the iTunes Store, follow these steps:

1. Open the iTunes Store app and use any method outlined in earlier tasks to locate a selection that you might want to buy.

2. Tap the item to see detailed information about it, as shown in **Figure 12-6.**

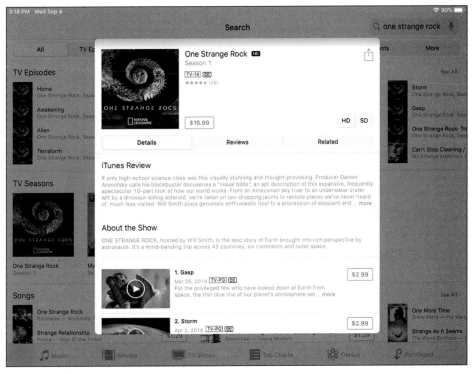

FIGURE 12-6

3. For a TV show, tap an episode to get further information (refer to Figure 12-6). If you're looking at a music selection, tap the track number or name of a selection to play a preview. For a movie or audiobook selection, tap the Trailers Play button (movies) shown in **Figure 12-7.**

Tap to buy

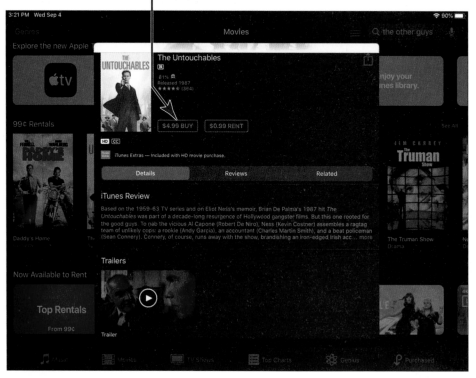

FIGURE 12-7

Buy a Selection

To buy a selection:

1. When you find an item that you want to buy, tap the button that shows either the price (if it's a selection available for purchase; see Figure 12-7) or the button labeled "Get" (if it's a selection available for free).

TIP

If you want to buy music, you can open the description page for an album and tap the album price, or buy individual songs rather than the entire album. Tap the price for a song and then proceed to purchase it.

2. When the dialog box appears at the bottom of the screen, tap Purchase, type your password in the Password field on the next screen, and then tap Sign In to buy the item. Alternatively, use Touch ID if you have it enabled for iTunes and App Store purchases. The dialog box will display "Pay with Touch ID" if you do.

3. The item begins downloading, and the cost, if any, is automatically charged to your account. When the download finishes, tap OK in the Purchase Complete message, and you can then view the content using the Music or TV app, depending on the type of content it is.

Rent Movies

In the case of movies, you can either rent or buy content. If you rent, which is less expensive but only a one-time deal, you have 30 days from the time you rent the item to begin watching it. After you have begun to watch it, you have 24 hours from that time left to watch it on the same device, as many times as you like.

To rent movies:

1. With the iTunes Store open, tap the Movies button.

2. Locate the movie you want to rent and tap it.

3. In the detailed description of the movie that appears, tap the Rent button (if it's available for rental); see **Figure 12-8.**

4. When the dialog box appears at the bottom of the screen, tap Rent, type your password in the Password field on the next screen, and then tap Sign In to rent the item. Alternatively, use Touch ID if you have it enabled for iTunes and App Store purchases. The dialog box will display "Pay with Touch ID" if you do. The movie begins to download to your iPad immediately, and your account is charged the rental fee.

5. After the download is complete, you can use the TV app to watch it. (See Chapter 16 to read about how this app works.)

Tap to rent

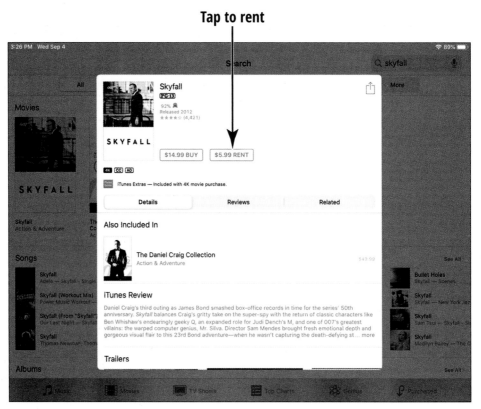

FIGURE 12-8

Use Apple Pay and Wallet

Apple is the creator of a relatively new, and increasingly popular, method of paying for items by using your iPad (or other Apple devices). It's called Apple Pay. Fancied as a mobile wallet, this service uses the Touch ID feature in your iPad's Home button to identify you and any credit cards you've stored at the iTunes Store to make payments via a feature called Wallet.

Your credit card information isn't stored on your phone or iPad, and Apple doesn't know a thing about your purchases. In addition, Apple considers Apple Pay safer because the store cashier doesn't even have to know your name.

To set up Apple Pay, go to Settings and tap Wallet & Apple Pay. Add information about a credit card. When you want to initiate a purchase, there's a shortcut you can use to bring up Apple Pay quickly: Double-tap the Home button when the lock screen is displayed on your device. This action opens Apple Pay with your default card ready to be used. (You can easily switch cards by tapping your other cards at the bottom of the screen.) If you're device is already unlocked, just tap the Wallet app to use Apple Pay. You can also change settings, set your default card, and add and delete cards from within the Wallet app itself.

For more information on Apple Pay, check out `http://www.apple.com/apple-pay`.

Set Up Family Sharing

Family Sharing is a feature that allows as many as six people in your family to share whatever anybody in the group has purchased from the iTunes, Apple Books, and App Stores even though you don't share Apple IDs. Your family must all use the same credit card to purchase items (tied to whichever Apple ID is managing the family), but you can approve purchases by children under 13 years of age. Start by turning on Family Sharing:

1. Tap Settings and then tap the Apple ID at the top of the screen.
2. Tap Set Up Family Sharing.
3. Tap Get Started. On the next screen, you can add a photo for your family. Tap Continue.
4. On the Share Purchases screen, tap Share Purchases from a different account to use another Apple account.
5. Tap Continue and check the payment method that you want to use. Tap Continue.
6. On the next screen, tap Add Family Member. Enter the person's name (assuming that this person is listed in your contacts) or email address. An invitation is sent to the person's email. When the invitation is accepted, the person is added to your family.

TECHNICAL
STUFF
The payment method for this family is displayed under Shared Payment Method in the Family Sharing screen (Settings⇨Apple ID⇨Family Sharing⇨Purchase Sharing). All those involved in a family have to use a single payment method for family purchases.

There's also an option called Create a Child Account. When you click Add Family Member in the Family Sharing window, click Create a Child Account and enter information to create the ID. The child's account is automatically added to your Family and retains the child status until he or she turns 13. If a child accesses iTunes to buy something, he or she is prompted to ask permission. You get an Ask to Buy notification on your iPad as well as via email. You can then accept or decline the purchase, giving you control over family spending in the iTunes Store.

IN THIS CHAPTER

» **Discover e-reading**

» **Find books**

» **Navigate and search a book**

» **Make it easier to read your e-books**

» **Set reading goals**

Chapter **13**

Reading Books

A traditional e-reader is a device that's used primarily to read the electronic version of books, magazines, and newspapers. Apple has touted the iPad as a great e-reader, and although it isn't a traditional e-reader device like the Kindle Paperwhite, you don't want to miss this cool functionality.

Apple's free app that turns your iPad into an e-reader is Apple Books (formerly known as iBooks), which also enables you to buy and download books (and audiobooks) from the Apple Books Store (offering millions of books and growing by the day). You can also use one of several other free e-reader apps — for example, Kindle or Nook. Then you can download books to your iPad from a variety of online sources, such as Amazon and Google, so that you can read to your heart's content.

In this chapter, you discover the options available for reading material and how to buy books. You also learn how to navigate a book or periodical and adjust the brightness and type, as well as how to search books and organize your Apple Books libraries.

Find Books with Apple Books

When you buy a book online (or get one of many free publications), it downloads to your iPad in a few seconds (or minutes, depending on your Internet connection speed and the size of the files) using a Wi-Fi or cellular connection.

1. To shop using Apple Books, tap the Apple Books application icon to open it. (It's on your first Home screen and looks like a white book against an orange background; it's also simply labeled Books.)

2. Tap the Book Store tab at the bottom of the screen.

3. In the Book Store, shown in **Figure 13-1,** featured titles and suggestions (based on your past reading habits and searches) are shown. You can do any of the following to find a book:

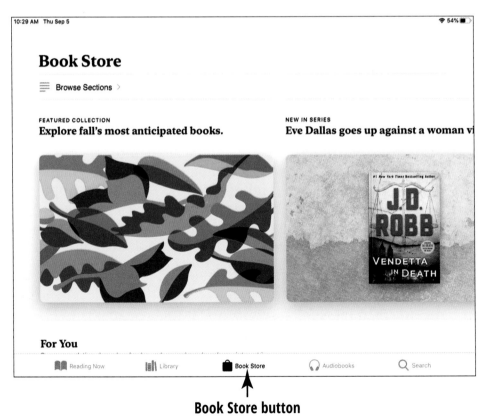

Book Store button

FIGURE 13-1

- Swipe left or right to see and read articles and suggestions for the latest books in various categories, such as Trending (ten popular books, as shown in **Figure 13-2**), Featured Collection, and the like.

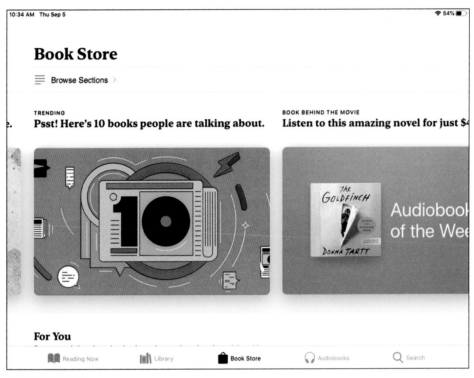

FIGURE 13-2

- Scroll down on the Book Store's main page to see links to popular categories of books, as shown in **Figure 13-3**. Tap a category to view those selections.

- Scroll down to Top Charts to view both Paid and Free books listed on top bestseller lists. Tap the See All button under Top Charts to focus on books that are the latest hits.

- Swipe further down the screen to find a list of Genres. Tap All Genres to see everything the Book Store has to offer.

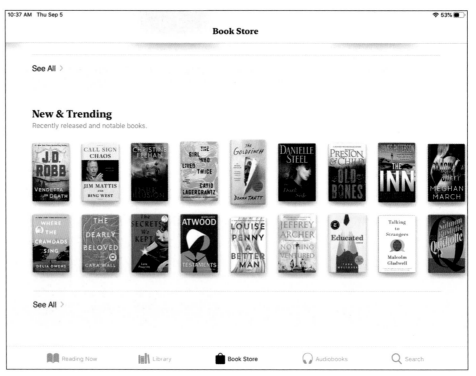

FIGURE 13-3

- On the main screen of the Book Store, tap the Browse Sections button under "Book Store" (at the top of the Book Store screen, if you've scrolled down) to open the Browse Sections menu, shown in **Figure 13-4**. From here you can easily scroll up and down the screen to browse book store sections and genres. Swipe the Browse menu from right to left to close it.

- Tap a suggested selection or featured book to read more information about it.

- Tap the Search button in the bottom-right of the screen, tap in the Search field that appears, and then type a search word or phrase using the onscreen keyboard.

TIP

Many books let you download free samples before you buy. You get to read several pages of the book to see whether it appeals to you, and it doesn't cost you a dime! Look for the Sample button when you view book details. (The button usually is below the price of the book.)

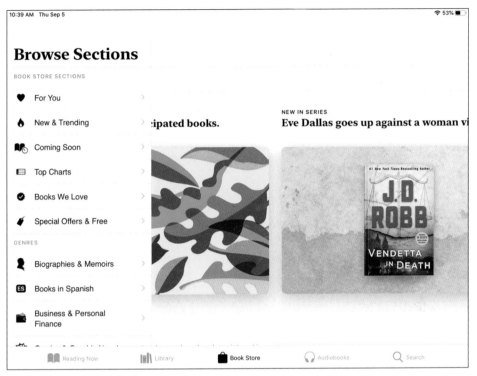

Browse Sections

BOOK STORE SECTIONS

♥   For You   >

◊   New & Trending   >   :ipated books.

📚   Coming Soon   >

▤   Top Charts   >

✿   Books We Love   >

✦   Special Offers & Free   >

GENRES

♟   Biographies & Memoirs   >

ES   Books in Spanish   >

💼   Business & Personal
     Finance   >

NEW IN SERIES
Eve Dallas goes up against a woman vi

📖 Reading Now   📚 Library   🛍 Book Store   🎧 Audiobooks   🔍 Search

FIGURE 13-4

Explore Other E-Book Sources

Beyond using Apple Books, the iPad is capable of using other e-reader apps to read book content from other bookstores. You first have to download another e-reader application, such as Kindle from Amazon or the Barnes & Noble Nook reader from the App Store (see Chapter 7 for how to download apps). You can also download a non-vendor-specific app such as Bluefire Reader, which handles ePub and PDF formats, as well as the format that most public libraries use (protected PDF). Then use the app's features to search for, purchase, and download content.

The Kindle e-reader application is shown in **Figure 13-5.** After downloading the free app from the App Store, you just open the app and enter the email address and password associated with your Amazon account. Any content you've already bought from the Amazon.com Kindle Store from your computer or Kindle Fire tablet is archived online and can be placed on your Kindle Home page on the iPad for you to read anytime you like. Tap the Downloaded tab (upper-right) to see titles stored on your iPad rather than in Amazon's Cloud library. To enhance your reading experience, you can change the background to a sepia tone or change the font. To delete a book from this reader, press and hold the title with your finger, and the Remove from Device button appears within a menu; simply tap the button to remove the book from your iPad.

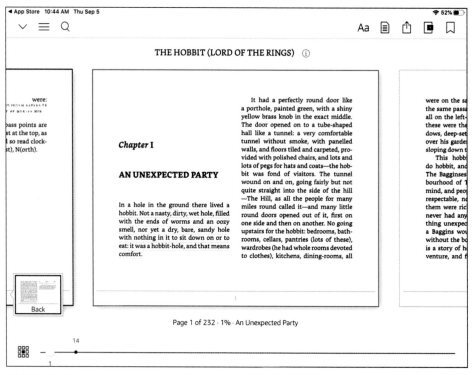

FIGURE 13-5

TIP

E-books are everywhere! You can get content from a variety of other sources, such as Project Gutenberg, Google Play, and some publishers like Baen. Download the content using your computer, if you like, and then just add the items to Books in iTunes and sync them to your iPad. You can also open items from a web link or email, and they're copied to Apple Books for you. You can also set up iCloud so that books are pushed across your Apple devices or you can place them in an online storage service (such as Drop-box or Google Drive) and access them from there.

TECHNICAL STUFF

E-books come in different formats, and Apple Books won't work with formats other than ePub or PDF. (For example, it can't use such formats as the Kindle's Mobi and AZW.)

Buy Books

If you've set up an account with iTunes, you can buy books at the Apple Books Store using the Apple Books app. (See Chapter 3 for more about iTunes.)

1. Open Apple Books, tap Book Store, and begin looking for a book.

2. When you find a book in the Book Store, you can buy it by tapping it and then tapping the Buy | Price button or the Get button (if it's free), as shown in **Figure 13-6**.

TIP

You may also tap the Want to Read button if you'd like to keep this book in mind for a future purchase, or tap Sample to download a few pages to read before you commit your hard-earned dollars to it.

3. When the dialog box appears in the center of the screen, tap Purchase, type your password in the Password field on the next screen, and then tap Sign In to buy the book. Alternatively, use Touch ID or Face ID if you have it enabled for iTunes and App Store purchases (and if your iPad supports it, of course).

4. The book begins downloading, and the cost, if any, is automatically charged to your account. When the download finishes, tap OK in the Purchase Complete message, and you can find your new purchase by tapping the Library button at the bottom of the screen.

Buy/Get button

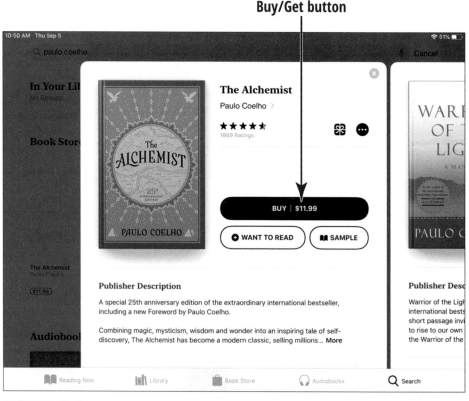

FIGURE 13-6

TIP

Books that you've downloaded to your computer can be accessed from any Apple device through iCloud. Content can also be synced with your iPad by using the Lightning to USB Cable and your iTunes account, or by using the wireless iTunes Wi-Fi Sync setting on the General Settings menu. See Chapter 3 for more about syncing.

Navigate a Book

Getting around in Apple Books is half the fun!

1. Open Apple Books and, if your Library (which looks a tiny bit like a bookshelf) isn't already displayed, tap the Library button at the bottom of the screen.

2. Tap a book to open it. The book opens to its title page or the last spot you read on any compatible device, as shown in **Figure 13-7.**

Table of Contents button

| 11:05 AM Sep 5 | | 🔋 49% ▪ |
| < ≣ Augustine, St. | St. Augustine's Confessions AA Q 🔖 |

were more or less than was said of him; and I weighed every word of his very attentively, but of the matter I was careless and scornful. And verily with the sweetness of his discourse I was much delighted: which, however it were more learned, yet was it not so pleasing and inveigling as Faustus his was, the manner of the oratory I mean, though for the matter there was no comparison. For Faustus did but rove up and down amongst his Manichean fallacies; but Ambrose taught salvation most soundly. But salvation is far enough from sinners, such as I was at that instant; and yet I drew by little and little nearer toward it; but how, I knew not.

XIV

Upon his hearing of St. Ambrose, he by little and little falls off from his errors

FOR though I took little heed to hearken to what he spake, but merely to the way how he delivered them: (for that empty care was now only left in me, I despairing utterly to find a way how man should come unto thee): yet together with his words which I liked, the things also themselves which I neglected, stole in upon my mind; for I knew not how to part them: and whilst I opened my heart to entertain, how eloquently he expressed it, there also entered with it, only by degrees, how truly he proved it. For first of all the things began to appear unto me as possible to be defended: and the Catholic faith, in defence of which I thought nothing could be answered to the Manichees' arguments, I now concluded with myself, might well be maintained without absurdity: especially after I had heard one or two hard places of the Old Testament resolved now and then; which when I understood literally, I was slain. Many places therefore of those

Back to page 352   404 of 727

405 of 727   3 pages left in this chapter

↑
Slider

FIGURE 13-7

3. Take any of these actions to navigate the book:

- To go to the book's Table of Contents: Tap the Table of Contents button at the top of the page (refer to Figure 13-7) and then tap the name of a chapter to go to it (see **Figure 13-8**).

  If you don't see the Table of Contents button, simply tap the screen once to display the navigation controls.

- To turn to the next page: Place your finger anywhere along the right edge of the page and tap or flick to the left.

TIP

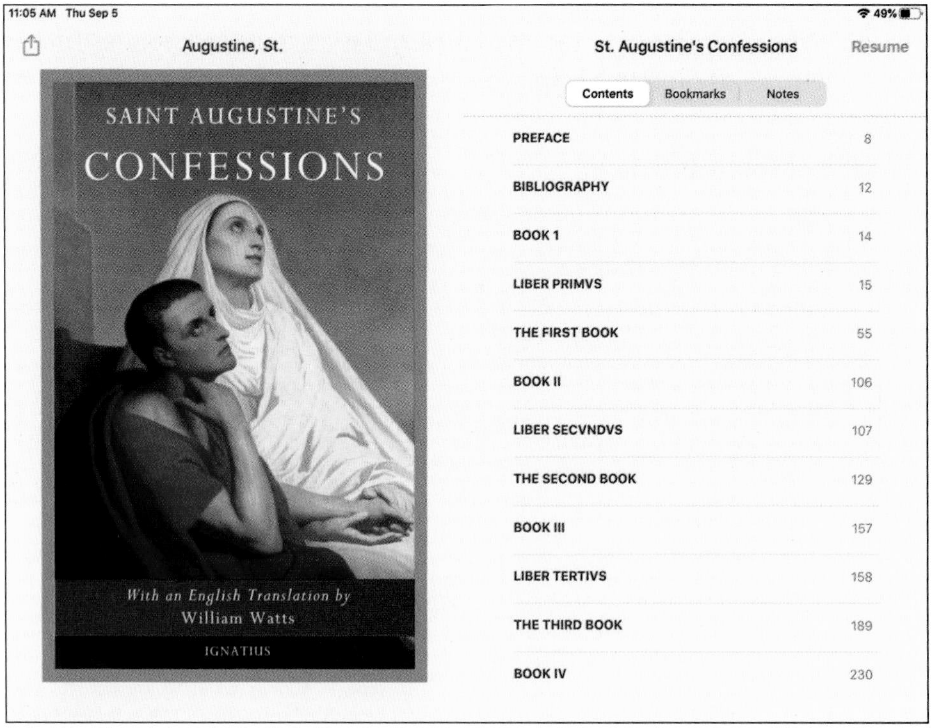

11:05 AM Thu Sep 5
49%
Augustine, St.
St. Augustine's Confessions
Resume
Contents
Bookmarks
Notes
SAINT AUGUSTINE'S
CONFESSIONS
With an English Translation by
William Watts
IGNATIUS
PREFACE 8
BIBLIOGRAPHY 12
BOOK 1 14
LIBER PRIMVS 15
THE FIRST BOOK 55
BOOK II 106
LIBER SECVNDVS 107
THE SECOND BOOK 129
BOOK III 157
LIBER TERTIVS 158
THE THIRD BOOK 189
BOOK IV 230

FIGURE 13-8

- To turn to the preceding page: Place your finger anywhere on the left edge of a page and tap or flick to the right.
- To move to another page in the book: Tap and drag the slider at the bottom of the page (refer to Figure 13-7) to the right or left.

TIP

To return to the Library to view another book at any time, tap the Back button, which looks like a left-pointing arrow and is found in the upper-left corner of the screen. If the button isn't visible, tap anywhere on the page, and the button and other tools appear.

Adjust Brightness in Apple Books

Apple Books offers an adjustable brightness setting that you can use to make your book pages more comfortable to read.

1. With a book open, tap the Display Settings button (looks like aA), shown in **Figure 13-9**.

Brightness slider

Display Settings button

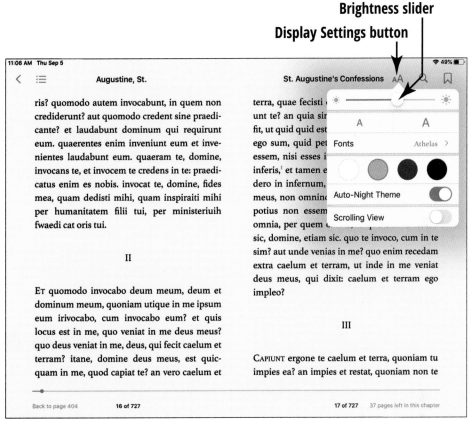

FIGURE 13-9

2. On the Brightness setting that appears at the top (refer to Figure 13-9), tap and drag the slider to the right to make the screen brighter, or to the left to dim it.

3. Tap anywhere on the page to close the Display Settings dialog box.

TIP

Experiment with the brightness level that works for you, or try out the Sepia setting, which you find by tapping the sepia-colored circle in the Display Settings dialog box. Bright-white screens are commonly thought to be hard on the eyes, so setting the brightness halfway relative to its default setting or less is probably a good idea (and saves on battery life).

Change the Font Size and Type

If the type on your screen is a bit small for you to make out, you can change to a larger font size or choose a different font for readability.

1. With a book open, tap the Display Settings button (refer to Figure 13-9).

2. In the dialog box that appears (shown in **Figure 13-10**), tap the button with a smaller A, on the left, to use smaller text, or the button with the larger A, on the right, to use larger text.

3. Tap the Fonts button. The list of fonts shown in **Figure 13-11** appears.

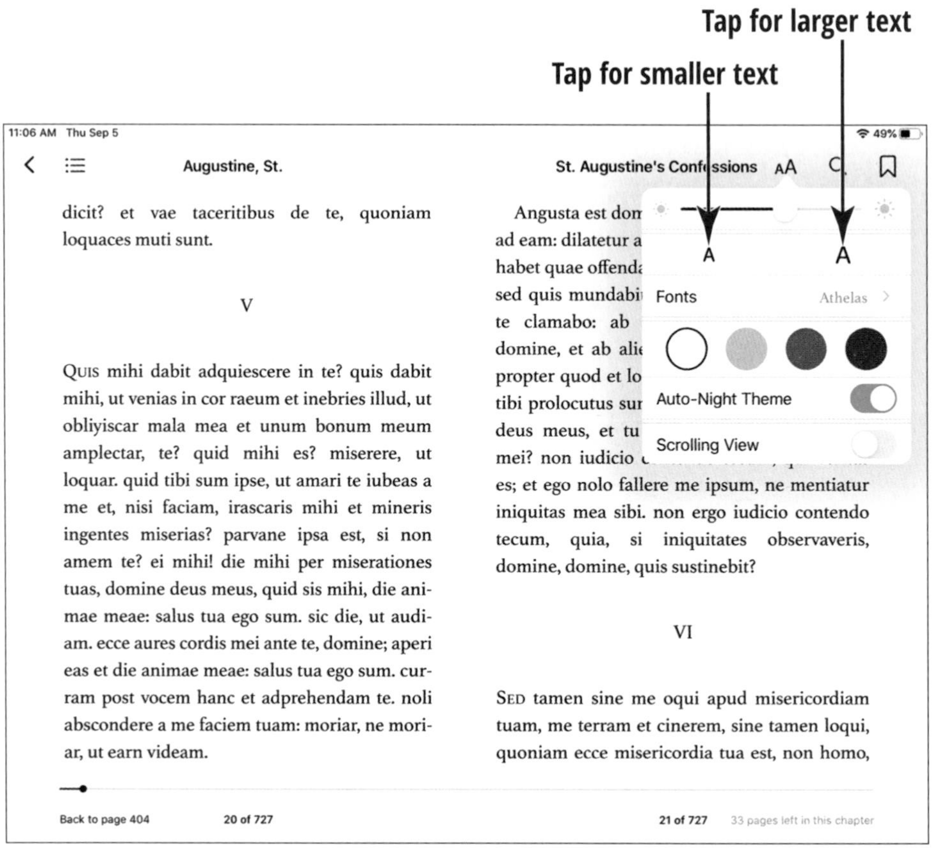

Tap for larger text

Tap for smaller text

FIGURE 13-10

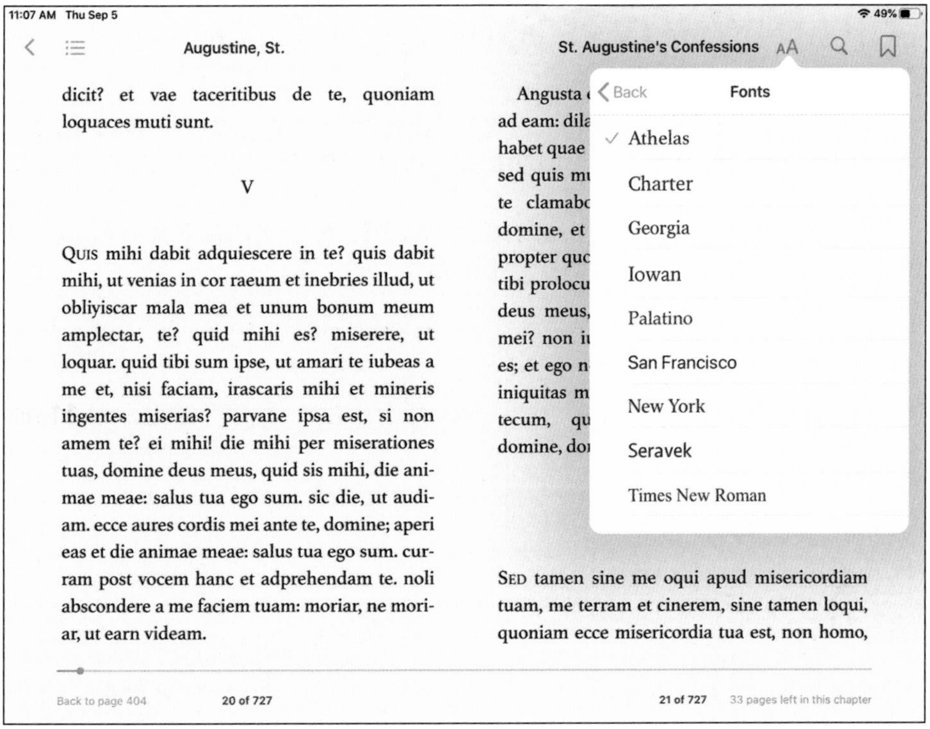

dicit? et vae taceritibus de te, quoniam loquaces muti sunt.

V

Quis mihi dabit adquiescere in te? quis dabit mihi, ut venias in cor raeum et inebries illud, ut obliyiscar mala mea et unum bonum meum amplectar, te? quid mihi es? miserere, ut loquar. quid tibi sum ipse, ut amari te iubeas a me et, nisi faciam, irascaris mihi et mineris ingentes miserias? parvane ipsa est, si non amem te? ei mihi! die mihi per miserationes tuas, domine deus meus, quid sis mihi, die ani- mae meae: salus tua ego sum. sic die, ut audi- am. ecce aures cordis mei ante te, domine; aperi eas et die animae meae: salus tua ego sum. cur- ram post vocem hanc et adprehendam te. noli abscondere a me faciem tuam: moriar, ne mori- ar, ut earn videam.

Angusta   < Back   Fonts
ad eam: dila
habet quae   ✓ Athelas
sed quis mu
te clamabc   Charter
domine, et
propter quc   Georgia
tibi prolocu
deus meus,   Iowan
mei? non ii
es; et ego n   Palatino
iniquitas m
tecum, qu   San Francisco
domine, doi
     New York

     Seravek

     Times New Roman

Sed tamen sine me oqui apud misericordiam tuam, me terram et cinerem, sine tamen loqui, quoniam ecce misericordia tua est, non homo,

FIGURE 13-11

4. Tap a font name to select it. The font changes on the book page.

5. If you want a sepia tint on the pages, which can be easier on the eye, tap the Back button in the upper-left of the Fonts list to go back to the Display Settings dialog box, and then tap one of the screen color options (the colored circles) to activate it.

6. Tap outside the Display Settings dialog box to return to your book.

Some fonts appear a bit larger on your screen than others because of their design. If you want the largest font, use Iowan.

TIP

Search in Your Book

You may want to find certain sentences or references in your book. Apple Books has a built-in Search feature that makes it simple.

1. With a book displayed, tap the Search button shown in **Figure 13-12**. The onscreen keyboard appears.

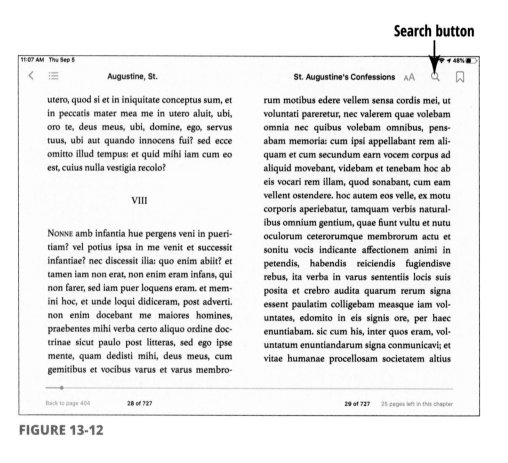

Search button

FIGURE 13-12

2. Enter a search term and then tap the Search key on the keyboard. Apple Books searches for any matching entries.

3. Use your finger to scroll down the entries (see **Figure 13-13**).

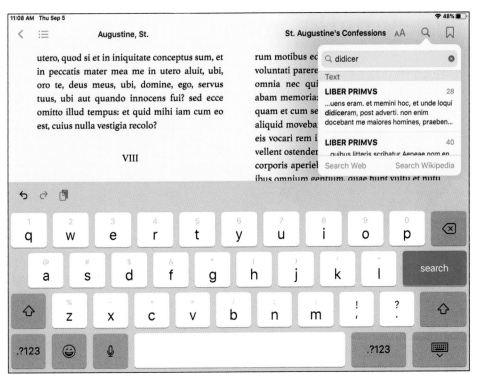

FIGURE 13-13

4. Flick your finger to scroll down the search results and then use either the Search Web or Search Wikipedia button at the bottom of the Search dialog box if you want to search for information about the search term online. Tap a result and you're taken to the page containing that result with a highlight applied to it.

TIP

You can also search for other instances of a particular word while in the book pages by pressing your finger on the word for just a moment and then releasing. A toolbar will appear. Tap Search to find your word.

Use Bookmarks and Highlights

Bookmarks and highlights in your e-books operate like favorite sites that you save in your web browser: They enable you to revisit a favorite passage or refresh your memory about a character or plot point.

1. To bookmark a page, display that page and tap the Bookmark button in the top-right corner (see **Figure 13-14**).

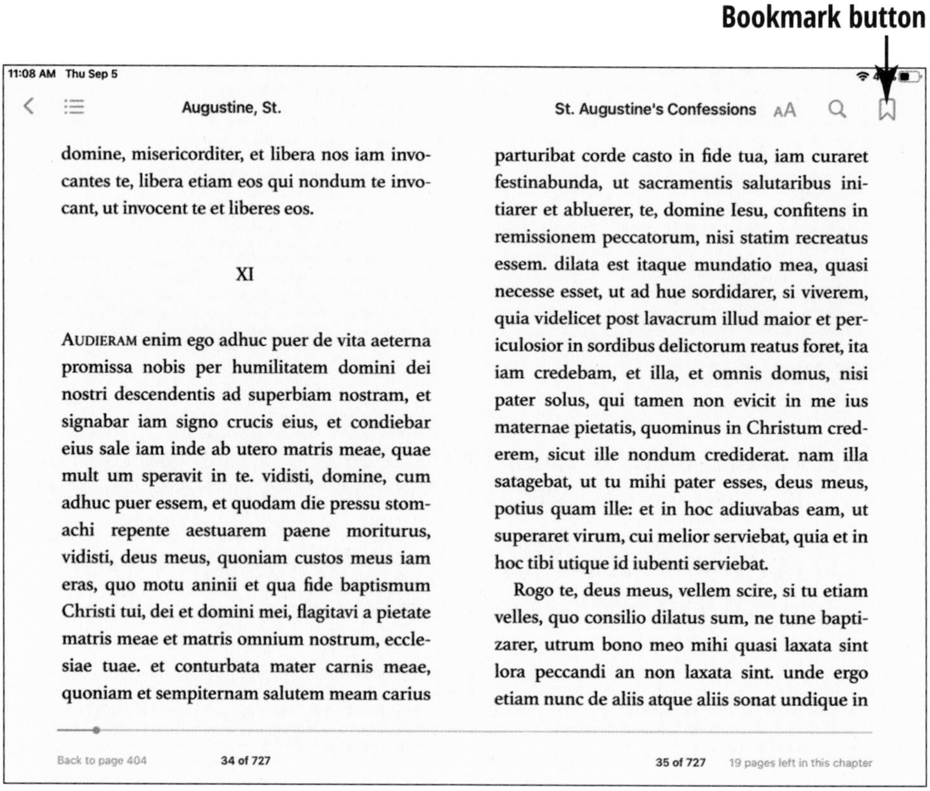

Bookmark button

FIGURE 13-14

2. To highlight a word or phrase, press and release a word and the toolbar shown in **Figure 13-15** appears.

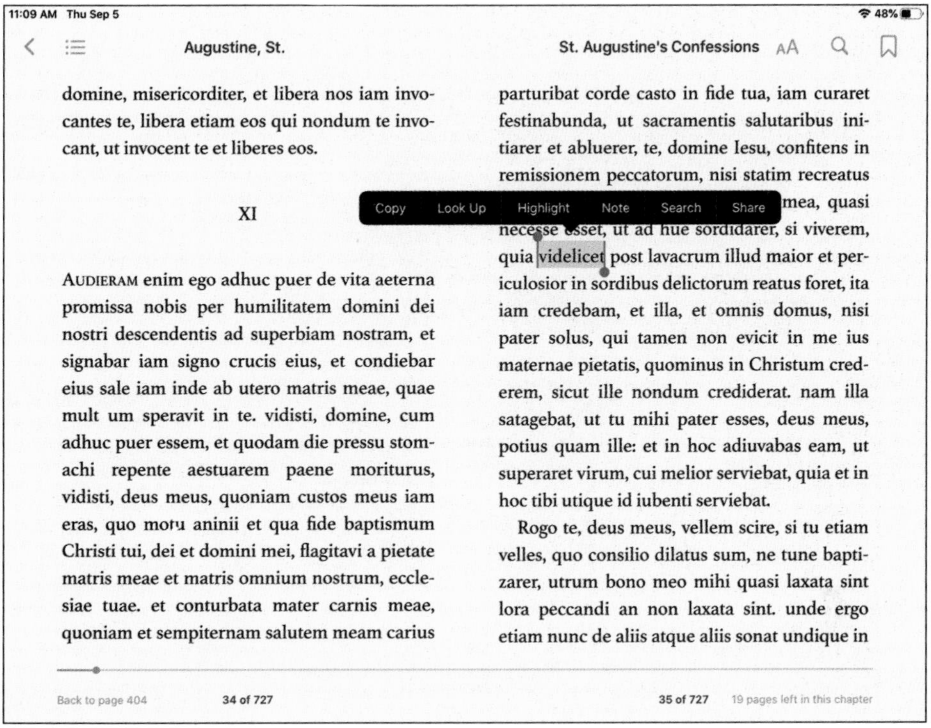
11:09 AM Thu Sep 5
48%
Augustine, St.
St. Augustine's Confessions
AA
domine, misericorditer, et libera nos iam invocantes te, libera etiam eos qui nondum te invocant, ut invocent te et liberes eos.
XI
AUDIERAM enim ego adhuc puer de vita aeterna promissa nobis per humilitatem domini dei nostri descendentis ad superbiam nostram, et signabar iam signo crucis eius, et condiebar eius sale iam inde ab utero matris meae, quae mult um speravit in te. vidisti, domine, cum adhuc puer essem, et quodam die pressu stomachi repente aestuarem paene moriturus, vidisti, deus meus, quoniam custos meus iam eras, quo motu aninii et qua fide baptismum Christi tui, dei et domini mei, flagitavi a pietate matris meae et matris omnium nostrum, ecclesiae tuae. et conturbata mater carnis meae, quoniam et sempiternam salutem meam carius
parturibat corde casto in fide tua, iam curaret festinabunda, ut sacramentis salutaribus initiarer et abluerer, te, domine Iesu, confitens in remissionem peccatorum, nisi statim recreatus
Copy
Look Up
Highlight
Note
Search
Share
mea, quasi
necesse esset, ut ad hue sordidarer, si viverem, quia videlicet post lavacrum illud maior et periculosior in sordibus delictorum reatus foret, ita iam credebam, et illa, et omnis domus, nisi pater solus, qui tamen non evicit in me ius maternae pietatis, quominus in Christum crederem, sicut ille nondum crediderat. nam illa satagebat, ut tu mihi pater esses, deus meus, potius quam ille: et in hoc adiuvabas eam, ut superaret virum, cui melior serviebat, quia et in hoc tibi utique id iubenti serviebat.
Rogo te, deus meus, vellem scire, si tu etiam velles, quo consilio dilatus sum, ne tune baptizarer, utrum bono meo mihi quasi laxata sint lora peccandi an non laxata sint. unde ergo etiam nunc de aliis atque aliis sonat undique in
Back to page 404
34 of 727
35 of 727
19 pages left in this chapter

FIGURE 13-15

3. Tap the Highlight button. A colored highlight is placed on the word, and the toolbar shown in **Figure 13-16** appears.

4. Tap one of these four buttons (from left to right):

   - Colors: Displays a menu of colors that you can tap to change the highlight color as well as an underline option.
   - Remove Highlight (looks like a trashcan): Removes the highlight.
   - Note: Lets you add a note to the item.
   - Share: Allows you to share the highlighted text with others via AirDrop, Messages, Mail, Notes, Twitter, or Facebook, or to copy the text.

5. You can also tap the arrow button at the right side of the toolbar to access Copy, Look Up, Highlight, and Note tools. Tap outside the highlighted text to close the toolbar.

‹ ☰   Augustine, St.   St. Augustine's Confessions AA 🔍 🔖

domine, misericorditer, et libera nos iam invocantes te, libera etiam eos qui nondum te invocant, ut invocent te et liberes eos.

XI

AUDIERAM enim ego adhuc puer de vita aeterna
promissa nobis per humilitatem domini dei
nostri descendentis ad superbiam nostram, et
signabar iam signo crucis eius, et condiebar
eius sale iam inde ab utero matris meae, quae
mult um speravit in te. vidisti, domine, cum
adhuc puer essem, et quodam die pressu stomachi repente aestuarem paene moriturus,
vidisti, deus meus, quoniam custos meus iam
eras, quo motu aninii et qua fide baptismum
Christi tui, dei et domini mei, flagitavi a pietate
matris meae et matris omnium nostrum, ecclesiae tuae. et conturbata mater carnis meae,
quoniam et sempiternam salutem meam carius

parturibat corde casto in fide tua, iam curaret
festinabunda, ut sacramentis salutaribus initiarer et abluerer, te, domine Iesu, confitens in
remissionem peccatorum, nisi statim recreatus
◯ 🗑 💬 ⬆️ › mundatio mea, quasi
necesse esset, ut ad huc sordidarer, si viverem,
quia videlicet post lavacrum illud maior et periculosior in sordibus delictorum reatus foret, ita
iam credebam, et illa, et omnis domus, nisi
pater solus, qui tamen non evicit in me ius
maternae pietatis, quominus in Christum crederem, sicut ille nondum crediderat. nam illa
satagebat, ut tu mihi pater esses, deus meus,
potius quam ille: et in hoc adiuvabas eam, ut
superaret virum, cui melior serviebat, quia et in
hoc tibi utique id iubenti serviebat.

Rogo te, deus meus, vellem scire, si tu etiam
velles, quo consilio dilatus sum, ne tune baptizarer, utrum bono meo mihi quasi laxata sint
lora peccandi an non laxata sint. unde ergo
etiam nunc de aliis atque aliis sonat undique in

FIGURE 13-16

6. To go to a list of bookmarks and notes (including highlighted text),
tap the Table of Contents button in the upper left of the screen.

7. In the Table of Contents, tap the Bookmarks tab shown in
Figure 13-17; all bookmarks are displayed. If you want to see
highlighted text and associated notes, you display the Notes tab.

8. Tap a bookmark in the bookmark list to go to that location in the
book.

TIP

Apple Books automatically bookmarks where you left off reading
in a book so that you don't have to mark your place manually.
If you use any other device registered to your iTunes or iCloud
account, you also pick up where you left off reading.

Bookmarks tab

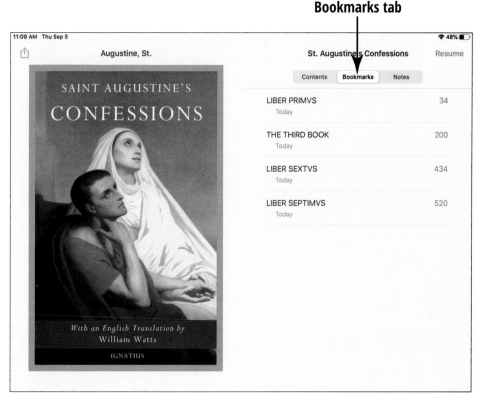

FIGURE 13-17

Set Reading Goals

iPad OS 13 introduces a new feature to Apple Books to help us stay on top of our daily reading: Reading Goals. This feature allows you to set a specific amount of time you'd like to spend reading each day, and it will keep track of the time for you. You can also set goals for the number of books you'd like to finish reading in a year.

1. Tap the Reading Now button in the lower-left and then swipe down to the Reading Goals section. The section is divided into two parts: one for Today's Reading and another for Books Read This Year.

2. Tap the Today's Reading area to adjust your goal or to share your progress with a significant other. To adjust your reading goal time, tap the Adjust Goal button, scroll up or down to select a new time in the menu provided, and tap the screen outside of the menu to exit it. Tap the small X in the upper-right to return to the Reading Goals section.

3. Tap the Books Read This Year area to adjust your goal or to share your progress. To adjust your goal for number of books read in a year, tap the Adjust Goal button, scroll up or down to select a number of books, and tap the screen outside of the menu to exit it. Tap the small X in the upper-right to return to the Reading Goals section.

Chapter **14**

Enjoying Music and Podcasts

PadOS includes an app called Music that allows you to take advantage of your iPad's amazing little sound system to play your favorite music or other audio files.

In this chapter, you get acquainted with the Music app and its features that allow you to sort and find music and control playback. You also get an overview of AirPlay for accessing and playing your music over a home network or over any connected device (this also works with videos and photos). Finally, I introduce you to Podcasts for your listening pleasure.

View the Library Contents

The Library in Music contains the music or other audio files that you've placed on your iPad, either by purchasing them through the iTunes Store or copying them from your computer. The following steps show you how to work with those files on your iPad:

1. Tap the Music app, located in the Dock on the Home screen, and the Music window opens, as shown **Figure 14-1.**

FIGURE 14-1

2. Tap the Library button in the upper-left corner and tap a category (see **Figure 14-2**) to view music by Recently Added, Playlists, Artists, Albums, Songs, or Downloaded Music. Tap Library in the upper-left corner again to return to the screen you were on.

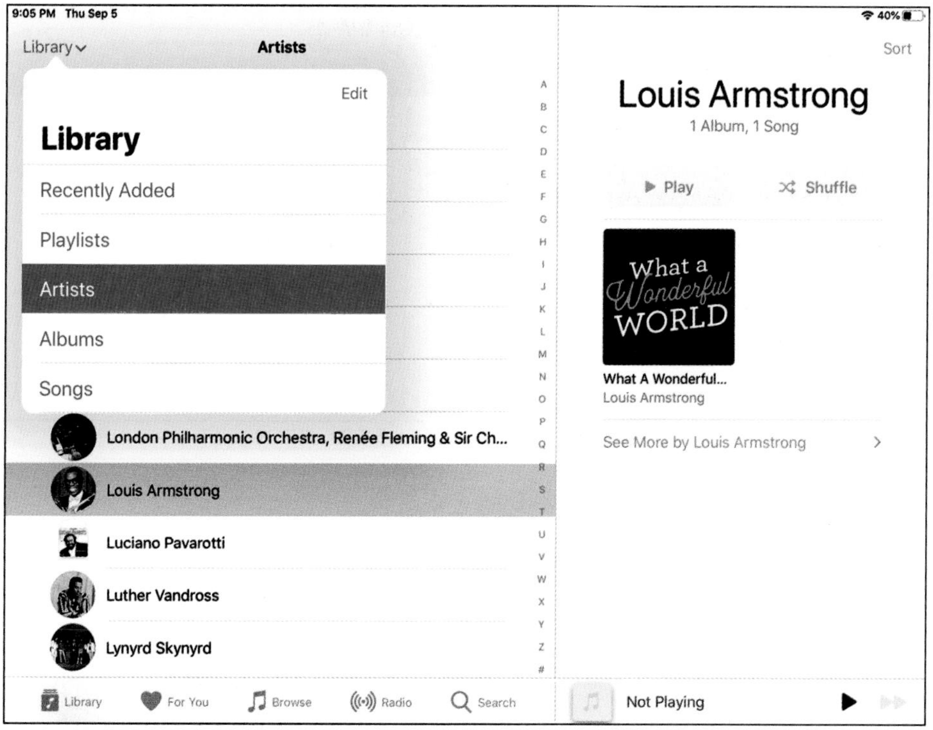

9:05 PM Thu Sep 5
40%
Library
Artists
Sort
Edit
Library
Recently Added
Playlists
Artists
Albums
Songs
London Philharmonic Orchestra, Renée Fleming & Sir Ch...
Louis Armstrong
Luciano Pavarotti
Luther Vandross
Lynyrd Skynyrd
Louis Armstrong
1 Album, 1 Song
Play
Shuffle
What a Wonderful WORLD
What A Wonderful...
Louis Armstrong
See More by Louis Armstrong
Library
For You
Browse
Radio
Search
Not Playing

FIGURE 14-2

TIP

iTunes has several free items that you can download and use to play around with the features in Music. You can also sync content (such as iTunes Smart Playlists stored on your computer or other Apple devices) to your iPad, and play it using the Music app. (See Chapter 3 for more about syncing and Chapter 12 for more about getting content from the iTunes Store.)

3. Tap Edit in the upper-right corner of the Library list to edit the list of categories, as seen in **Figure 14-3.** Tap the check box to the left of categories that you'd like to sort your Music Library by; uncheck those you don't want to use.
4. Tap Done when you're finished.

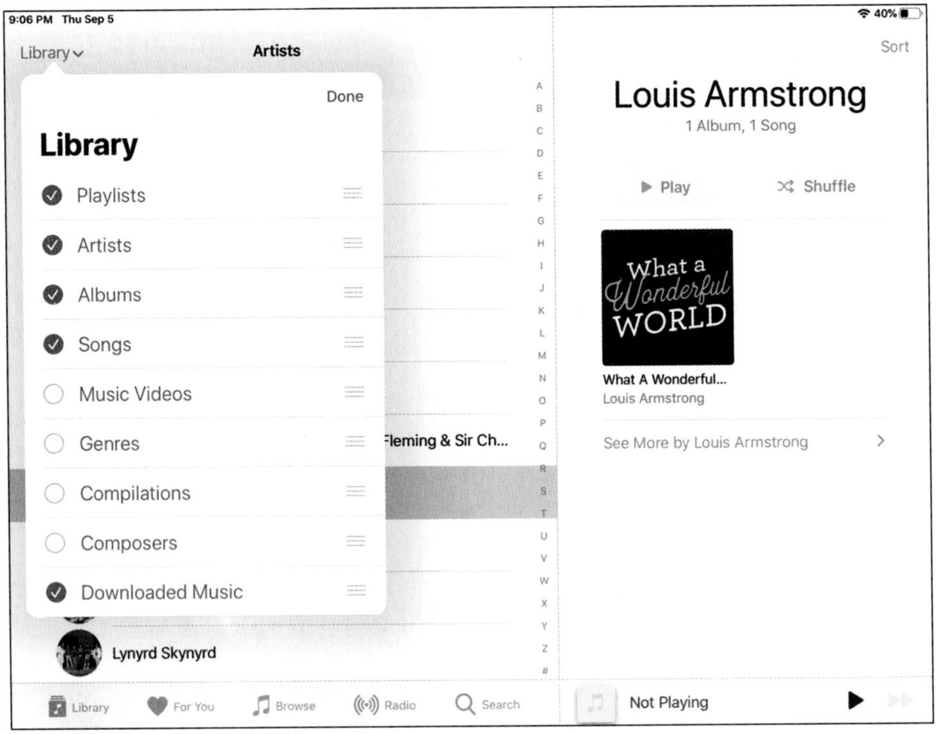

FIGURE 14-3

Apple offers a service called iTunes Match. (Visit `https://support.apple.com/en-us/HT204146` for more information.) You pay $24.99 per year for the capability to match the music you've bought from other providers (and stored in the iTunes Library on your computer) to what's in the iTunes Library. If there's a match (and there usually is), that content is added to your iTunes Library on iCloud. Then, using iCloud, you can sync the content among all your Apple devices. Is this service worth $24.99 a year? That's entirely up to you, my friend. However, for a few bucks more, you can have the benefits of iTunes Match plus access to millions of songs across all of your Apple devices using another Apple service: Apple Music. There's more about Apple Music later in this chapter.

Create Playlists

You can create your own playlists to put tracks from various sources into collections of your choosing:

1. Tap the Playlists category in the Library list.

2. Tap the New button in the upper-right corner. In the dialog box that appears (see **Figure 14-4**), tap Playlist Name and enter a title for the playlist.

3. Tap Add Music, search for music by artist, title, or lyrics, or tap Library and browse to what you're looking for.

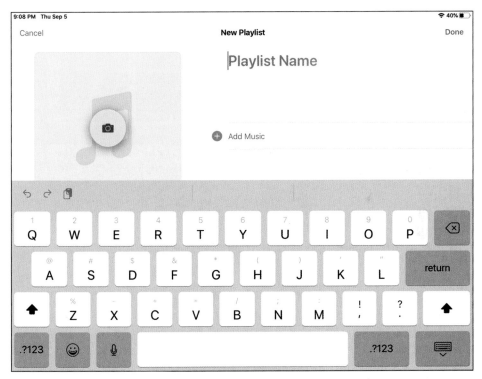

FIGURE 14-4

4. In the list of selections that appears (see **Figure 14-5**), tap the plus sign to the right of each item you want to include (for individual songs or entire albums). Continue until you've selected all the songs you want to add to the playlist.

Tap here

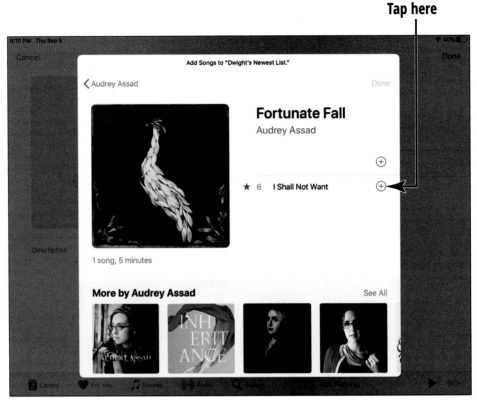

FIGURE 14-5

5. Tap the Done button and then tap Done on the next screen to return to the Playlists screen.

6. Your playlist appears in the list, and you can now play it by tapping the list name and then tapping a track to play it.

TIP

To search for and play a song in your music libraries from your Home screen (without even opening the Music app), use the Spotlight Search feature. From your first Home screen, you can swipe down from the screen outside the Dock and enter the name of the song in the Search field. A list of search results appears. Just tap the Play button and rock on!

Search for Music

You can search for an item in your Music Library by using the Search feature:

1. With Music open, tap the Search button at the bottom of the screen. The Search screen appears showing Recent Searches and Trending Searches, along with a Search field at the top of the screen. Tap either the Your Library tab to search for songs stored on your iPad, or tap Apple Music to search the Apple Music library. You may search for items in Apple Music, but you must be subscribed to play selections from it.

2. Enter a search term in the Search field. Results are displayed, narrowing as you type, as shown in **Figure 14-6.**

3. Tap an item to play it.

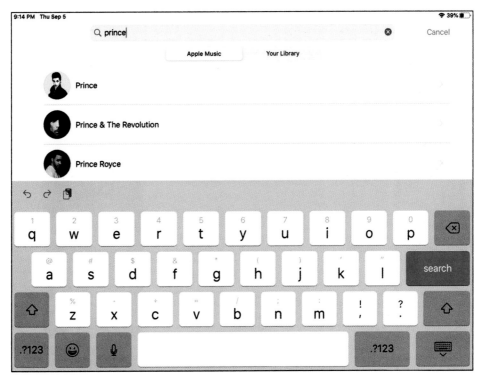

FIGURE 14-6

You can enter an artist's name, a lyricist's or a composer's name, or a word from the item's title, or even lyrics in the Search field to find what you're looking for.

Play Music

After you know how to find your music, you can have some real fun by playing it!

You can use Siri to play music hands-free. Just press and hold the Home button, and when Siri appears, say something like "Play 'L.A. Woman'" or "Play 'Fields of Gold.'"

To play music on your iPad, follow these steps:

1. Locate the music that you want by using the methods described in previous tasks in this chapter.

2. Tap the item you want to play. If you're displaying the Songs category, you don't have to tap an album to open a song; you need only tap a song to play it. If you're using any other categories, you have to tap items, such as albums (or multiple songs from one artist), to find the song you want to hear.

Home Sharing is a feature of iTunes that you can use to share music among up to five devices that have Home Sharing turned on. After Home Sharing is set up via iTunes, any of your devices can stream music and videos to other devices, and you can even click and drag content between devices using iTunes. For more about Home Sharing, visit this site: https://support.apple.com/en-us/HT202190.

3. Tap the item you want to play from the list that appears; it begins to play (see **Figure 14-7**).

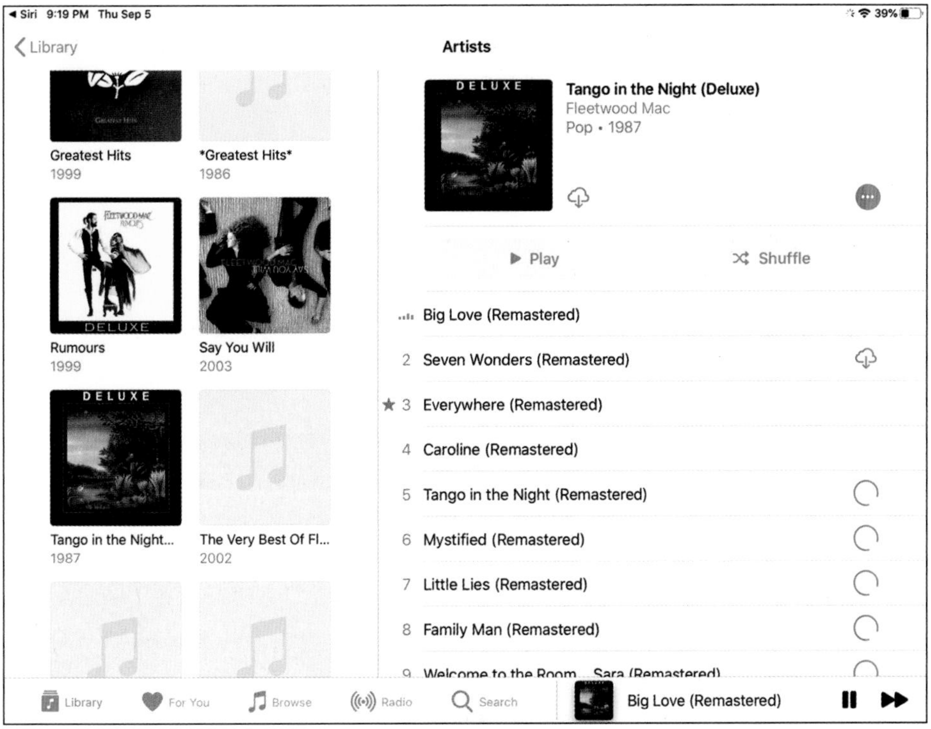

FIGURE 14-7

4. Tap the currently playing song title in the lower right of the screen to open it, displaying playback controls. Use the Previous and Next buttons at the bottom of the screen shown in **Figure 14-8** to navigate the audio file that's playing:

   • The Previous button takes you back to the beginning of the item that's playing if you tap it or rewinds the song if you press and hold it.

   • The Next button takes you to the next item if you tap it or fast-forwards the song if you press and hold it.

   Use the Volume slider on the bottom of the screen (or the Volume buttons on the side of your iPad) to increase or decrease the volume.

5. Tap the Pause button to pause playback. Tap the button again to resume playing.

   TIP

   You can also use music controls for music that's playing from the lock screen.

FIGURE 14-8

6. Tap and drag the red line (it appears gray until you touch it) near the middle of the screen (underneath the album art) that indicates the current playback location. Drag the line to the left or right to "scrub" to another location in the song.

7. Do you like to sing along but sometimes flub the words? Tap the Lyrics button in the lower-left (looks like a speech box with a quotation mark in it), and if the song is from the Apple Music library, the lyrics will scroll up the screen in sync with the song, as shown in **Figure 14-9**. You can swipe through the lyrics, or if you tap a lyric, Music will jump to that point in the song.

8. If you don't like what's playing, here's how to make another selection: Drag down from the top of the playback controls screen to view other selections in the album that's playing.

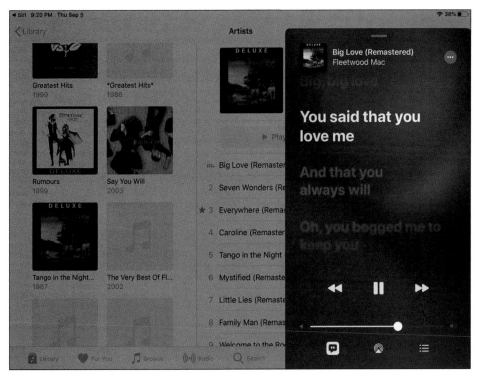

FIGURE 14-9

TIP

Family Sharing allows up to six members of your family to share purchased content even if they don't share the same iTunes account. You can set up Family Sharing under iCloud in Settings. See Chapter 12 for more about Family Sharing.

Shuffle Music

If you want to play a random selection of the music in an album on your iPad, you can use the Shuffle feature.

1. Tap the name of the currently playing song at the bottom of the screen.

2. Tap the Menu button in the lower-right (it looks like three dots and three lines stacked).

3. Tap the Shuffle button located to the right of Up Next, which looks like two lines crossing to form an X. Your content plays in random order.

4. Tap the Repeat button to play the songs over again continuously.

Use AirPlay

The AirPlay streaming technology is built into the iPad, iPod touch, Macs, PCs running iTunes, and iPhone. Streaming technology allows you to send media files from one device that supports AirPlay to be played on another. For example, you can send a movie that you've purchased on your iPad or a slideshow of your photos to be played on your Apple TV, then control the TV playback from your iPad. You can also send music to be played over compatible speakers, such as Apple's HomePod (go to http://www.apple.com/homepod for more information). Check out the Apple TV Remote app in the App Store, which you can use to control your Apple TV from your iPad.

To stream music via AirPlay on your iPad with another AirPlay-enabled device on your network or in close proximity, tap the AirPlay button (looks like a pyramid with sound waves emanating from it) at the bottom-center of the playback control screen while listening to a song. Then select the AirPlay device to stream the content to or choose your iPad to move the playback back to it.

TIP

If you get a bit antsy watching a long movie, one of the beauties of AirPlay is that you can still use your iPad to check email, browse photos or the Internet, or check your calendar while the media file is playing on the other device.

Find and Subscribe to Podcasts

First, what the heck is a podcast? A podcast is sort of like a radio show that you can listen to at any time. You'll find podcasts covering just about any subject imaginable, including news, sports, gardening, cooking, education, comedy, religion, and so much more. The Podcasts app is the vehicle by which you'll find and listen to podcasts on your iPad.

To search Apple's massive library of podcasts and subscribe to them (which is free, by the way):

1. Tap the Podcasts icon on the home screen to open it.

2. There are three ways to discover podcasts:

- Tap Browse at the bottom of the screen and then tap Featured. There you'll find podcasts that are featured by the good folks at Apple, as shown in **Figure 14-10**.

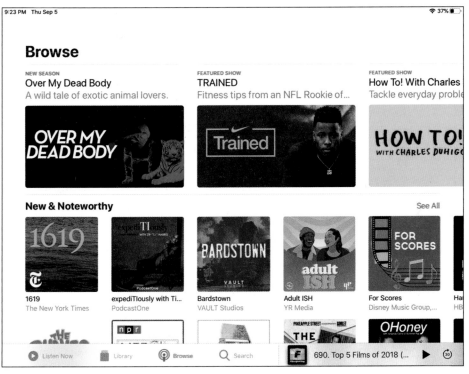

FIGURE 14-10

- Tap Browse at the bottom of the screen and swipe down to Top Shows or Top Episodes. Tap See All and you'll be greeted with lists of the most popular podcasts. Tap the All Categories button in the upper-right corner to sift through the podcasts based on the category (such as Arts, Health & Fitness, or Music).

- Tap Search and then tap the Search field at the top of the screen. When the keyboard appears, type the name or subject of a podcast to see a list of results.

3. When you find a podcast that intrigues you, tap its name to see its information page, which will be similar to the one in **Figure 14-11**.

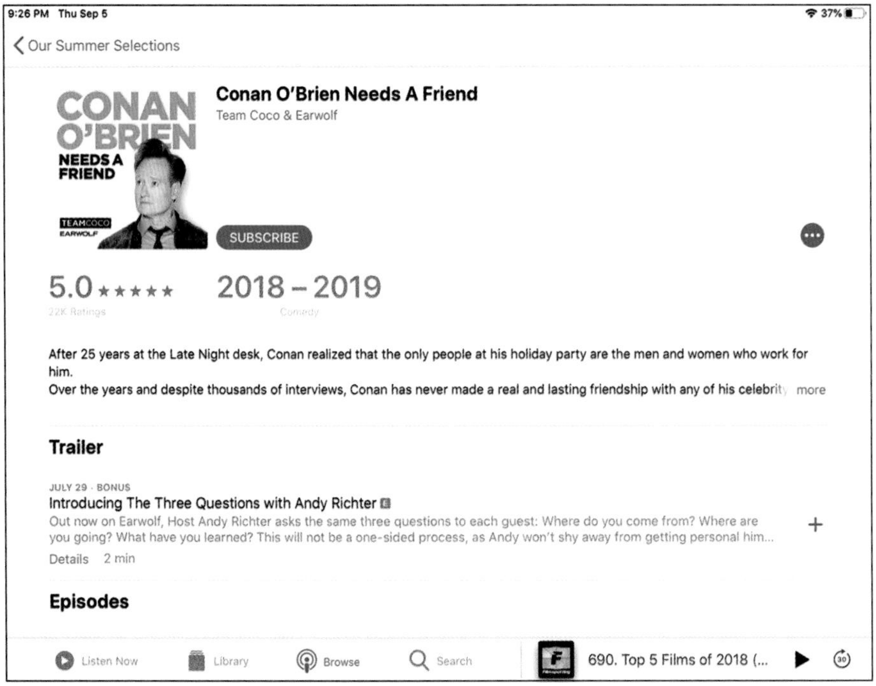

FIGURE 14-11

4. Tap the Subscribe button. The podcast now appears in the Library section of the app, and the newest episode will be downloaded to your iPad.

5. Tap Library in the toolbar at the bottom of the screen, tap Shows on the left, and then tap the name of the podcast you subscribed to and view its information screen.

6. Tap the More button on the right (looks like a circle containing three dots) and then tap the Settings icon (looks like a gear) to see the settings for the podcast. From here (see **Figure 14-12**), you can customize how the podcast downloads and organizes episodes. Tap Done in the upper-right corner when you're finished with the Settings options.

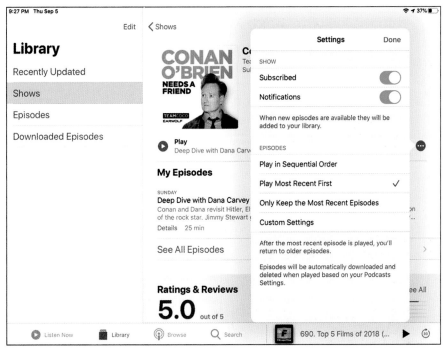

FIGURE 14-12

Play Podcasts

Playing podcasts is a breeze and works very much like playing audio files in the Music app.

1. Open the Podcasts app and tap Library at the bottom of the screen.

2. Tap the name of the podcast you'd like to listen to.

3. Tap the episode you want to play. The episode begins playing; you can see the currently playing episode near the bottom of the screen, just above the toolbar.

4. Tap the currently playing episode in the lower right of the screen to open the playback controls

5. Drag the line in the middle of the screen to scrub to a different part of the episode or tap the Rewind or Fast Forward buttons to the left and right of the Pause/Play button, respectively.

6. Adjust the playback speed by tapping the 1x icon in the lower left of the Play controls. Each tap increases or decreases playback speed.

7. Adjust the volume by dragging the Volume slider near the bottom of the screen or using the Volume buttons on the side of your iPad.

TIP

Tap the Listen Now button in the toolbar at the bottom of the app's screen to see a list of the newest episodes that have been automatically downloaded to your iPad.

Chapter **15**

Taking and Sharing Photos

With its gorgeous screen, the iPad is a natural for taking and viewing photos. It supports most common photo formats, such as JPEG, TIFF, and PNG. You can shoot your photos by using the built-in cameras in iPad with built-in square or panorama modes. With recent iPad models, you can edit your images using smart adjustment filters. You can also sync photos from your computer, save images that you find online to your iPad, or receive them by email, MMS, or iMessage.

The Photo Sharing feature lets you share groups of photos with people using iCloud on an iPadOS device, iOS device, or on a Mac or Windows computer with iCloud access. Your iCloud Photo Library makes all this storage and sharing easy.

When you have taken or downloaded photos to play with, the Photos app lets you organize photos and view photos in albums, one by one, or in a slideshow. You can also view photos by the years in which they were taken, with images divided into collections by the location or time you took them. With iPadOS 13, videos and live photos will play as you browse through Photos, making it a more dynamic and interesting experience. You can also AirDrop, email, message, or tweet a photo to a friend, print it, share it via AirPlay, or post it to Facebook.

Finally, you can create time-lapse videos with the Camera app, allowing you to record a sequence in time, such as a flower opening as the sun warms it or your grandchild stirring from sleep. You can read about all these features in this chapter.

Take Pictures with the iPad Cameras

The cameras in the iPad are just begging to be used, no matter which model you have!

TIP

To go to the camera with the lock screen displayed, swipe down from the right corner of the screen and tap the Camera app icon in the Control Center to go directly to the Camera app. You can also swipe from right to left in Notification Center to access Camera.

1. Tap the Camera app icon on the Home screen to open the app.

2. If the camera type on the lower-right side of the screen (see **Figure 15-1**) is set to Video or something other than Photo, swipe to choose Photo (the still camera).

TIP

iPad's front- and rear-facing cameras allow you to capture photos and video (see Chapter 16 for more about the video features) and share them with family and friends. Newer models offer incredible cameras, and up to 12-megapixel with iPad Pro, with such features as

» Autofocus

» Automatic image stabilization to avoid fuzzy moving targets

» True Tone Flash (with iPad Pro), a sensor that tells iPad when a flash is needed

FIGURE 15-1

The following are options for taking pictures after you've opened the Camera app:

» You can set the Pano (for panorama) and Square options using the camera type control below the Capture button (the large white or red circle, depending on the image type selected). These controls let you create square images like those you see on the popular Instagram site. With Pano selected, tap to begin to take a picture and pan across a view and then tap Done to capture a panoramic display.

» If your iPad supports it, tap the Flash button (looks like a lightning bolt) when using the rear camera and then select a flash option:

- On, if your lighting is dim enough to require a flash
- Off, if you don't want iPad to use a flash
- Auto, if you want to let iPad decide for you

- To use the High Dynamic Range or HDR feature, tap the HDR setting and tap to turn it on. This feature uses several images, some underexposed and some overexposed, and combines the best ones into one image, sometimes providing a more finely detailed picture.

HDR pictures can be very large in file size, meaning they'll take up more of your iPad's memory than standard pictures.

- If you want a time delay before the camera snaps the picture, tap the Time Delay button (looks like a timer), then tap 3s or 10s for a 3- or 10-second delay, respectively.

- Tap the Live button (looks like concentric circles) to take Live Photos. As opposed to freezing a single moment in time, Live Photos lets you capture three-second moving images, which can create some truly beautiful photos. Be sure to hold your iPhone still for at least three seconds so that you don't move too soon and cause part of your Live Photo to show the movement of your iPhone as you get into position for the picture.

- Move the camera around until you find a pleasing image. You can do a couple of things at this point to help you take your photo:

  - Tap the area of the grid where you want the camera to autofocus.

  - Place two fingers apart from each other on the screen and then pinch them together (still touching the screen) to display a digital zoom control. Drag the circle in the zoom bar to the left to zoom in or out on the image.

- Tap the Capture button; you've just taken a picture, and it's stored in the Photos app gallery automatically.

You can also use a Volume button (located on the right side of your iPad) to capture a picture or start or stop video camera recording.

» Tap the Switch Camera button above the Capture button to switch between the front camera and rear camera. You can then take selfies (pictures of yourself), so go ahead and tap the Capture button to take another picture.

» To view the last photo taken, tap the thumbnail of the latest image directly beneath the Capture button; the Photos app opens and displays the photo.

» While viewing the image in Photos, tap the Share button (it's the box with an arrow coming out of it, located near the upper-right corner of the screen) to display a menu that allows you to AirDrop, email, or instant message the photo, assign it to a contact, use it as iPad wallpaper, tweet it, post it to Facebook, share via iCloud Photo Sharing or Flickr, or print it (see **Figure 15-2**).

FIGURE 15-2

>> You can tap images to select more than one.

>> To delete the image, have it displayed and tap the Trash button in the bottom-right corner of the screen. Tap Delete Photo in the confirming menu that appears.

You can use the iCloud Photo Sharing feature to automatically sync your photos across various devices. Turn on iCloud Photo Sharing by tapping Settings on the Home screen, tapping Photos, and then toggling the iCloud Photos switch to On (green).

View an Album

The Photos app organizes your pictures into albums, using such criteria as the folder or album on your computer from which you synced the photos or photos captured using the iPad camera (saved in the Camera Roll album). You may also have albums for images that you synced from other devices through iTunes or shared via Photos.

To view your albums:

1. Tap the Photos app icon on the Home screen.

2. Tap the Albums button at the bottom of the screen to display your albums, as shown in **Figure 15-3**.

3. Tap an album. The photos in it are displayed.

You can associate photos with faces and events. When you do, additional tabs appear at the bottom of the screen when you display an album containing that type of photo.

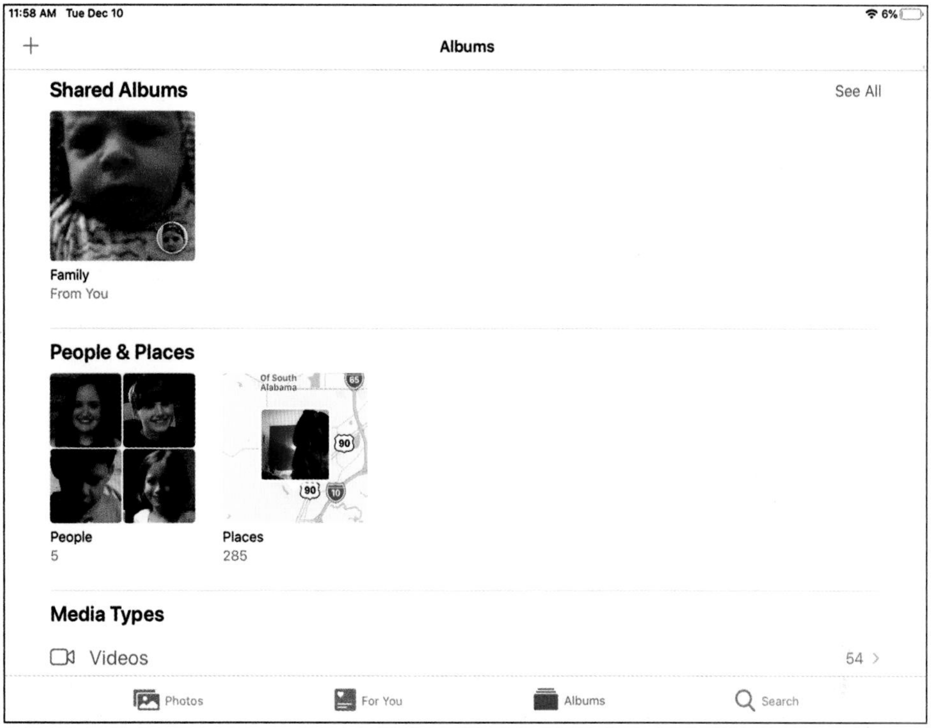

FIGURE 15-3

View Individual Photos

You can view photos individually by opening them from within an album.

To view individual photos:

1. Tap the Photos app icon on the Home screen.

2. Tap Albums (refer to Figure 15-3).

3. Tap an album to open it; then, to view a photo, tap it. The picture expands, as shown in **Figure 15-4**.

4. Flick your finger to the left or right to scroll through the album to look at the individual photos in it.

FIGURE 15-4

5. You can tap the Back button in the upper-left corner (looks like a left-pointing arrow) and then the Albums button to return to the Album view.

You can place a photo on a person's information record in Contacts. For more about how to do this, see Chapter 8.

Edit Photos

iPad Photos isn't Photoshop, but it does provide some tools for editing photos. To edit photos:

1. Tap the Photos app on the Home screen to open it.
2. Locate and display a photo you want to edit.

3. Tap the Edit button in the upper right of the screen; the Edit Photo screen shown in **Figure 15-5** appears.

Filters

Adjustments

Auto-enhance

Crop

FIGURE 15-5

4. At this point, you can take several possible actions with these tools:

- **Crop:** To crop the photo to a portion of its original area, tap the Crop button. You can then tap any corner of the image and drag inward or outward to remove areas of the photo. Tap Crop and then Save to apply your changes.

- **Filters:** Apply any of nine filters (such as Vivid, Mono, or Noir) to change the look and feel of your image. These effects adjust the brightness of your image or apply a black-and-white tone to your color photos. Tap the Filters button in the middle of the tools on the left side of the screen and scroll to view available filters. Tap one and then tap Apply to apply the effect to your image.

- **Adjustments:** Swipe the options to the right of the screen to see adjustment options such as Light, Color, or B&W. There are a slew of tools that you can use to tweak contrast, color intensity, shadows, and more.

- **Auto-enhance:** The icon for this feature looks like a magic wand, and it pretty much works like one. Tapping the wand allows your iPhone to apply automatic adjustments to your photos exposure, saturation, contract, and so on.

5. If you're pleased with your edits, tap the Done button. A copy of the edited photo is saved.

TIP

Each of the editing features has a Cancel button. If you don't like the changes you made, tap this button to stop making changes before you save the image.

Organize Photos

You'll probably want to organize your photos to make it simpler to find what you're looking for:

1. If you want to create your own album, open the Recents album.

2. Tap the Select button in the top-right corner and then tap individual photos to select them. Small check marks appear on the selected photos (see **Figure 15-6**).

3. Tap the Share button (box containing an upward-pointing arrow) in the upper-left corner of the screen, tap Add to Album, and then tap the New Album option.

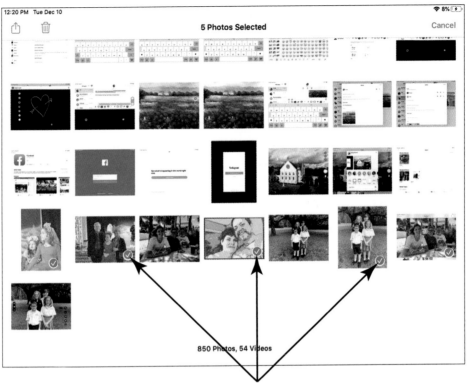

Check marks show selected items

FIGURE 15-6

TIP

If you've already created albums, you can choose to add the photo to an existing album at this point.

4. Enter a name for a new album and then tap Save. If you create a new album, it appears in the Photos main screen with the other albums that are displayed.

TIP

You can also choose several other Share options or Delete when you've selected photos in Step 2 of this task. This allows you to share or delete multiple photos at a time.

Share Photos with Mail, Twitter, or Facebook

You can easily share photos stored on your iPad by sending them as email attachments, as a text message, by posting them to Facebook, sharing them via iCloud Photo Sharing or Flickr, or as tweets on Twitter.

To share photos:

1. Tap the Photos app icon on the Home screen.

2. Tap the Photos or Albums button and locate the photo you want to share.

3. Tap the photo to select it and then tap the Share button. (It looks like a box with an arrow jumping out of it.) The menu shown in **Figure 15-7** appears. Tap to select additional photos, if you want them.

4. Tap the Mail, Message, Twitter, iCloud Photo Sharing, Facebook, Flickr, or any other option you'd like to use.

5. In the message form that appears, make any modifications that apply in the To, Cc/Bcc, or Subject fields and then type a message for email or enter your Facebook posting or Twitter tweet.

6. Tap the Send or Post button, and the message and photo are sent or posted.

TIP

You can also copy and paste a photo into documents, such as those created in the Pages word-processor app. To do this, tap a photo in Photos and tap Share. Tap the Copy command. In the destination app, press and hold the screen and tap Paste.

FIGURE 15-7

Share a Photo Using AirDrop

AirDrop provides a way to share content, such as photos with others who are nearby and who have an AirDrop-enabled device (iPhones, iPads, and more recent Macs that can run macOS 10.10 or later).

Follow the steps in the previous task to locate a photo you want to share.

1. Tap the Share button.

2. If an AirDrop-enabled device is in your immediate vicinity (such as within 30 feet or so), you see the device listed in the Tap to share with AirDrop section directly underneath the selected image (see **Figure 15-8**). Tap the device name and your photo is sent to the other device.

AirDrop-enabled devices nearby

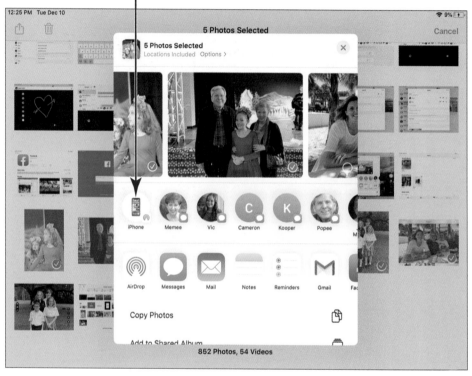

FIGURE 15-8

Other iOS or iPadOS devices must have AirDrop enabled to use this feature. To enable AirDrop, open the Control Center (swipe up from the bottom of any screen) and tap AirDrop, shown in **Figure 15-9**. Choose Contacts Only or Everyone to specify whom you can use AirDrop with.

TIP

Tap to enable/disable AirDrop

FIGURE 15-9

Share Photos Using iCloud Photo Sharing

iCloud Photo Sharing allows you to automatically share photos using your iCloud account:

1. Open the Photos app.

2. Select a photo or photos you would like to share, and tap the Share button in the upper-right.

3. In the Share screen that opens, tap Add to Shared Album.

4. Enter a comment if you like (see **Figure 15-10**) and then tap Post. The photos are posted to your iCloud Photo Library.

FIGURE 15-10

Print Photos

If you have a printer that's compatible with Apple's AirPrint technology, you can print photos from your iPad.

1. With Photos open, locate the photo you want to print and tap it to maximize it.

2. Tap the Share button. On the menu that appears, scroll to near the bottom of the list of options and then tap Print.

3. In the Printer Options dialog box that appears (see **Figure 15-11**), tap an available printer in the list or Select Printer. iPad presents you with a list of any compatible wireless printers on your local network.

4. Tap the plus or minus symbols in the Copy field to set the number of copies to print.

5. Tap the Print button, and your photo is sent to the printer.

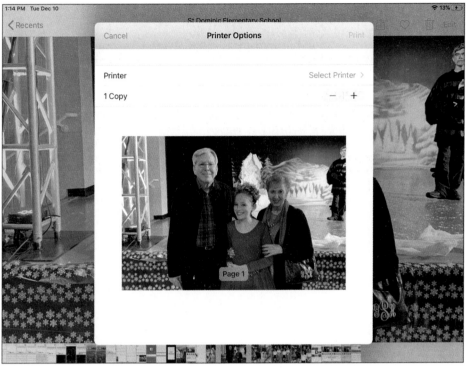

FIGURE 15-11

Delete Photos

You may find that it's time to get rid of some of those old photos of the family reunion or the last community center project. If the photos weren't transferred from your computer, but instead were taken, downloaded, or captured as screenshots on the iPad, you can delete them.

1. Tap the Photos app icon on the Home screen.

2. Tap the Albums tab and then tap an album to open it.

3. Locate and tap on a photo that you want to delete and then tap the Trash icon. In the confirming dialog box that appears, tap the Delete Photo button to finish the deletion.

WARNING

If you delete a photo in Photo Sharing, it is deleted on all devices that you shared it with.

TIP

If you'd like to recover a photo you've deleted, tap the Albums tab, swipe to the bottom of the page, and tap Recently Deleted. Tap the photo you want to retrieve, tap the Recover button in the lower-right corner, and then tap the Recover Photo button when prompted. Be aware that photos only stay in the Recently Deleted album for 30 days from the date they were originally deleted. After that, they're gone for good.

Chapter **16**

Creating and Watching Videos

Using the TV app (formerly known as Videos), you can watch downloaded movies or TV shows, as well as media that you've synced from iCloud on your Mac or PC, and even media that's provided from other content providers, such as cable and streaming video services. The TV app aims to be your one-stop shop for your viewing pleasure.

In addition, iPads sport both a front and rear video camera that you can use to capture your own videos, which iPadOS now allows you to edit in the same way you can edit photos: You can apply adjustments, filters, and crop your videos. Speaking of editing, you can also download the iMovie app for iPad (a more limited version of the longtime mainstay on Mac computers) that allows you to do an editing deep-dive with the capability to add titles, music, transitions, and much more. Newer iPad Pro models sport cameras that support up to 4K video, which produces rich detail with 8 million pixels per frame. The latest iPad and iPad mini models support HD video up to 1080p.

A few other features of video in newer iPad models include image stabilization to avoid the shakes when recording, more frames shot per second for smoother video, and continuous autofocus video (iPad Pro models only), which means that your iPad Pro continually autofocuses as you're recording.

In this chapter, I explain all about shooting and watching video content from a variety of sources. For practice, you may want to refer to Chapter 12 first to find out how to purchase or download one of many available TV shows or movies from the iTunes Store.

Capture Your Own Videos with the Built-In Cameras

The camera lens that comes on newer iPads has perks for photographers, including a large aperture and highly accurate sensor, which make for better images all around. In addition, auto image stabilization makes up for any shakiness in the hands holding the iPad, and autofocus has sped up thanks to the fast processors being used. For videographers, you'll appreciate a fast frames-per-second capability as well as a slow-motion feature.

1. To capture a video, tap the Camera app on the Home screen. With an iPad, two video cameras are available for capturing video, one from the front and one from the back of the device. (See more about this topic in the next task.)

2. The Camera app opens (see **Figure 16-1**). Tap and slide the camera-type options on the lower-right of the screen until Video is selected and you see the red Record button. This button is how you switch from the still camera to the video camera.

3. If you want to switch between the front and back cameras, tap the Switch Camera button above the Record button (refer to Figure 16-1).

4. Tap the red Record button to begin recording the video. (The red dot in the middle of this button turns into a red square when the camera is recording.) The duration of your recording is displayed at the top of the screen. Use the Zoom slider (see Figure 16-1) to zoom in and

out if you need to get closer to or farther away from your subject. When you're finished, tap the Record button again. Your new video is now listed under the Record button. Tap the video to play it, share it, or delete it. In the future, you can find and play the video in your Camera Roll or in the Videos album when you open the Photos app.

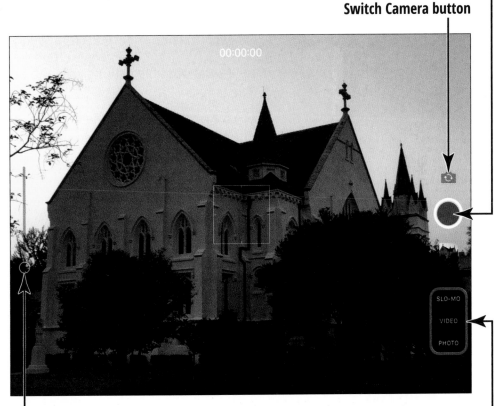

Record button

Switch Camera button

Zoom slider

Camera-type options

FIGURE 16-1

TIP

Before you start recording, remember where the camera lens is — while holding the iPad and panning, you can easily put your fingers directly over the lens! Also, you can't pause your recording; when you stop, your video is saved, and when you start recording, you're creating a new video file.

Edit Videos

The iPadOS Photos app isn't as full featured as Apple's Final Cut or Adobe's Premier, but it does provide some tools for editing videos.

1. Tap the Photos app (where your videos are stored) on the Home screen, locate your video, and tap to open it.

2. Tap the Edit button in the upper-right corner of the screen; the Edit Photo screen appears. The one shown in **Figure 16-2** is for a video shot in Landscape mode.

3. At this point, you can take several possible actions with the tools provided:

   - **Crop:** To crop the video to a portion of its original area, tap the Crop button. You can then tap any corner of the image and drag inward or outward to remove areas of the video. Tap Crop and then Save to apply your changes.

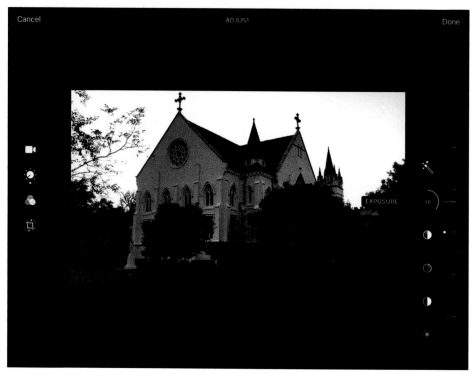

FIGURE 16-2

- **Filters:** Apply any of nine filters (such as Vivid, Mono, or Noir) to change the look of your video images. These effects adjust the brightness of your video or apply a black-and-white tone to your color videos. Tap the Filters button on the left side of the screen and then scroll through the list on the right side to view available filters. Tap one to apply the effect to your video.

- **Adjustments:** Tap Light, Color, or B&W to access a slew of tools that you can use to tweak contrast, color intensity, shadows, and more.

- **Auto-enhance:** The icon for this feature looks like a magic wand, and it pretty much works like one. Tapping the wand allows your iPad to apply automatic adjustments to your video's exposure, saturation, contrast, and so on.

- **Trim:** Use the trim tool to remove parts of your video you no longer want to view.

4. If you're pleased with your edits, tap the Done button. A copy of the edited video is saved.

TIP

Each of the editing features has a Cancel button. If you don't like the changes you made, tap this button (in the upper-left corner) to stop making changes before you save the image. How about if you make changes you later regret? Just open the video and tap Edit, then tap the red Revert button in the upper-right to discard changes to the original.

Play Movies or TV Shows with TV

Open the TV app for the first time, and you'll be greeted with a Welcome screen. Tap Continue, and you'll be asked to sign in to your television provider.

Signing in will allow you to use the TV app to access content in other apps, if such services are supported by your TV provider. This way, you need to use only the TV app to access content and sign in, as opposed to having multiple apps to juggle and sign in to.

TIP

Should you decide to skip signing in to your TV provider and worry about it later (or if you've already opened the TV app and cruised right past this part), you can access the same options by going to Settings⇨TV Provider, tapping the name of your provider, and then entering your account information.

The TV app offers a couple of ways to view movies and TV shows: via third-party providers or items you've purchased or rented from the iTunes Store.

To access content from third-party providers like NBC, ABC, PBS, and more, tap the Watch Now button in the bottom left of your screen (see **Figure 16-3**). Swipe to see hit shows and browse by genres like Comedy, Action, and others.

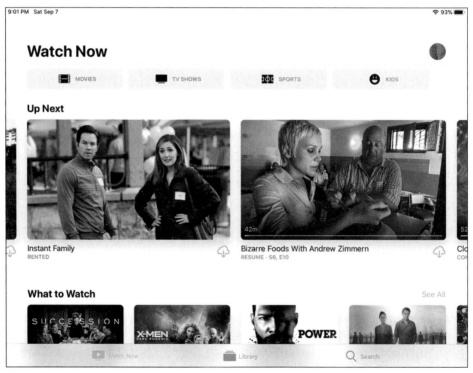

FIGURE 16-3

Tap on a show that interests you and then tap an episode to see a description, like I've done in **Figure 16-4.** Tap Play, and if you have the app that supports the video, it will open automatically. You may be prompted to connect apps from providers like PBS and ABC to the TV app so that you can watch their videos in TV. If you want to do so, tap Connect, but if not, just tap Not Now. If you don't have the app installed that you need to watch the video, you'll be asked if you'd like to download and install it, as shown in **Figure 16-5**.

FIGURE 16-4

If your iPad is on the same Wi-Fi network as your computer and both are running iTunes, with the iPad and iTunes set to use the same Home Sharing account, you see the Shared List. With this setup, you can stream videos from iTunes on your computer to your iPad.

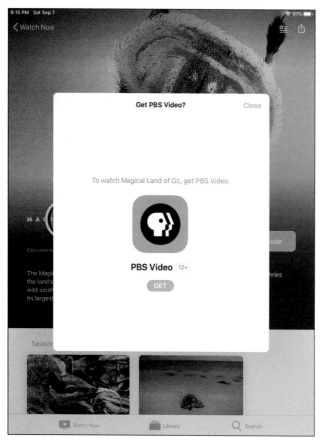

FIGURE 16-5

To access video you've purchased or rented from the iTunes Store, follow these steps:

1. Tap the TV app icon on the Home screen to open the application and then tap Library at the bottom of the screen.

2. On a screen like the one in **Figure 16-6**, tap a selection from within the categories listed and then tap the video you want to watch. You can also tap the Library button in the upper left to view items in select categories, such as Rentals, TV Shows, or Movies, depending on the content you've downloaded.

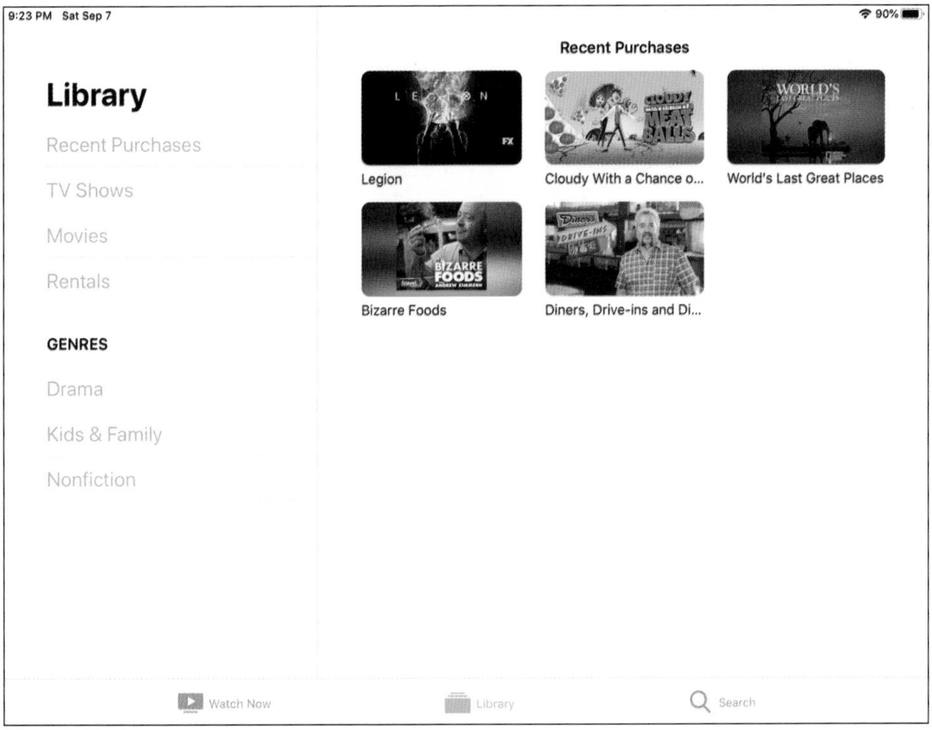

Recent Purchases

Library

Recent Purchases

TV Shows

Legion   Cloudy With a Chance o...   World's Last Great Places

Movies

Rentals

Bizarre Foods   Diners, Drive-ins and Di...

GENRES

Drama

Kids & Family

Nonfiction

▶ Watch Now   📚 Library   🔍 Search

FIGURE 16-6

Information about the movie or TV show episodes appears, as shown in **Figure 16-7**.

3. For TV Shows, tap the episode that you'd like to play; for Movies, the Play button appears right on the description screen. Tap the Play button, and the movie or TV show begins playing (see **Figure 16-8**). (If you see a small, cloud-shaped icon instead of a Play button, tap it, and the content is downloaded from iCloud.)

TECHNICAL STUFF

The progress of the playback is displayed on the Progress bar showing how many minutes you've viewed and how many remain. If you don't see the bar, tap the screen once to display it briefly, along with a set of playback tools at the bottom of the screen.

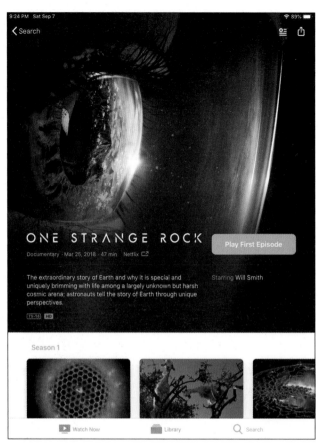

FIGURE 16-7

4. With the playback tools displayed, take any of these actions:

- Tap the Pause button to pause playback.

- Tap either Go to Previous Chapter or Go to Next Chapter to move to a different location in the video playback.

TIP

If a video has chapter support, another button called Scenes appears here for displaying all chapters so that you can move more easily from one to another.

- Tap the circular button on the Volume slider and drag the button left or right to decrease or increase the volume, respectively.

TIP

If your controls disappear during playback, just tap the screen, and they'll reappear.

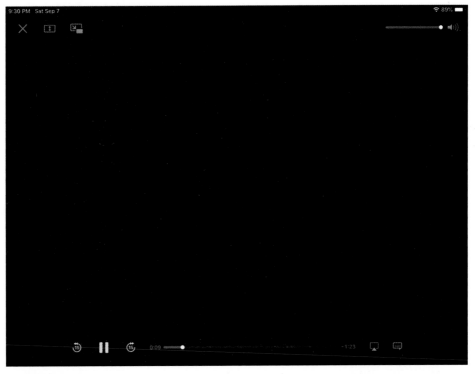

FIGURE 16-8

5. To stop the video and return to the information screen, tap the Done button to the left of the Progress bar.

If you've watched a video and stopped it before the end, it opens by default to the last location where you were viewing. To start a video from the beginning, tap and drag the circular button (the *playhead*) on the Progress bar all the way to the left.

TIP

Turn On Closed-Captioning

iTunes and iPad offer support for closed-captioning and subtitles. Look for the CC logo on media that you download to use this feature.

Video you record on your iPad won't have closed-captioning capability.

TECHNICAL STUFF

If a movie has either closed-captioning or subtitles, you can turn on the feature in iPad.

1. Begin by tapping the Settings icon on the Home screen.

2. Tap Accessibility, scroll down, and tap Subtitles & Captioning.

3. On the menu that displays, tap the Closed Captions + SDH switch to turn on the feature (the switch toggles to green). Now when you play a movie with closed-captioning, you can tap the Audio and Subtitles button to the left of the playback controls to manage these features. Tap the Style option to see and control how your subtitles will appear on screen.

Delete a Video from the iPad

You can buy videos directly from your iPad, or you can sync via iCloud or iTunes to place content you've bought or created on another device on your iPad.

When you want to get rid of video content on your iPad because it's a memory hog, you can delete it:

1. Open the TV app and go to the TV show or movie you want to delete.

2. Tap the Downloaded button (looks like a rectangle containing a check mark), shown in **Figure 16-9**.

3. Tap Remove Download in the options that appear, and the downloaded video will be deleted from your iPad.

If you buy a video using iTunes, sync to download it to your iPad, and then delete it from your iPad, it's still saved in your iTunes Library. You can sync your computer and iPad again to download the video again. Remember, however, that rented movies, when deleted, are gone with the wind. Also, video doesn't sync to iCloud as photos and music do.

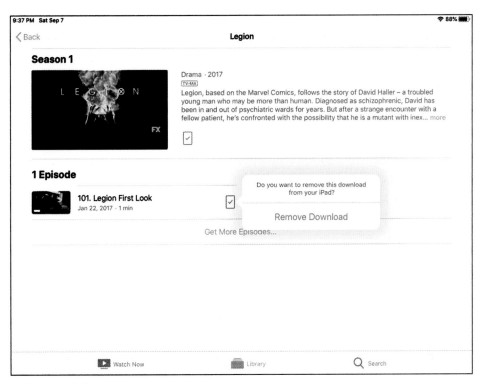

FIGURE 16-9

TIP

iPad has a much smaller storage capacity than your typical computer, so downloading lots of TV shows or movies can fill its storage area quickly. If you don't want to view an item again, delete it to free up space.

4

Living with Your iPad

IN THIS CHAPTER

» Add calendar events

» Create repeating events

» Create a calendar account

» Use a family calendar

» Delete an event

» Display and delete clocks

» Set alarms and alerts

» Use Stopwatch and Timer

Chapter **17**

Keeping on Schedule with Calendar and Clock

Whether you're retired or still working, you have a busy life full of activities (even busier if you're retired, for some unfathomable reason). You may need a way to keep on top of all those activities and appointments. The Calendar app on your iPad is a simple, elegant, electronic daybook that helps you do just that.

In addition to being able to enter events and view them in a list or by the day, week, or month, you can set up Calendar to send alerts to remind you of your obligations and search for events by keywords. You can even set up repeating events, such as birthdays, monthly get-togethers with the girls or guys, or weekly babysitting appointments with your grandchild. To help you coordinate calendars on multiple devices, you can also sync events with other calendar accounts. And by taking advantage of the Family Sharing feature, you can create a Family calendar that everybody in your family can view and add events to.

Another preinstalled app that can help you stay on schedule is Clock. Though simple to use, Clock helps you view the time in multiple locations, set alarms, check yourself with a stopwatch feature, and use a timer.

In this chapter, you master the simple procedures for getting around your calendar, creating a Family calendar, entering and editing events, setting up alerts, syncing, and searching. You also discover the simple ins and outs of using Clock.

View Your Calendar

Calendar offers several ways to view your schedule:

1. Start by tapping the Calendar app icon on the Home screen to open it. Depending on what you last had open and the orientation in which you're holding your iPad, you may see today's calendar, List view, the year, the month, the week, an open event, or the Search screen with search results displayed.

2. Tap the Today button at the bottom of the screen to display Today's view (if it isn't already displayed) and then tap the Search button to see all scheduled events for that day. The Today view with Search open, shown in **Figure 17-1**, displays your daily appointments for every day in a list, with times listed on the left. Tap an event in the list to get more event details or tap the Cancel button (upper-right) to exit Search.

TIP

If you'd like to display events only from a particular calendar, such as the Birthday or US Holidays calendars, tap the Calendars button at the bottom of the screen and select a calendar to view by tapping the circle(s) to the left of the listed calendar(s).

3. Tap the Week button to view all events for the current week. In this view, appointments appear against the times listed along the left side of the screen.

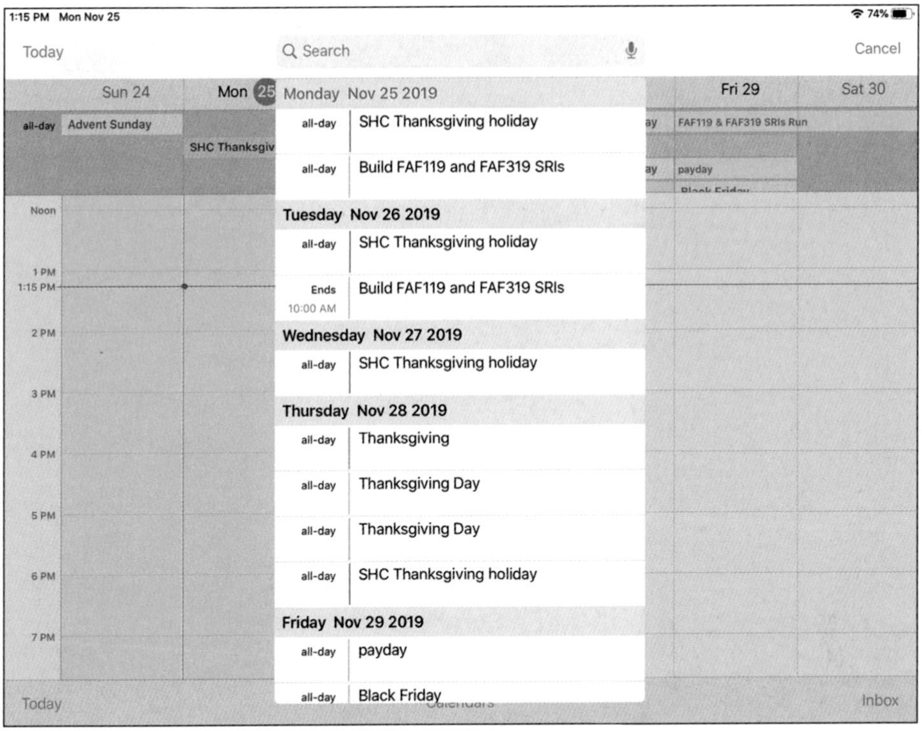

FIGURE 17-1

4. Tap the Month button to get an overview of your busy month (see **Figure 17-2**). In this view, you see the name and timing of each event.

5. Tap the Year button to see all months in the year so you can quickly move to one, as shown in **Figure 17-3**.

6. In any calendar view, tap the Search button to see List view, which lists all your commitments in a drop-down list.

7. To move from one month or year to the next (depending on which view you're in), you can also scroll up or down the screen with your finger.

8. To jump back to today, tap the Today button in the bottom-left corner of the screen. The month containing the current day is displayed.

Tap to select a view

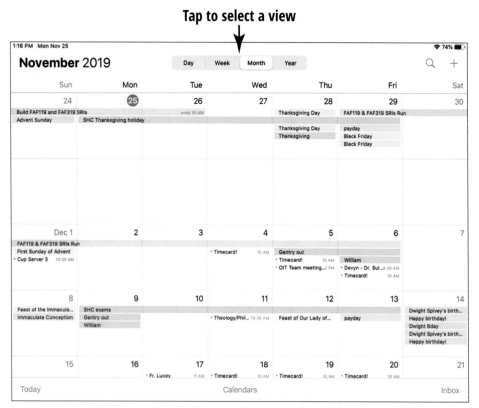

FIGURE 17-2

Calendar looks slightly different when you hold your iPad in portrait and landscape orientations. Turn your iPad in both directions to see which orientation you prefer to work in, and make sure to try this with each view option.

TIP

To view any invitation that you accepted, which placed an event on your calendar, tap Inbox in the lower-right corner and a list of invitations is displayed. You can use text within emails (such as a date, flight number, or phone number) to add an event to Calendar. Tap Done in the upper right of the window or tap outside the Inbox window to return to the calendar.

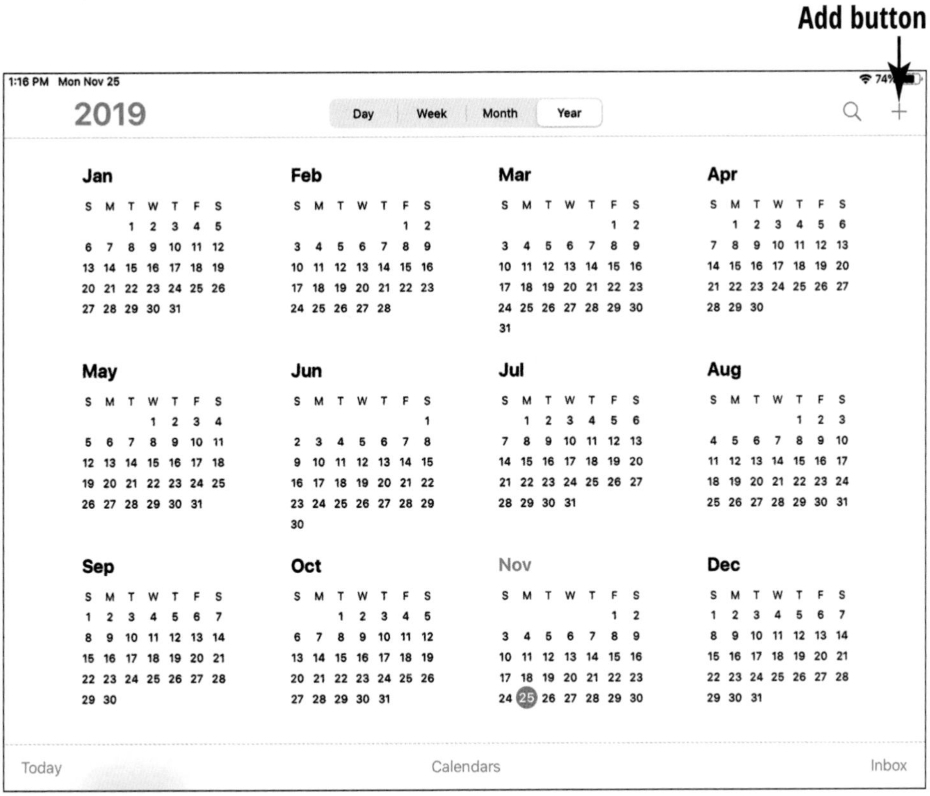

Add button

FIGURE 17-3

Add Calendar Events

To add events to your calendar:

1. With any view displayed, tap the Add button (which looks like a plus symbol) in the upper-right corner of the screen to add an event (refer to Figure 17-3). The New Event dialog box appears.

2. Enter a title for the event and, if you want, a location.

3. Tap the All-day switch to turn it on for an all-day event, or tap the Starts and Ends fields to set start and end times for the event. As shown in **Figure 17-4,** the scrolling setting for day, hour, and minute appears.

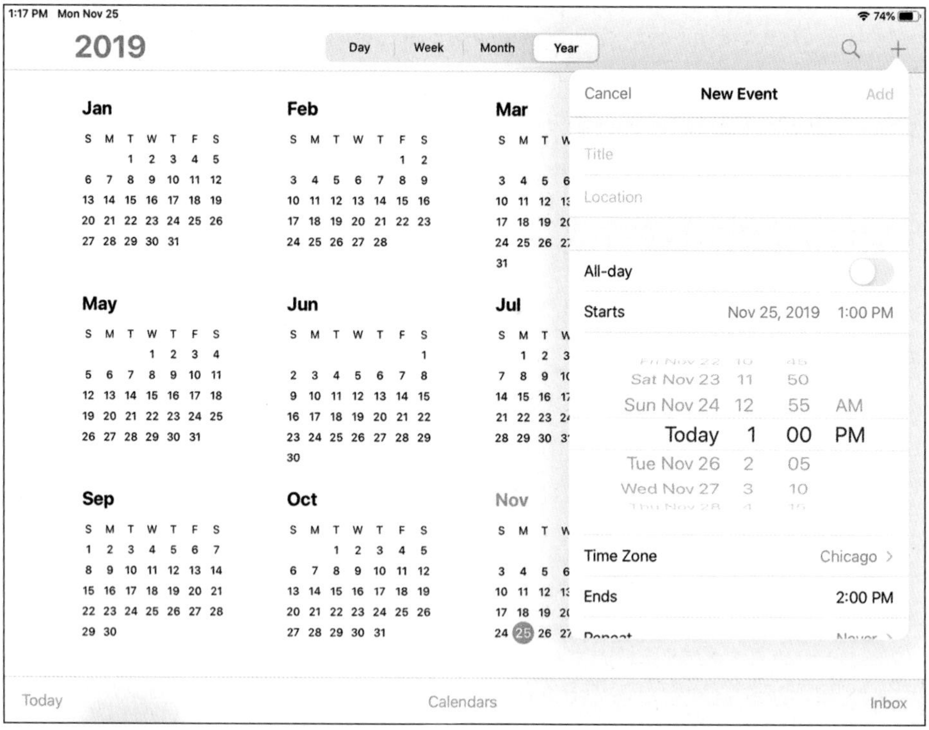

FIGURE 17-4

4. Place your finger on the date, hour, minute, or AM/PM column and move your finger to scroll up or down.

5. If you want to add notes, use your finger to scroll down in the New Event dialog box and tap in the Notes field. Type your note and then tap the Add button to save the event.

TIP

You can edit any event at any time by simply tapping it in any view of your calendar. When the details are displayed, tap Edit in the upper-right corner. The Edit Event dialog box appears, offering the same settings as the New Event dialog box. Tap the Done button to save your changes or Cancel to return to your calendar without saving any changes.

Add Events with Siri

Play around with this feature and Calendar; it's a lot of fun!

1. Press and hold the Home button (Top button for iPad Pro models) or say "Hey Siri."

2. Speak a command, such as "Hey Siri. Create a meeting on October 3 at 2:30 p.m."

3. When Siri asks you whether you're ready to schedule the event, say "Yes." The event is added to Calendar.

TIP

You can schedule an event with Siri in several ways:

» Say "Create event." Siri asks you first for a date and then for a time.

» Say "I have a meeting with John on April 1." Siri may respond by saying "I don't find a meeting with John on April 1; shall I create it?" You can say "Yes" to have Siri create it.

Create Repeating Events

If you want an event to repeat, such as a weekly or monthly appointment, you can set a repeating event.

1. With any view displayed, tap the Add button to add an event. The New Event dialog box (refer to Figure 17-4) appears.

2. Enter a title and location for the event and set the start and end dates and times, as shown in the earlier section, "Add Calendar Events."

3. Scroll down the page, if necessary, and then tap the Repeat field; the Repeat dialog box, shown in **Figure 17-5,** is displayed.

4. Tap a preset time interval — Every Day, Week, 2 Weeks, Month, or Year — and you return to the New Event dialog box. Tap Custom and make the appropriate settings if you want to set any other interval, such as every two months on the 6th of the month.

5. Should you like to set an expiration date for the repeated event, tap End Repeat and make the necessary settings.

6. Tap Done and you'll return to the Calendar.

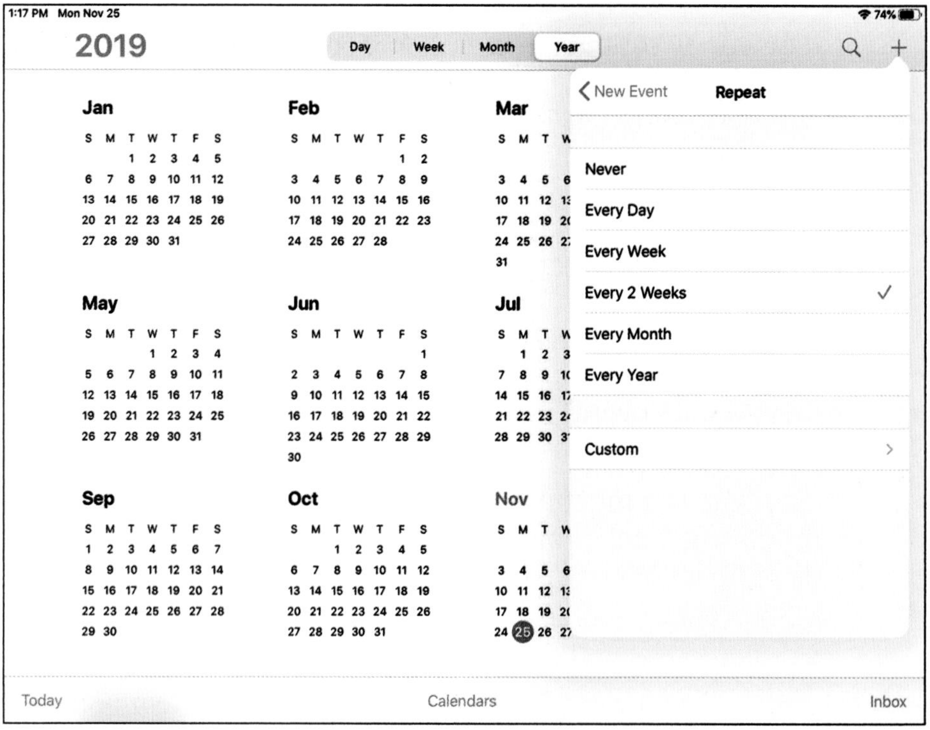

FIGURE 17-5

View an Event

Tap an event anywhere — on a Day view, Week view, Month view, or List view — to see its details. To make changes to the event you're viewing, tap the Edit button in the upper-left corner.

Add Alerts

If you want your iPad to alert you when an event is coming up, you can use the Alert feature.

1. Tap the Settings icon on the Home screen and choose Sounds.

2. Scroll down to Calendar Alerts and tap it; then tap any Alert Tone, which causes iPad to play the tone for you. After you've chosen the alert tone you want, tap Sounds to return to Sounds settings. Press the Home

button (or swipe up from the bottom of the screen for iPad Pro models), then tap Calendar, and create an event in your calendar or open an existing one for editing, as covered in earlier tasks in this chapter.

3. In the New Event (refer to Figure 17-4) or Edit Event dialog box, tap the Alert field. The Event Alert dialog box appears, as shown in **Figure 17-6.**

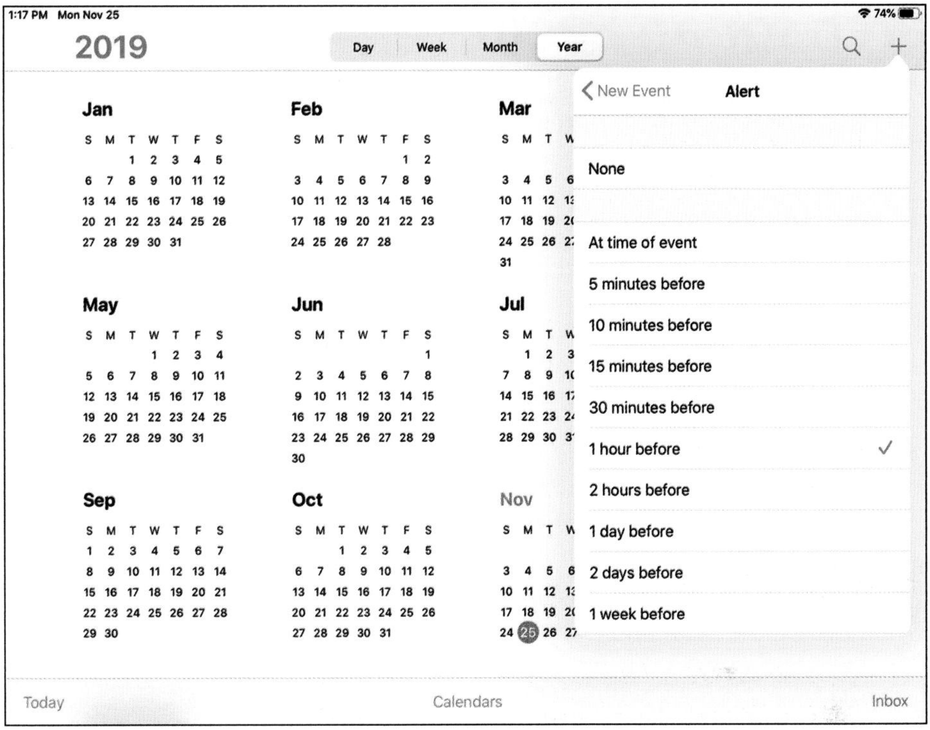

FIGURE 17-6

4. Tap any preset interval, from 5 Minutes to 2 Days Before or At Time of Event, and you'll return to the New Event or Edit Event dialog box.

5. Tap Done in the Edit Event dialog box or Add in the New Event dialog box to save all settings.

If you work for an organization that uses a Microsoft Exchange account, you can set up your iPad to receive and respond to invitations from colleagues in your company. When somebody sends an invitation that you accept, it appears on your calendar. Check with your company network administrator (who will jump at the

TIP

chance to get her hands on your iPad) or the iPad User Guide to set up this feature if it sounds useful to you.

iCloud offers individuals functionality similar to Microsoft Exchange.

TIP

Search for an Event

1. With Calendar open in any view, tap the Search button in the top-right corner.

2. Tap the Search field to display the onscreen keyboard.

3. Type a word or words to search by and then tap the Search key. While you type, the Results dialog box appears, as shown in **Figure 17-7.**

4. Tap any result to display the event details.

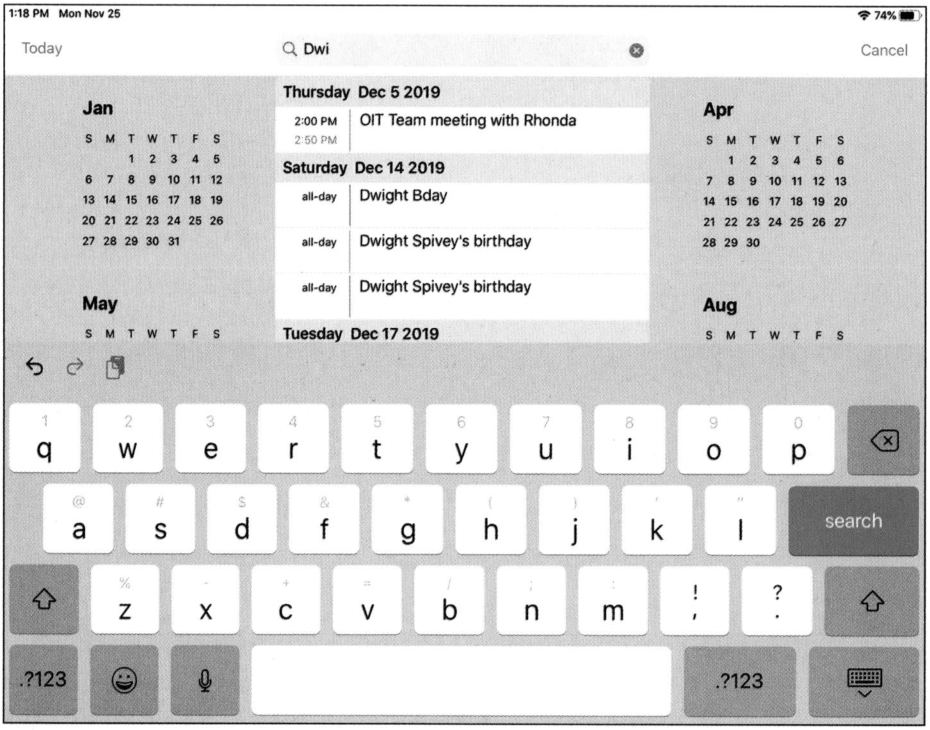

FIGURE 17-7

Create a Calendar Account

If you use a calendar available from an online service, such as Yahoo! or Google, you can subscribe to that calendar to read events saved there on your iPad.

1. Tap the Settings icon on the Home screen to get started.

2. Tap the Passwords & Accounts option.

3. Tap Add Account and the Add Account options, shown in **Figure 17-8,** appear.

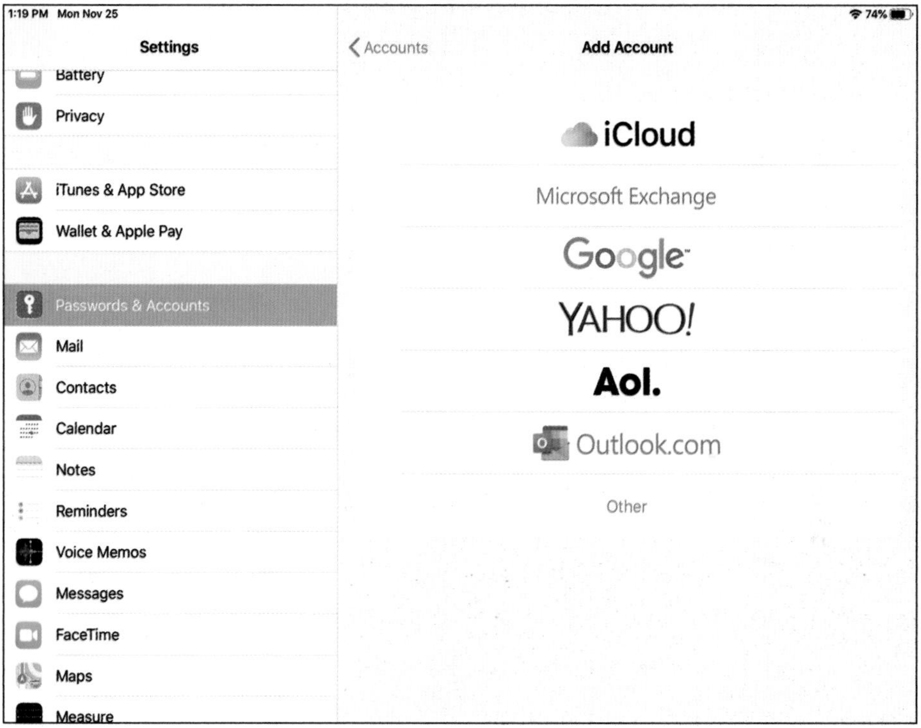

FIGURE 17-8

4. Tap a selection, such as Outlook.com, Google, or Yahoo!, depending on the calendar service you'd like to use.

Turn on Calendars for other accounts that aren't listed by tapping Other.

TIP

5. In the next screen that appears (see **Figure 17-9**), enter your account information for the service (the screen you see will vary, depending on the service you selected in Step 4). If you don't yet have an account for the service, there will be a way on the screen for you to create a new account.

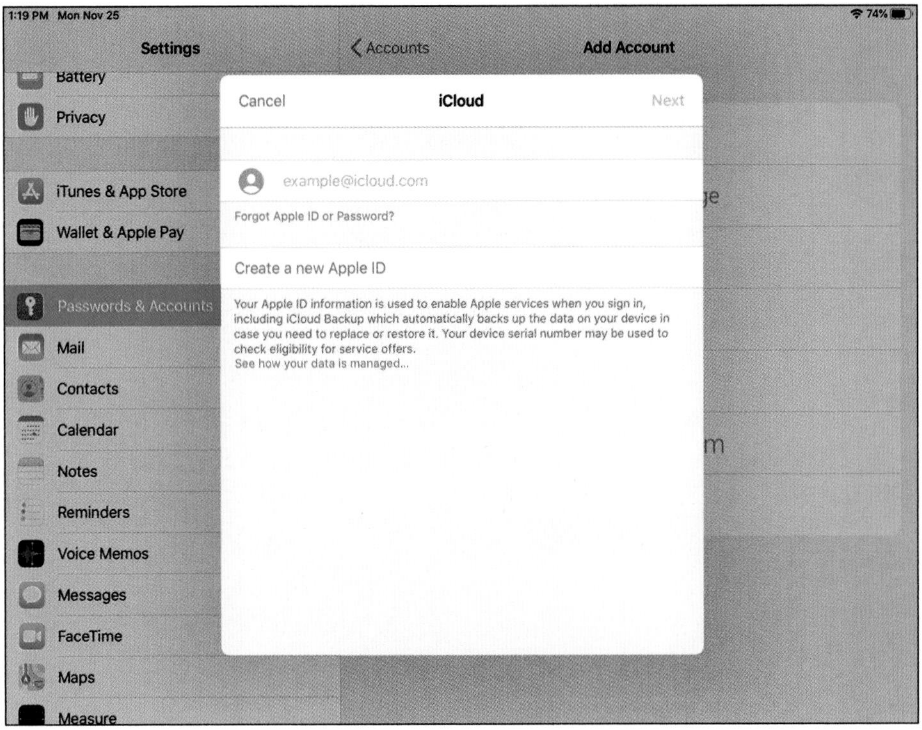

FIGURE 17-9

6. Tap Next. iPad verifies your account information.

7. On the following screen (see **Figure 17-10**), tap the On/Off switch for the Calendars field; your iPad retrieves data from your calendar at the interval you have set to fetch data. Tap Save to save your account settings.

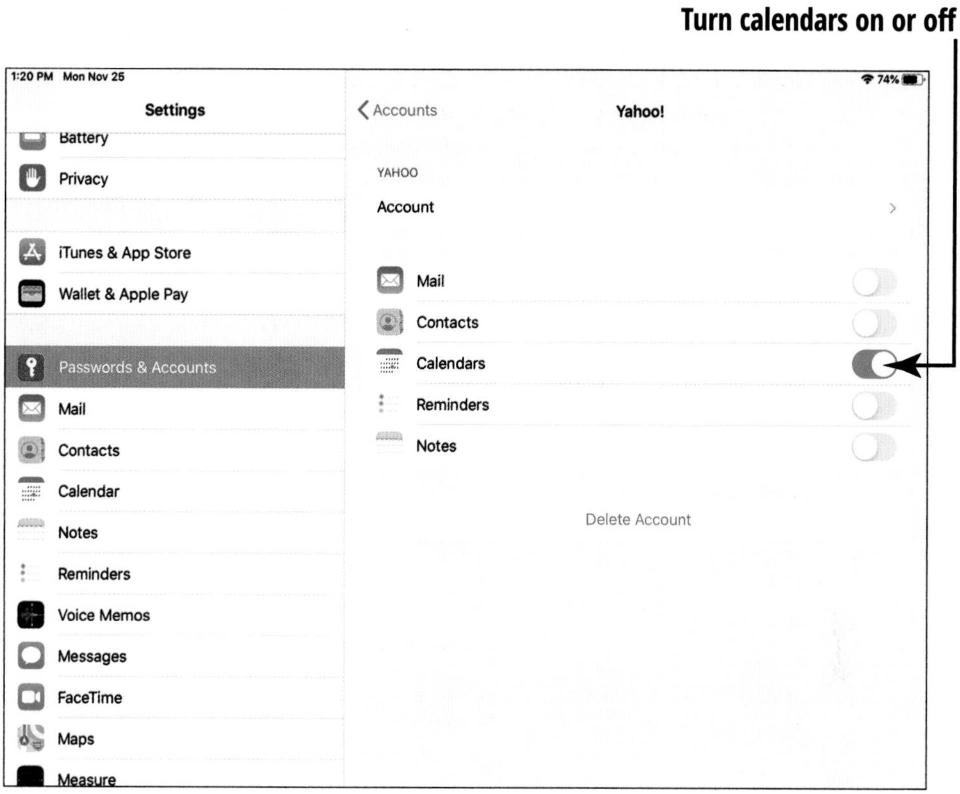

Turn calendars on or off

FIGURE 17-10

Use a Family Calendar

If you set up the Family Sharing feature (see Chapter 12 for how to do this), you create a Family calendar that you can use to share family events with up to five other people. After you set up Family Sharing, you have to make sure that the Calendar Sharing feature is on.

1. Tap Settings on the Home screen.

2. Tap the Apple ID (you may need to swipe up to see it on the left) and check that Family Sharing is set up (see **Figure 17-11**). You'll see Family Sharing rather than Set Up Family Sharing if it has been set up. If you see Set Up Family Sharing, go to Chapter 12 for instructions on setting up Family Sharing.

3. Tap iCloud. In the iCloud settings, tap the switch for Calendars to turn it on if it isn't already on.

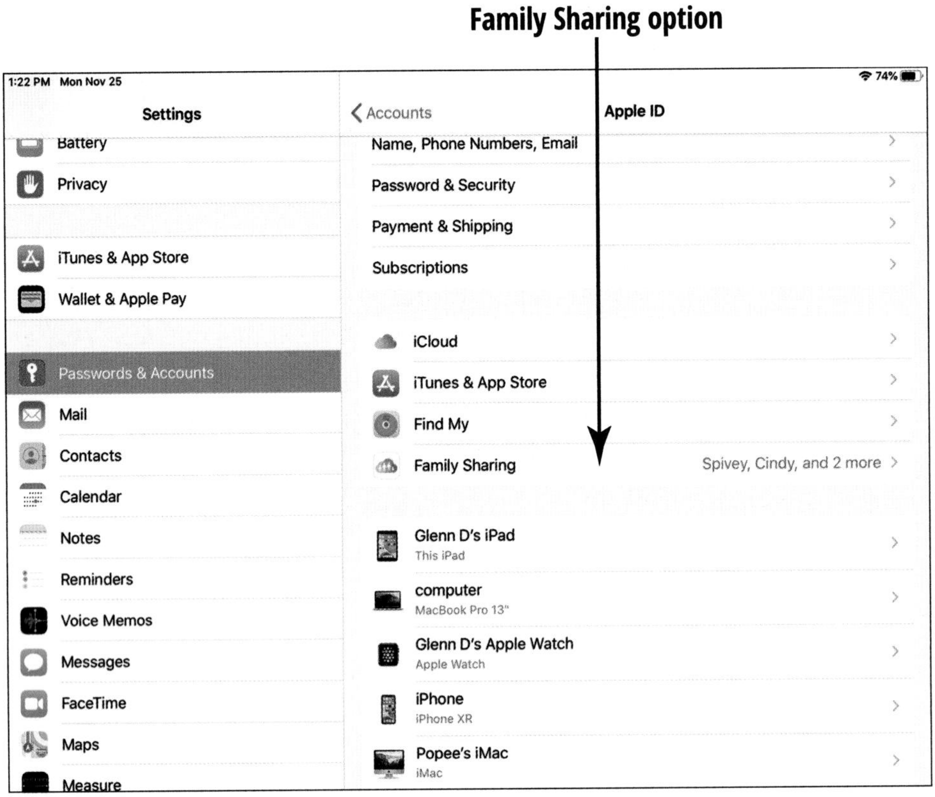

FIGURE 17-11

4. Now tap the Home button or swipe up from the bottom of the screen (iPad Pro models) and then tap Calendar to open the app. Tap the Calendars button at the bottom-center of the screen. Scroll down, and in the Show Calendars dialog box that appears, make sure that Family is selected. Tap Done in the upper-right corner of the Show Calendars dialog box when finished.

5. Now when you create a new event in the New Event dialog box, tap Calendar and choose Family or Show All Calendars. The details of events contain a notation that an event is from the Family calendar.

TIP

If you store birthdays for people in the Contacts app, by default the Calendar app then displays these when the day comes around so that you won't forget to pass on your congratulations! You can turn off this feature by tapping Calendars in the Calendar app and deselecting Birthday Calendar.

Delete an Event

When an upcoming luncheon or meeting is canceled, you may want to delete the appointment.

1. With Calendar open, tap an event.

2. Tap Delete Event at the bottom of the screen (see **Figure 17-12**), and then tap Delete Event again to confirm (or Cancel to reconsider).

3. If this is a repeating event, you have the option to delete this instance of the event or this and all future instances of the event. Tap the button for the option you prefer. The event is deleted, and you return to Calendar view.

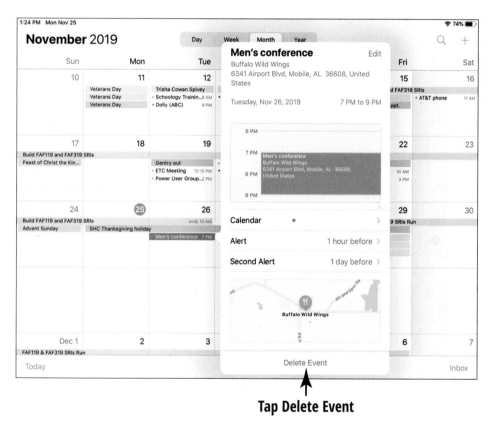

Tap Delete Event

FIGURE 17-12

TIP If an event is moved but not canceled, you don't have to delete the old one and create a new one. Simply edit the existing event to change the day and time in the Event dialog box.

Display Clock

Clock is a preinstalled app that resides on the Home screen along with other preinstalled apps, such as Apple Books and Camera.

1. Tap the Clock app to open it. If this is the first time you've opened Clock you'll see the World Clock tab (see **Figure 17-13**).

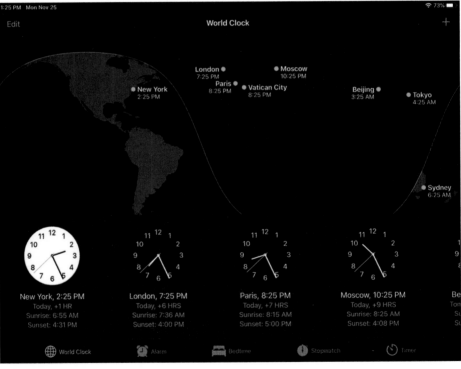

FIGURE 17-13

2. You can add a clock for many (but not all) locations around the world. With Clock displayed, tap the Add button (looks like a plus symbol) in the upper-right corner.

3. Tap a city on the list or tap a letter on the right side to display locations that begin with that letter (see **Figure 17-14**) and then tap a city. You can also tap in the Search field and begin to type a city name to find and tap a city. The clock appears in the last slot at the bottom.

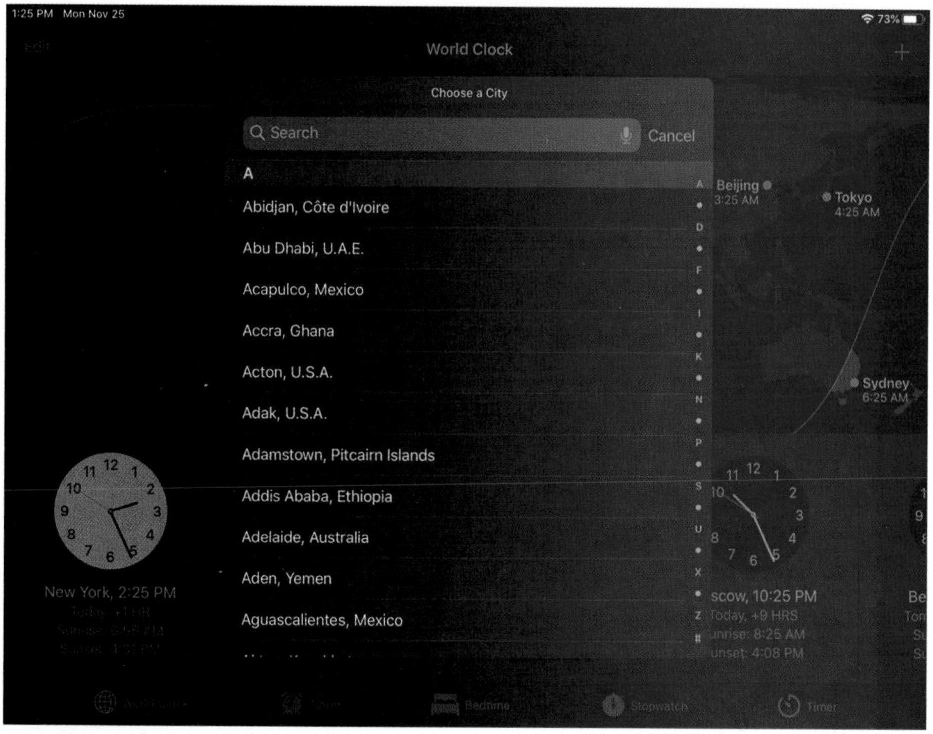

FIGURE 17-14

Delete a Clock

Maybe you no longer need to know what time it is in San Francisco, which is one of the default clocks on your iPad. You can delete that clock if you want:

1. To remove a location, tap the Edit button in the top-left corner of the World Clock screen.

2. Tap the minus symbol next to a location to delete it (see **Figure 17-15**).

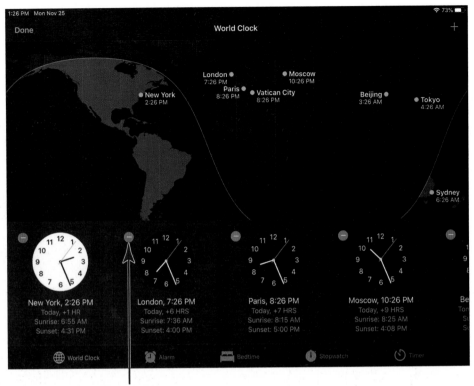

Delete button

FIGURE 17-15

Set an Alarm

It seems like nobody has a bedside alarm clock anymore; everyone uses their smart device instead. Here's how you set an alarm:

1. With the Clock app displayed, tap the Alarm tab.

2. Tap the Add button (the + in the upper-right corner). In the Add Alarm dialog box shown in **Figure 17-16**, take any of the following actions, tapping Back after you make each setting to return to the Add Alarm dialog box:

    -   Tap Repeat if you want the alarm to repeat at a regular interval, such as every Monday or every Sunday.

    -   Tap Label if you want to name the alarm, such as "Take Pill" or "Call Glenn."

- Tap Sound to choose the tune the alarm will play.

- Tap the On/Off switch for Snooze if you want to use the Snooze feature.

FIGURE 17-16

3. Place your finger on any of the three columns of sliding numbers at the top of the dialog box and scroll to set the time you want the alarm to occur (don't forget to verify AM or PM!); then tap Save. The alarm appears in the Alarm tab.

TIP To delete an alarm, tap the Alarm tab and tap Edit. All alarms appear. Tap the red circle with a minus in it, and the alarm is deleted. Be careful: When you tap the Delete button, the alarm is unretrievable and will need to be recreated from scratch if you mistakenly removed it.

Set Bedtime and Waking Alerts

The Clock can also help you develop better sleeping habits by allowing you to set bedtime and wake alerts and keeping track of your sleep habits.

1. Tap the Bedtime button at the bottom of the Clock app screen.

2. If this is your first time to open the Bedtime feature, tap Get Started and answer the questions you're asked to help configure the Bedtime settings.

3. When you've completed the initial configuration, you will see a screen displaying your bedtime and waking hours (see **Figure 17-17**).

4. You can manually change the bedtime by pressing the button that looks like a moon and dragging it around the clock face. You can do the same for the wake time by pressing and dragging the button that looks like a bell. To keep the same amount of sleep time, you can press and drag the orange band.

FIGURE 17-17

5. Tap the Options button in the upper-left corner to reconfigure the settings for Bedtime (see **Figure 17-18**). You can adjust the days the Bedtime feature is used, the reminder time, enable/disable the Do Not Disturb During Bedtime feature, set the Wake Up Sound, and the volume for the Wake Up Sound. Tap Done when finished (or Cancel if you didn't make any changes).

6. Tap the Bedtime toggle switch to Off (white) to disable or On (green) to enable.

FIGURE 17-18

Use Stopwatch and Timer

Sometimes life seems like a countdown or a ticking clock counting the minutes you've spent on a certain activity. You can use the Timer and Stopwatch tabs of the Clock app to do a countdown to a specific time, such as the moment when your chocolate chip cookies are done cooking or to time an activity, such as reading.

These two work very similarly: Tap the Stopwatch or Timer tab from Clock's screen and then tap the Start button (see **Figure 17-19**). When you set the Timer, iPad uses a sound to notify you when time's up. When you start the Stopwatch, you have to tap the Stop button when the activity is done.

TIP

Stopwatch allows you to log intermediate timings, such as a lap in the pool or the periods of a timed game. With Stopwatch running, just tap the Lap button, and the first interval of time is recorded. Tap Lap again to record a second interval, and so on.

Start button

FIGURE 17-19

IN THIS CHAPTER

» **Make and edit reminders and lists**

» **Schedule a reminder**

» **Sync reminders and lists**

» **Complete or delete reminders**

» **Set notification types**

» **View notifications**

» **Set up Do Not Disturb**

Chapter **18**

Working with Reminders and Notifications

The Reminders app and Notification Center features warm the hearts of those who need help remembering all the details of their lives.

Reminders is a kind of to-do list that lets you create tasks and set reminders so that you don't forget important commitments.

You can even be reminded to do things when you arrive at or leave a location, or receive a message from someone. For example, you can set a reminder so that, when your iPad detects that you've left the location of your golf game, an alert reminds you to pick up your grandchildren, or when you arrive at your cabin, iPad reminds you to turn on the water . . . you get the idea.

Notification Center allows you to review all the things you should be aware of in one place, such as mail messages, text messages, calendar appointments, and alerts.

If you occasionally need to escape all your obligations, try the Do Not Disturb feature. Turn this feature on, and you won't be bothered with alerts until you're ready to be.

In this chapter, you discover how to set up and view tasks in Reminders and how Notification Center can centralize all your alerts in one easy-to-find place.

Create a Reminder

Creating an event in Reminders is pretty darn simple:

1. Tap Reminders on the Home screen.

2. On the screen that appears, tap Reminders, and then tap the New Reminder button with a plus sign to the left of it at the bottom of the screen to add a task (see **Figure 18-1**). The onscreen keyboard appears.

3. Enter a task name or description using the onscreen keyboard, and then tap Done in the upper-right corner.

The following task shows how to add more specifics about an event for which you've created a reminder.

TIP

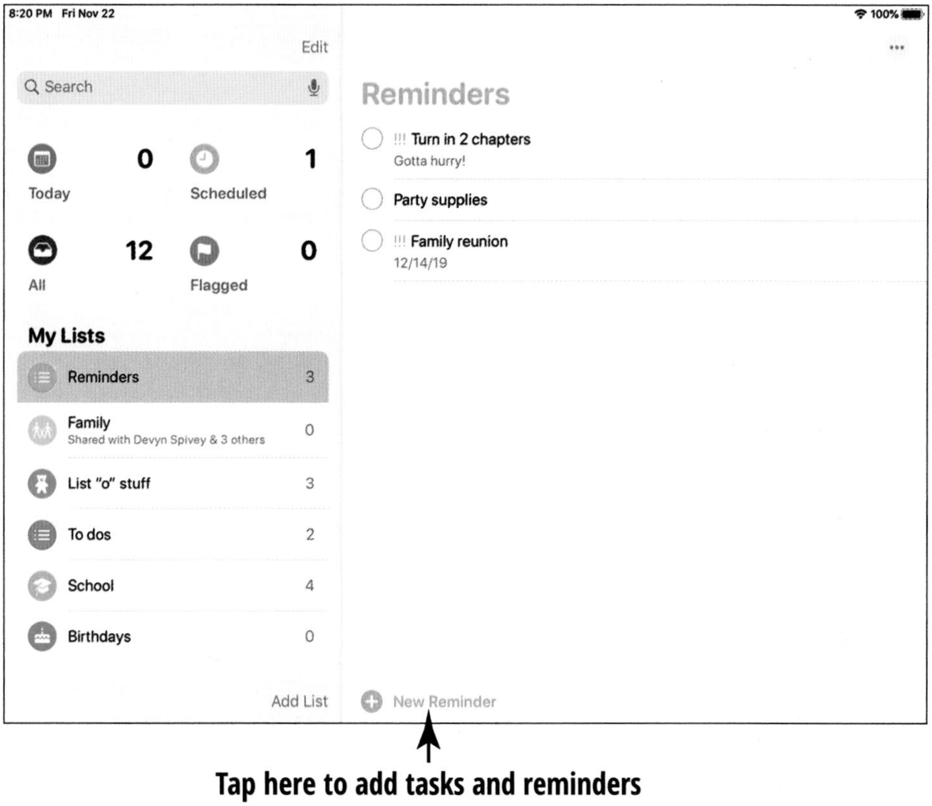

Edit   ...

Q Search   🎤

Reminders

📅	**0**	⏰	**1**
Today		Scheduled	
📦	**12**	🏳	**0**
All		Flagged	

○ **!!! Turn in 2 chapters**
Gotta hurry!

○ **Party supplies**

○ **!!! Family reunion**
12/14/19

My Lists

≡ Reminders		3
👥 Family Shared with Devyn Spivey & 3 others		0
🎃 List "o" stuff		3
≡ To dos		2
🎓 School		4
🎂 Birthdays		0

Add List   ⊕ New Reminder

↑

Tap here to add tasks and reminders

FIGURE 18-1

Edit Reminder Details

TIP

1. Tap a reminder and then tap the Details button (an i in a circle) that appears to the right of it to open the Details dialog box shown in **Figure 18-2**.

I deal with reminder settings in the following task.

2. Tap Notes and enter any notes about the event using the onscreen keyboard.

3. Toggle the Flagged switch to enable or disable a flag for the reminder. Swipe up or down within the Details dialog box if you don't see the Flagged switch (or any other options discussed in this section) upon first glance.

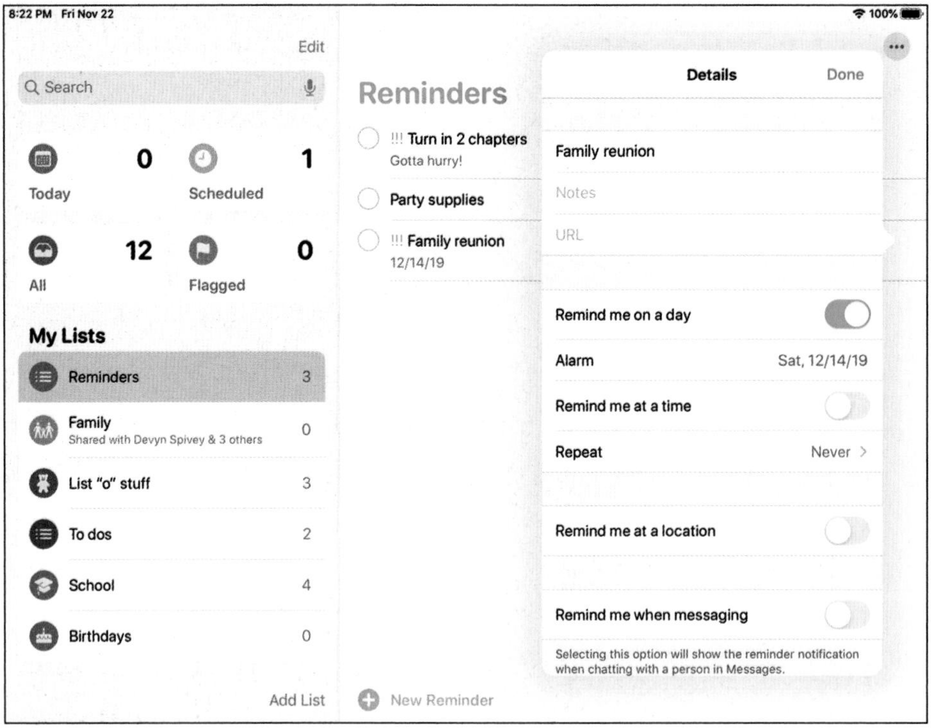

FIGURE 18-2

4. Tap Priority and then tap None, Low (!), Medium (!!), or High (!!!) from the choices that appear. Tap Details in the upper-left of the Priority dialog box to return to the Details screen.

TIP

With this version of the app, priority settings now display the associated number of exclamation points on a task in a list to remind you of its importance.

5. Tap List and then tap which list you want the reminder saved to, such as your calendar, iCloud, Exchange, or a category of reminders that you've created (see **Figure 18-3**). Tap Details in the upper-left of the Change List dialog box to return to the Details screen.

6. Tap Done in the upper-right of the Details dialog box to save the task.

TIP

Reminders in iOS 13 includes a quick toolbar that appears just above the keyboard, which allows you to quickly add a time, location, flags, or images to the reminder you've tapped in a list. Just tap the icon for whichever item you want to activate, and make the appropriate settings as prompted.

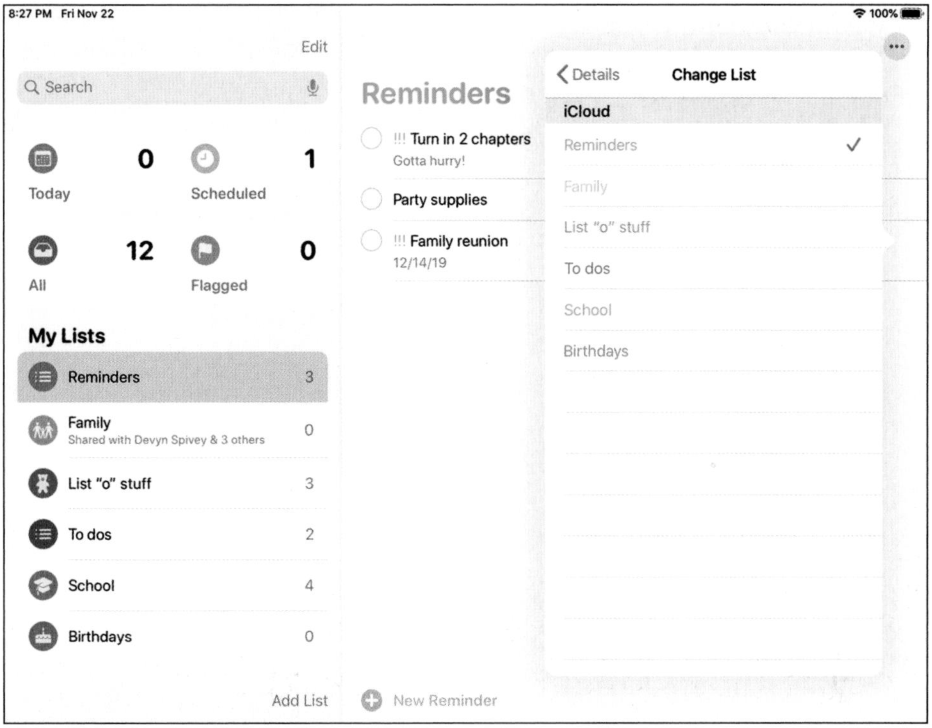

FIGURE 18-3

Schedule a Reminder by Time, Location, or When Messaging

One of the major purposes of Reminders is to remind you of upcoming tasks. To set options for a reminder, follow these steps:

1. Tap a task and then tap the Details button that appears to the right of the task.

2. In the dialog box that appears (refer to **Figure 18-2**), toggle the Remind me on a day switch to turn the feature On (green).

3. Tap the Alarm field that appears below this setting (see **Figure 18-4**) to display date settings.

4. Tap and flick the month, day, and year fields to set the correct date.

5. Toggle the Remind me at a time switch to On (green).

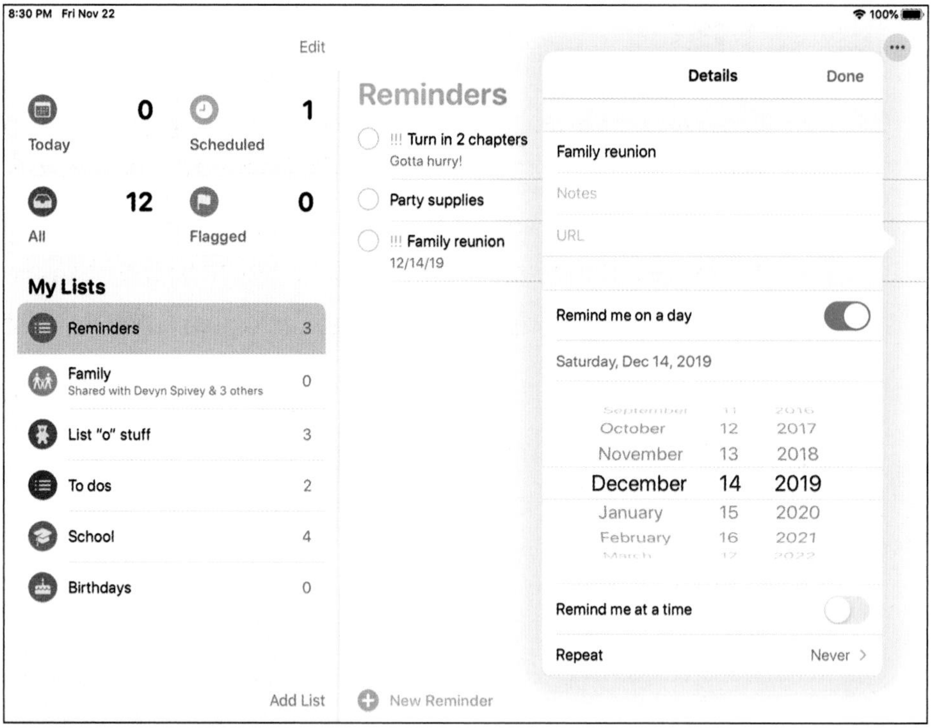

FIGURE 18-4

6. Tap and flick the hour, minutes, and AM/PM fields to scroll to the correct time for the reminder. Tap Repeat and select an appropriate option if this is something you frequently need to be reminded of.

7. Toggle the Remind me at a location switch to On and then tap the Location field. If prompted, tap Allow to let Reminders use your current location.

8. Use the field labeled Current Location to find your location or enter a location in the Search field. Tap Details in the upper-left corner of the Location dialog box to return to the task detail screen.

9. Toggle the Remind me when messaging switch to On and then tap Choose Person. Select a person or group from your Contacts. Using this option will cause you to be reminded of the item when you're engaged in messaging with the person or group selected.

10. Tap Done in the upper-right of the Details dialog box to save the settings for the reminder.

Create a List

You can create your own lists of tasks to help you keep different parts of your life organized and even edit the tasks on the list in List view.

1. Tap Reminders on the Home screen to open it. If a particular list is open, tap Lists in the upper-left corner to return to the List view.

2. Tap Add List at the bottom of the screen to display the New List form shown in **Figure 18-5**.

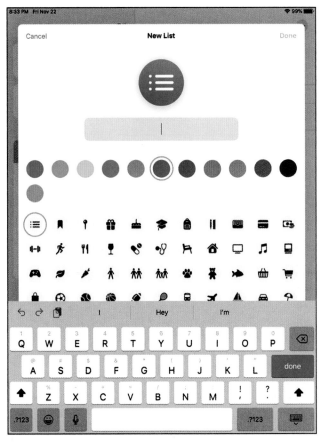

FIGURE 18-5

3. Tap the text field and then enter a name for the list.

4. Tap a color; the list name will appear in that color in List view.

5. Tap an icon to customize the icon for the list. This feature helps you to better organize your lists by using icons for birthdays, medications, groceries, and whole host of other occasions and subjects (see in **Figure 18-6**).

6. Tap Done in the upper-right corner to save the list. Tap the New Reminder button to enter a task.

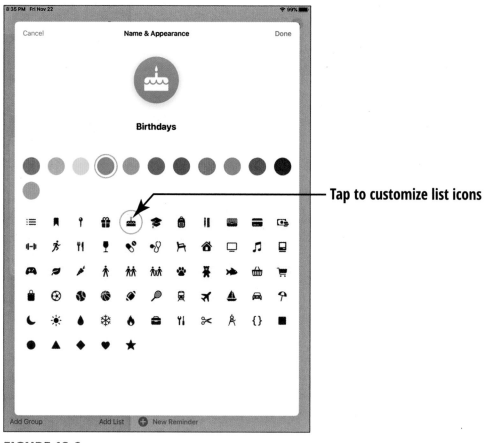

Tap to customize list icons

FIGURE 18-6

Sync with Other Devices and Calendars

To make all these settings work, you should set up your default Calendar in the Settings⇨Calendar settings and set up your iCloud account to enable Reminders (Settings⇨Apple ID [top of the screen]⇨iCloud).

TIP

Your default Calendar account is also your default Reminders account.

1. To determine which tasks are brought over from other calendars (such as Outlook), tap the Settings button on the Home screen.

2. Tap your Apple ID and then tap iCloud. In the dialog box that appears, be sure that Reminders is set to On (green).

3. In the main Settings list on the left, find and then tap Passwords & Accounts.

4. Tap the account you want to sync Reminders with and then toggle the Reminders switch to On, if available (shown in **Figure 18-7**).

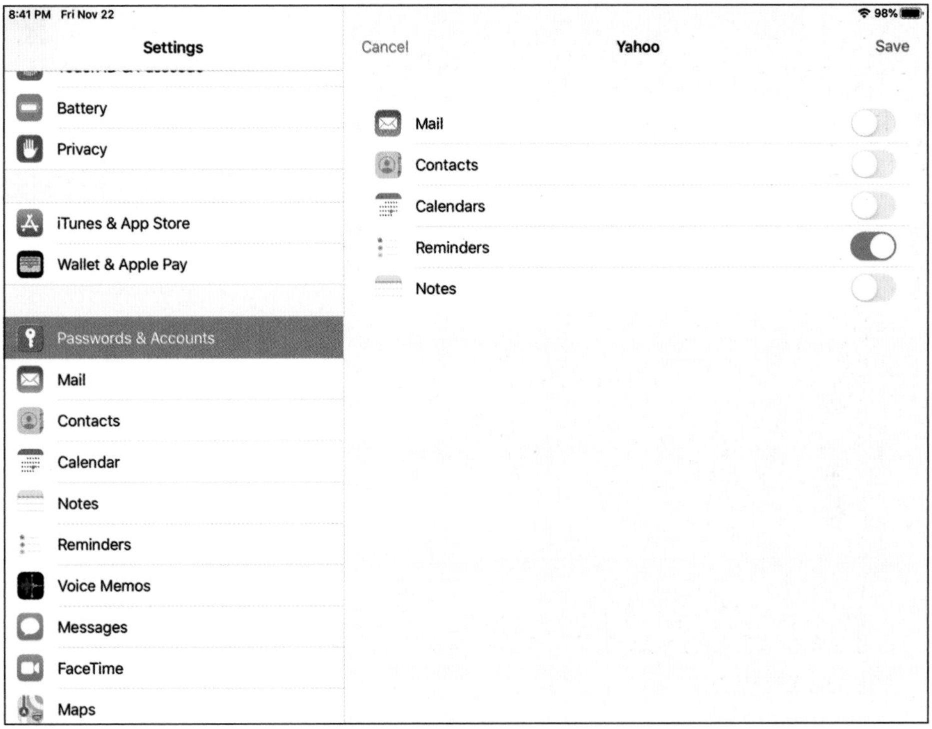

FIGURE 18-7

Mark as Complete or Delete a Reminder

You may want to mark a task as completed or just delete it entirely.

1. With Reminders open and a list of tasks displayed, tap the circle to the left of a task to mark it as complete. When you next open the list, the completed task will have been removed. To view completed tasks, tap the More button in the upper-right (looks like a gray circle containing three tiny dots) and tap Show Completed in the options (shown in **Figure 18-8**). To hide completed tasks, just tap the More button and then tap Hide Completed.

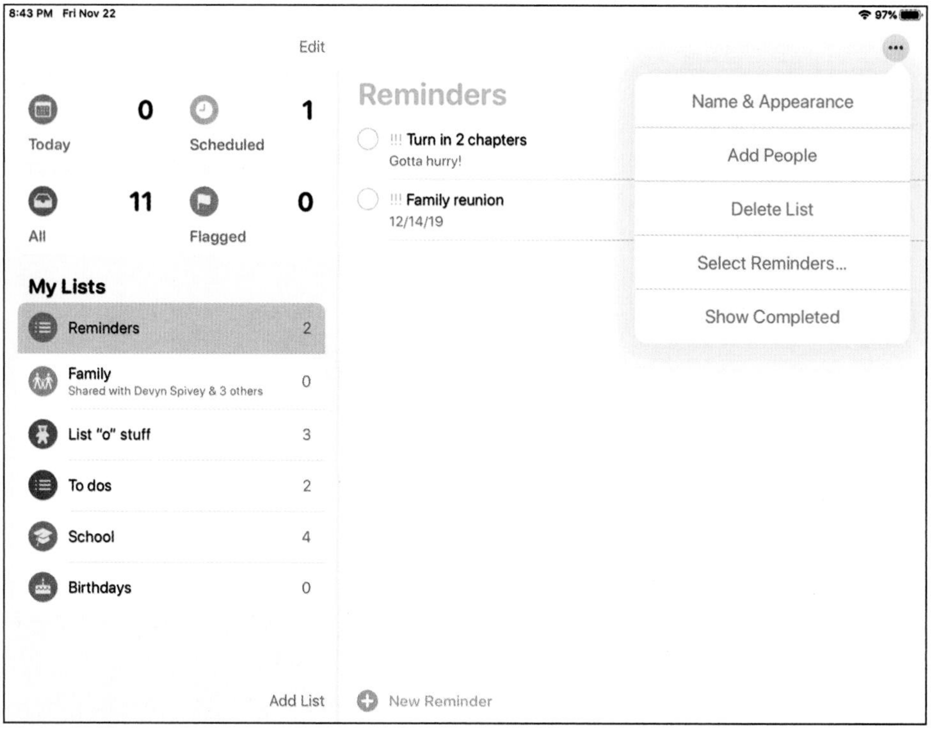

FIGURE 18-8

2. To delete a single task, with the list of tasks displayed, swipe the task you want to delete to the left. Tap the red Delete button to the right of the task (see **Figure 18-9**) and it will disappear from your list.

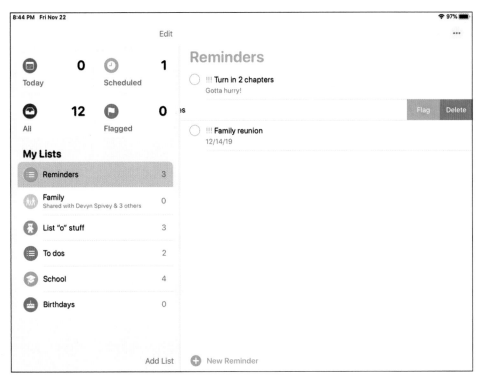

FIGURE 18-9

WARNING

Be aware that if you delete a task, it's gone for good. There is no area in Reminders to retrieve deleted tasks. If you simply want to remove the item from the list without deleting it entirely, be sure to mark it as completed, as instructed in Step 1.

3. To delete more than one task, with the list of tasks displayed, tap the More button and tap Select Reminders in the options. In the screen shown in **Figure 18-10**, tap the circle to the left of the tasks you want to select, then tap the Delete button in the lower-right corner.

Tap to select   Tap to delete

FIGURE 18-10

Set Notification Types

Notification Center is a list of various alerts and scheduled events; it even provides information (such as stock quotes) that you can display by swiping down from the top of your iPad screen. Notification Center is on by default, but you don't have to include every type of notification there if you don't want to. For example, you may never want to be notified of incoming messages but always want to have reminders listed here — it's up to you. Some Notification Center settings let you control what types of notifications are included:

1. Tap Settings and then tap Notifications.

2. In the settings that appear (see **Figure 18-11**), you see a list of items to be included in Notification Center. You can view the state of an item by reading it directly under the item's name. For example, under Accuweather in Figure 18-11, you read "Banners, Sounds, Badges," indicating the methods of notifications that are enabled for that app.

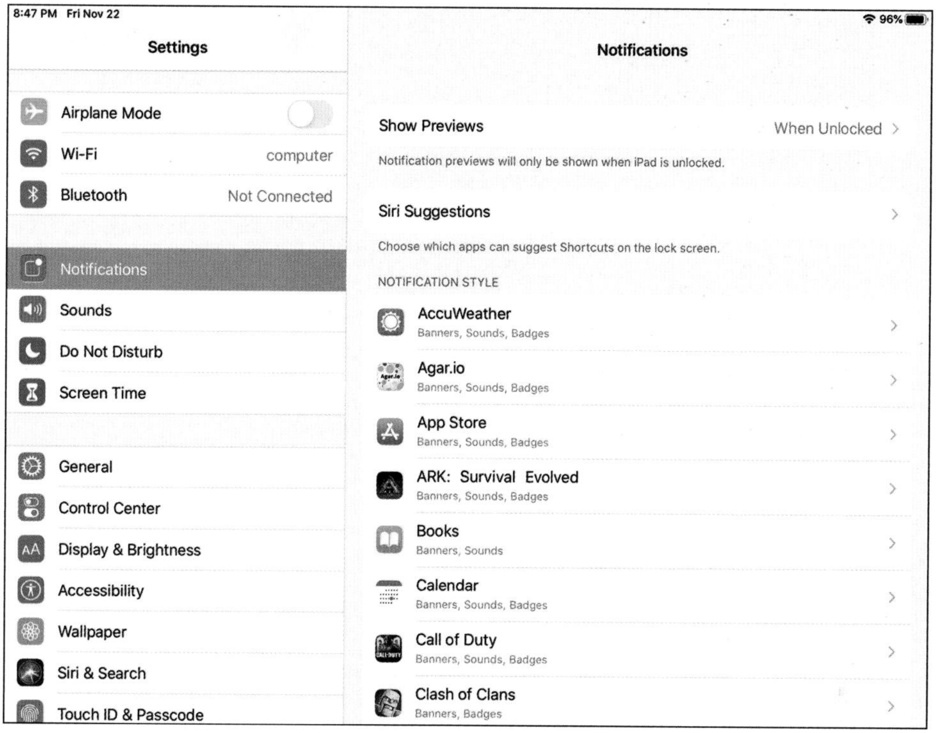

FIGURE 18-11

3. Tap any item. In the settings that appear, set an item's Allow Notifications switch (see **Figure 18-12**) to On or Off, to include or exclude it from Notification Center.

4. In the Alerts section, choose to display alerts on the Lock Screen, Notification Center, as Banners, or a combination of one or more. You may also decide to have no alerts appear when nothing is checked in the Alerts section.

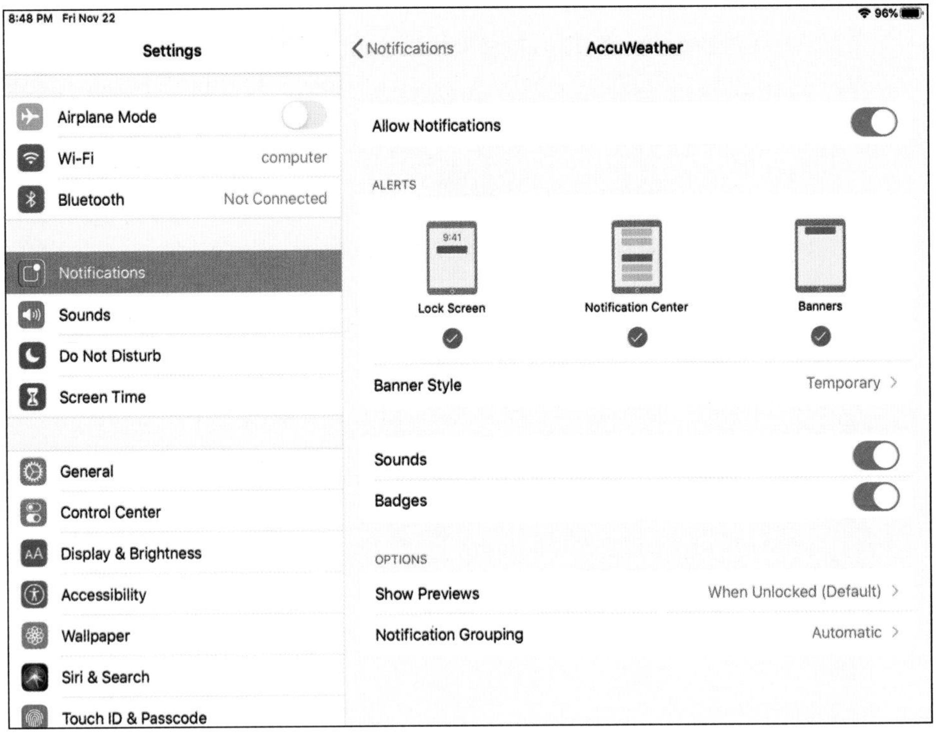

FIGURE 18-12

TIP

If you enable Banners, choose a style by tapping the Banner Style option. Banners will appear and then disappear automatically if you tap the Temporary style. If you choose Persistent, you have to take an action to dismiss the alert when it appears (such as swiping it up to dismiss it or tapping to view it). Tap the Back button in the upper-left to return to the previous screen.

5. Toggle the Sounds and Badges switches On or Off to suit your taste.

6. Tap Show Previews to determine when or if previews of notifica-tions should be shown on your iPad's screen. Options include When Unlocked (which is default), Always, or Never. Tap the name of the app at the top of the screen to go to the previous screen.

7. Select a Notification Grouping option. This feature allows you to group notifications if you like, which can keep things much cleaner, as opposed to seeing every single notification listed. Options include

- **Automatic**: Notifications are grouped according to their originating app, but they may also be sorted based on various criteria. For example, you may see more than one group for Mail if you receive multiple emails from an individual; those email notifications may merit their own grouping.

- **By App**: Notifications are grouped according to their originating app — period. You'll only see one grouping for the app, not multiple groups based on the varying criteria, as described for the Automatic setting.

- **Off**: All notifications for this app will be listed individually.

Tap the name of the app at the top of the screen to return to the previous screen.

8. Tap Notifications at the top of the screen to return to the main Notifications settings screen. When you've finished making settings, press the Home button or swipe up from the bottom of the screen (iPad Pro models only).

View Notification Center

After you've made settings for what should appear in Notification Center, you'll regularly want to take a look at those alerts and reminders.

1. From any screen, tap and hold your finger at the top of the screen and drag down to display Notification Center (see **Figure 18-13**).

Swipe from left-to-right on the date at the top of the Notification Center to view other notifications such as weather, reminders, Siri app suggestions, and more. Swipe from right-to-left on the date at the top to return to app notifications.

2. To close Notification Center, swipe upward from the bottom of the screen.

To determine what is displayed in Notification Center, see the previous task.

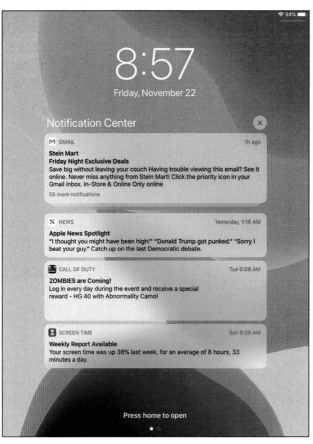

FIGURE 18-13

There are two sections in Notification Center for you to play with: Notification Center and Today.

1. Swipe down from the top of the screen to open Notification Center. Notifications are displayed by default.

2. Swipe from left to right on the date/time at the top of Notification Center to access the Today tab to view information in widgets that pertain to today, such as Reminders, weather, stock prices, Calendar items, and other items you've selected to display in Notification Center (see the preceding task).

TIP

You select which widgets appear in the Today tab by tapping the Edit button at the bottom of the Today screen and then selecting the items you want to see. Tap Done to return to the Today screen.

3. Swipe from right to left on the date/time at the top of Today tab to go back to the Notifications section to see all notifications that you set up in the Settings app. You'll see only notifications that you haven't responded to, deleted in the Notifications section, or haven't viewed in their originating app.

Get Some Rest with Do Not Disturb

Do Not Disturb is a simple but useful setting you can use to stop any alerts, text messages, and FaceTime calls from appearing or making a sound. You can make settings to allow calls from certain people or several repeat calls from the same person in a short time period to come through. (The assumption here is that such repeat calls may signal an emergency situation or urgent need to get through to you.)

1. Tap Settings and then tap Do Not Disturb.

2. Set the Do Not Disturb switch to On (green) to enable the feature.

3. In the other settings shown in **Figure 18-14**, do any of the following:

   • Toggle the Scheduled switch to On (green) to allow alerts during a specified time period to appear.

   • Tap Allow Calls From and then, from the next screen select Everyone, No One, Favorites, or Groups such as All Contacts.

   • Toggle the Repeated Calls switch to On to allow a second call from the same person in a three-minute time period to come through.

   • Choose to silence incoming calls and notifications Always or only While iPad is locked.

4. Press the Home button or swipe up from the bottom of the screen (iPad Pro models only) to return to the Home screen.

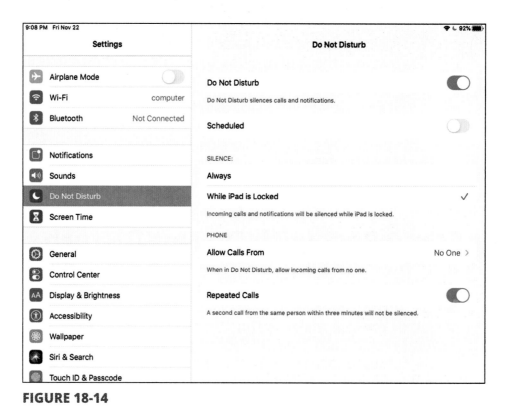

FIGURE 18-14

IN THIS CHAPTER

» Create notes

» Copy and paste

» Insert pictures

» Add drawings and text styles

» Create checklists

» Delete notes

Chapter **19**

Making Notes

N otes is the app that you can use to do everything from jotting down notes at meetings to keeping to-do lists. It isn't (yet) a robust word processor (such as Apple Pages or Microsoft Word), but for taking notes on the fly, jotting down shopping lists, or writing a few pages of your novel-in-progress while you sip a cup of coffee on your deck, it's becoming an increasingly useful tool with each new iteration.

In this chapter, you see how to enter and edit text in Notes and how to manage those notes by navigating among them, searching for content, or sharing or deleting them. I also help you explore the shortcut menu that allows you to create bulleted checklists, add pictures and drawings to notes, and apply styles to text in a note.

Open a Blank Note

To open a blank note:

1. To get started with Notes, tap the Notes app icon on the Home screen. If you've never used Notes, it opens with a blank Notes list displayed. (If you have used Notes, it opens to the last note you were working on. If that's the case, you may want to jump to the next task to display a new, blank note.) You see the view shown in **Figure 19-1**.

New Note button

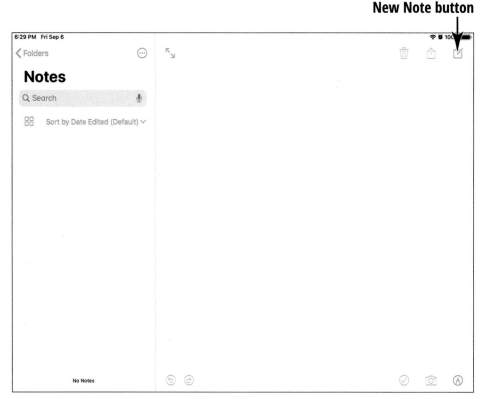

FIGURE 19-1

2. Tap the New Note button in the upper-right corner of the open note (looks like a piece of paper with a pencil writing on it; refer to Figure 19-1). A blank note opens and displays the onscreen keyboard, shown in **Figure 19-2**.

TIP

Notes can be shared among Apple devices via iCloud. In Settings, both devices must have Notes turned on under iCloud. New notes are shared instantaneously if both devices are connected to the Internet; this makes it easy to begin a note on one device and move to another device, picking up right where you left off.

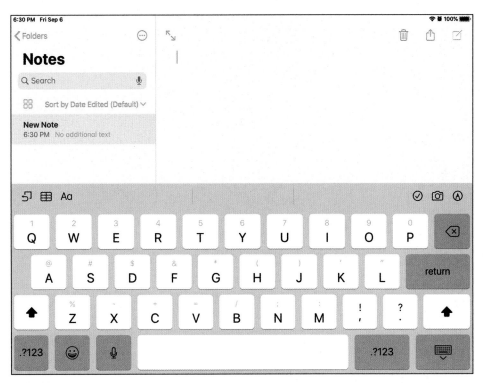

FIGURE 19-2

3. Tap keys on the keyboard to enter text or, with Siri enabled, tap the
Dictation key (the one with the microphone on it) to speak your text.
If you want to enter numbers or symbols, tap the key labeled .?123 on
the keyboard (refer to Figure 19-2). The numeric keyboard, shown in
Figure 19-3, appears. Whenever you want to return to the alphabetic
keyboard, tap the key labeled ABC.

When you have the numerical keyboard displayed (refer to
Figure 19-3), you can tap the key labeled #+= to access more
symbols, such as the percentage sign or the euro symbol, or
additional bracket styles.

TIP

Allow me to introduce you to a cool keyboard trick: the ability
to access alternate characters on a key with a simple pull-down.
For example, if you need to type the number 4, simply touch the
R key, pull down on it, and then release, as opposed to engaging
the numerical keyboard.

TIP

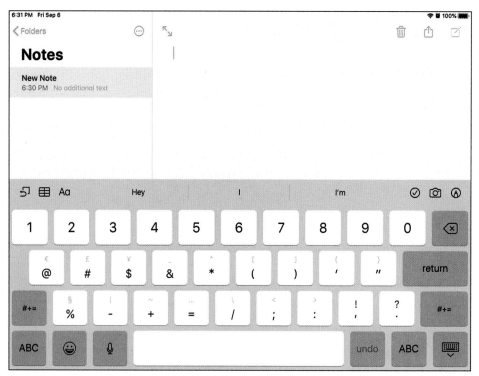

FIGURE 19-3

4. To capitalize a letter, tap the Shift key that looks like a bold, upward-facing arrow (refer to Figure 19-2) and then tap the letter. Tap the Shift key once again to turn the feature off.

TIP

You can activate the Enable Caps Lock feature in Settings ➪ General ➪ Keyboard so that you can then turn Caps Lock on by double-tapping the Shift key. (This upward-pointing arrow is available only in the alphabetic keyboard.)

5. When you want to start a new paragraph or a new item in a list, tap the Return key (refer to Figure 19-2).

6. To edit text, tap to the right of the text you want to edit and either use the Delete key (refer to Figure 19-2) to delete text to the left of the cursor or enter new text. No need to save a note — it's kept automatically until you delete it.

TIP

You can press a spot on your note and, from the menu that appears, choose Select or Select All. Then you can tap the button labeled BIU to apply bold, italic, or underline formatting.

Use Copy and Paste

The Notes app includes two essential editing tools that you're probably familiar with from using word processors: Copy and Paste.

TIP

1. With a note displayed, press and hold your finger on a word.

   To extend a selection to adjacent words, press one of the little handles that extend from an edge of the selection and drag to the left, right, up, or down.

2. Tap Select or Select All in the options that appear.

3. On the next toolbar that appears (see **Figure 19-4**), tap the Copy button.

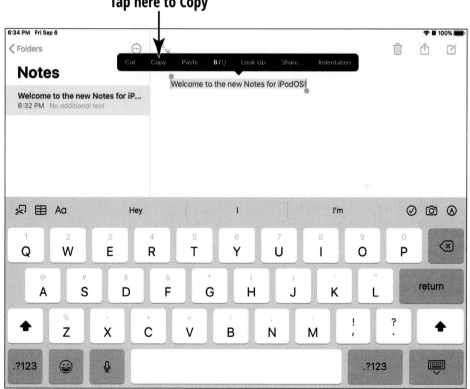

FIGURE 19-4

4. Tap in the document where you want the copied text to go and then press and hold your finger on the screen.

5. On the toolbar that appears (see **Figure 19-5**), tap the Paste button. The copied text appears (see **Figure 19-6**).

TIP

If you want to select all text in a note to either delete or copy it, tap the Select All button on the toolbar shown in Figure 19-5. All text is selected, and then you use the Cut or Copy command on the toolbar, as shown in Figure 19-4, to delete or copy the selected text. You can also tap the Delete key on the keyboard to delete selected text.

FIGURE 19-5

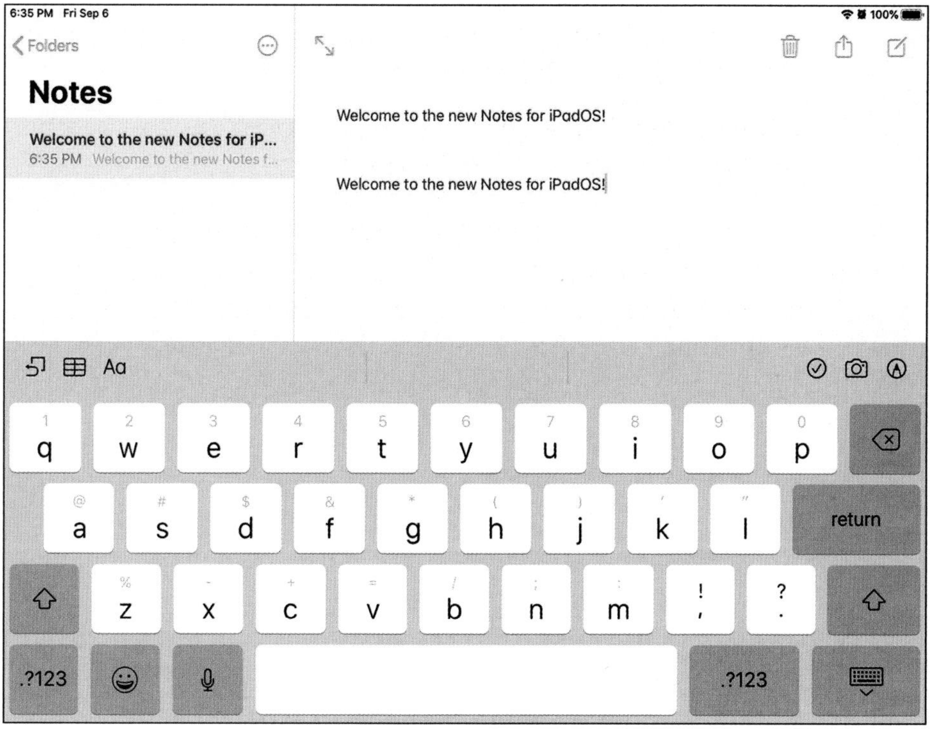

FIGURE 19-6

Insert a Picture

To insert a photo into a note:

1. Tap the Camera button on the top-right of the keyboard. In the menu that appears, tap Photo Library (see **Figure 19-7**).

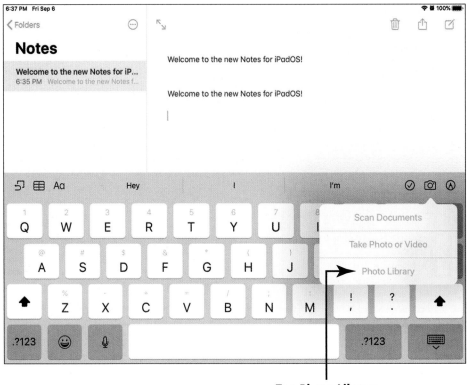

Tap Photo Library

FIGURE 19-7

2. Tap to choose the photos you want to insert, as shown in **Figure 19-8**.

3. Tap Done, and the photos are inserted into your note.

TIP

If you want to take a photo or video, tap Take Photo or Video in Step 2 and take a new photo or video. Tap Use Photo (lower-right corner) to insert it in your note, or tap Retake (lower-left corner) to start over.

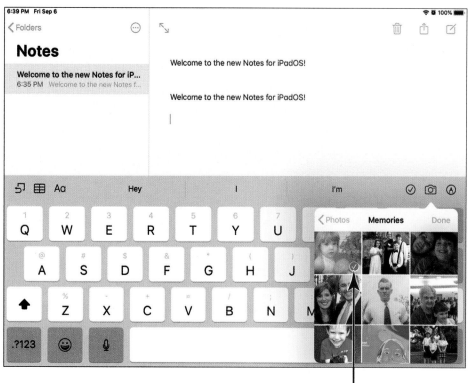

Selected photo

FIGURE 19-8

Add a Drawing

Notes has advanced to the point where you can now create a drawing to add to your note.

1. With a note open, tap the Add Sketch button on the top-right of the keyboard to display the shortcut toolbar and the drawing tools appear.

2. Tap a drawing tool (Pen, Marker, or Pencil). The selected tool will be the tallest among the group.

3. Tap a Color button in the color palette.

4. Tap a color and then draw on the screen using your finger (or with a stylus, such as an Apple Pencil), as shown in **Figure 19-9**.

FIGURE 19-9

5. When you've finished drawing, tap Done in the upper-left corner.

6. You can delete a drawing from a note by pressing the drawing until the toolbar appears. Tap the Delete button, shown in **Figure 19-10**, to remove the drawing.

Tapping the Ruler tool places a ruler-shaped item on screen that you can use to help you to draw straight lines.

TIP

Tap to delete

FIGURE 19-10

Apply a Text Style

Text styles, including Title, Heading, Subheading, Body, Mono-spaced, Bulleted List, Dashed List, and Numbered List, are available on the shortcut toolbar (which is just sitting on top of the onscreen keyboard). With a note open and the shortcut toolbar displayed, press on the text and choose Select or Select All.

Tap the Text Style tool on the shortcut bar (labeled with Aa) and then tap to choose a style from the options, shown in **Figure 19-11**.

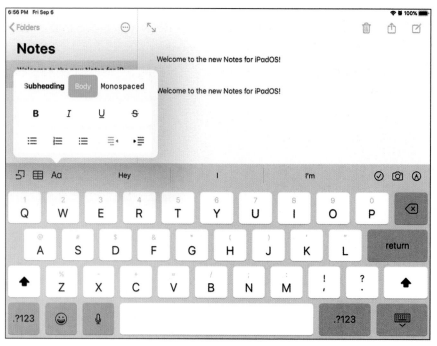

FIGURE 19-11

Notes is a very nice application and is getting better with every iOS iteration, but it's limited when compared to full-blown word processing apps. So if you've made some notes and want to graduate to building a more robust document in a word processor, you have a couple of options. One way is to download the Pages word-processor app for iPad from the App Store (if it's not already installed) and copy your note (using the copy-and-paste feature discussed earlier in this chapter). Alternatively, you can send the note to yourself in an email message, sync it to your computer, or use the Share button to send it your computer via AirDrop. Open the note and copy and paste its text into a full-fledged word processor, and you're good to go.

Create a Checklist

The Checklist formatting feature in Notes allows you to add circular buttons in front of text and then tap those buttons to check off completed items on a checklist.

1. With a note open, tap the Checklist button (the circle containing a check mark) in the shortcut toolbar at the top of the keyboard.

2. Enter text and press Return on the keyboard. A second checklist bullet appears.

3. When you're done entering Checklist items, tap the Checklist button again to turn the feature off.

TIP

You can apply the Checklist formatting to existing text if you press on the text, tap Select or Select All, and then tap the Checklist button.

Now that your checklist is completed, simply tap the circle next to completed items in the checklist to place a check in them, marking them complete, as shown in **Figure 19-12**.

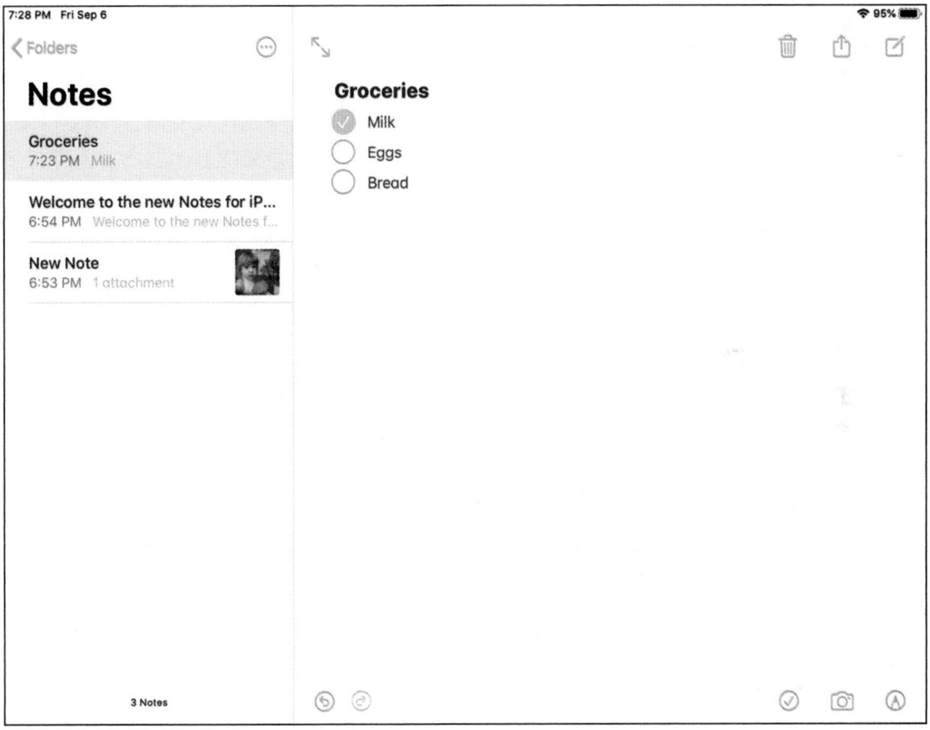

FIGURE 19-12

Delete a Note

There's no sense in letting your Notes list get cluttered, making it harder to find the ones you need. When you're done with a note, it's time to delete it.

1. Tap Notes on the Home screen to open Notes.

2. Tap a note in the Notes list to open it.

3. Tap the Trash button, as shown in the upper-right corner of Figure 19-12. The note is deleted.

An alternative method to delete a note is to swipe to the left on a note in the Notes list and then tap the Delete button that appears (it looks like a trash can). You could also move the note to another folder or lock the note to prevent it from being viewed. If you lock the note, you'll want to provide a password, and perhaps even use Touch ID or Face ID, to secure it from prying eyes.

TIP Should you like to retrieve a note you've deleted, tap the Back button in the upper-left corner of the screen until you get to the Folders list and then tap Recently Deleted. Tap the More button (a circle containing three dots) in the upper-right of the Recently Deleted list, choose Select Notes, tap the note or notes you'd like to recover, tap Move To in the lower-left corner, and then select a folder to relocate the selected items. Notes not removed from Recently Deleted will be permanently deleted in 30 days.

IN THIS CHAPTER

» **Reading the news**

» **Selecting Favorites**

» **Exploring channels and topics**

» **Finding news**

» **Saving and sharing news stories**

Chapter **20**

Getting the News You Need

The News app is a news aggregator, meaning that it gathers news stories that either match your news reading habits or match the channels and topics you've selected. You can choose which news sites are your favorites, search for news on a particular topic, and save news stories to read later. The News app also has a handy sidebar that makes it even easier to browse news sources, find articles, and more. In this chapter, you get an overview of all these features.

Read Your News

Whether kicking off your day or calling it a night, reading the news is a great way to catch up on world, national, and local events. Here's how to get the latest scoop on your iPad:

1. Tap the News app icon to get started. The first time you open it, you'll be asked a few questions to set up the app — customization of

notifications and whether to deliver news to your Inbox, for example. Continue through the initial screens until you get to the news stories.

TIP

When you first open News, it will ask your permission to access your location. The purpose of knowing your location is to provide more accurate searches and local weather information. If you prefer more accurate info and weather, tap Allow when prompted; if not, tap Don't Allow.

2. The layout of items in News varies depending on how you hold your iPad. In portrait mode, you'll see news articles and a Sidebar button that appears in the upper-left corner, which you can tap to view the new Sidebar. Viewing News in landscape mode automatically displays the Sidebar. Both views are displayed in **Figure 20-1.**

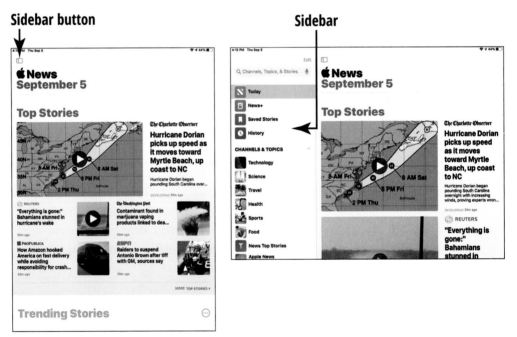

FIGURE 20-1

3. Swipe up or down on the screen to browse the stories of the day in categories like Trending Stories.

4. Tap a story to open it.

5. If you like a story, tap the Share button in the upper-right corner and then tap the Suggest More Like This option to help News understand which kinds of stories you enjoy (see **Figure 20-2**). If you dislike the story, tap the Suggest Less Like This option to discourage News from showing stories like it (also in Figure 20-2).

6. Tap the Text Size button in the upper-right corner to adjust text size for easier reading (refer to Figure 20-2). If you don't see it, simply swipe up or down on the screen until it appears.

7. Tap the Back button (left-pointing arrow) in the upper-left corner to go back to the news list (refer to Figure 20-2).

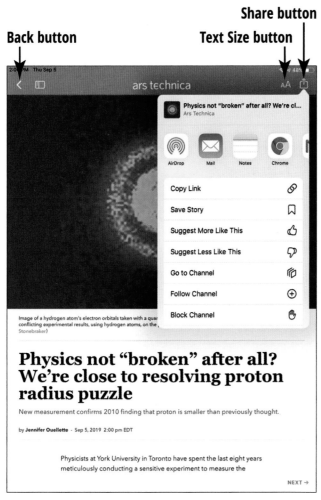

FIGURE 20-2

TIP

When you're reading a story you like, you can tap the Share button in the upper-right corner of the screen to share via Mail, Message, Twitter, Facebook, and a multitude of other options, as discussed later in this chapter.

See Who or What Is in the Spotlight

The Apple News Spotlight tab in the Sidebar features a topic or story of the day that Apple's News editors handpick for further exploration. The topic, one of which is illustrated in **Figure 20-3**, can be anything from as light as Emmy or Academy Award nominations to sports (the Super Bowl, for example) to heavier political fare.

FIGURE 20-3

Follow Favorite Channels and Topics

The Sidebar allows you to select the topics and channels you prefer to include in your News, as well as manage notifications from news sources.

1. With the News app open, access the Sidebar to view a list of news sources and other items, as shown in **Figure 20-4.** The Sidebar is divided into items or sources that you follow, items suggested by Siri based on popular categories or your own browsing history, stories you've saved, and your viewing history.

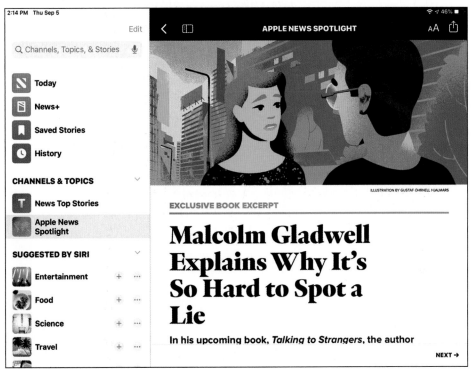

FIGURE 20-4

2. Scroll down the Sidebar to find suggestions from Siri based on your searches, favorite channels, and topics that appeal to you. You can also search for topics and channels using the search field at the top of the Sidebar.

3. Tap Edit above the Search field to edit the list of news sources you follow.

4. To delete an item, tap the red circle containing the "–" and then tap the Unfollow button that appears to the right (see **Figure 20-5**). You can also rearrange items in the list by dragging the bars to the right of an item up and down the list and dropping it where you like. Tap Done above the search bar when you finish editing the list.

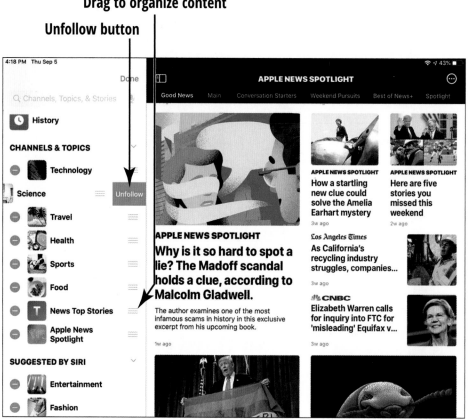

FIGURE 20-5

5. In the Suggested by Siri section, tap the + button to let News know which topics most interest you and to add the topic to your Channels & Topics list in the Sidebar (see **Figure 20-6**). If you don't care for a topic, tap the More button (looks like a gray circle containing three tiny red dots and is also seen in Figure 20-6) and tap Stop Suggesting or Block

Topic to keep News from bothering you with it. If you're ambivalent toward a particular topic, simply choose Stop Suggesting; News will occasionally offer you a story on the topic, but won't flood you with it or completely ignore it. Select Block Topic to prevent anything related to the topic from appearing in your News.

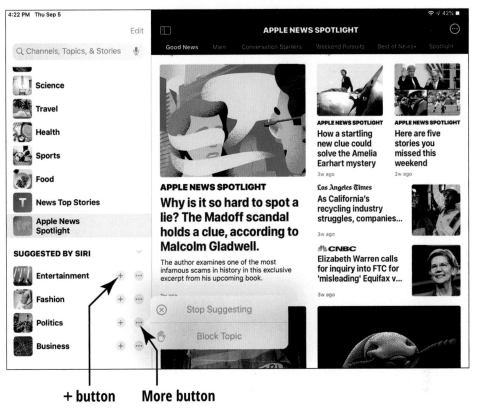

+ button **More button**

FIGURE 20-6

6. Scroll near the bottom of the Sidebar and tap the Discover Channels and Topics button to see a list of channels and topics you may designate as favorites, as shown in **Figure 20-7**.

7. Scroll up and down the page to find items that interest you and tap them to make them favorites. (The + on the icon will turn into a red circle containing a white check mark for favorites; tap again to remove a favorite.)

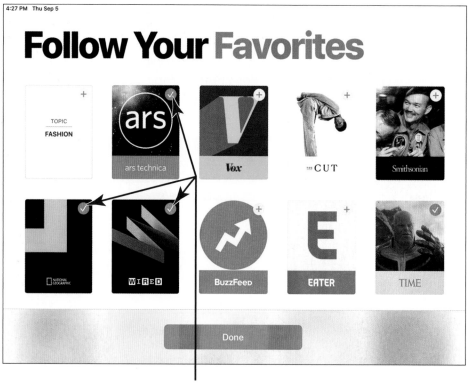

Favorites

FIGURE 20-7

8. Tap the red Done button at the bottom of the screen to quit browsing and return to the Sidebar.

9. Scroll near the bottom of the Sidebar to see Manage. Tap Notifications under Manage to scroll through a list of channels and toggle the switch to enable (green) or disable (white) notifications for a news outlet (as shown in **Figure 20-8**). Tap the Done button in the upper-right of the Notification window to exit Notifications.

TIP

You can preview stories before opening them, which saves some download time. In Settings, tap News and then be sure the Show Story Previews switch is set to On (which it is by default).

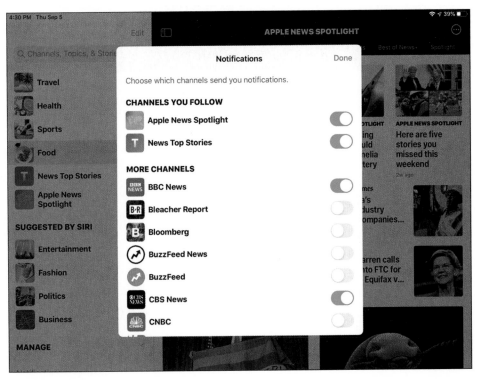

FIGURE 20-8

Chapter **21**

Using Utilities

U tilities are simple apps that can be very useful indeed to help with common tasks, such as recording ideas for your first novel or measuring the height of your dining room chairs.

In this chapter, I show you how to make recordings using the Voice Memos app, and how to take measurements with the Measure app in iPadOS. Also, in case you lose your iPad, I even tell you about a feature that helps you find it, activate it remotely, or even disable it if it has fallen into the wrong hands. Finally, I offer a quick introduction to the Home app, which enables you to set up and control all of your smart devices.

Record Voice Memos

Voice Memos is perhaps the most robust of the apps covered in this chapter, and it's also been redesigned for iPadOS. The app allows you to record memos, edit memos by trimming them down, share them by email or instant message with Messages, synchronize recordings and edits across Apple devices (iPad, iPhone, and Mac), and label recordings so that you find them easily.

To record voice memos, follow these steps:

1. Tap the Voice Memos icon to open the app.

2. In the Voice Memos app (see **Figure 21-1**), tap the red Record button at the bottom-left of the screen to record a memo.

   This button changes to a red Pause button when you're recording, and the screen changes to show you the recording in progress. A red line moving from right to left indicates that you're in recording mode (see **Figure 21-2**).

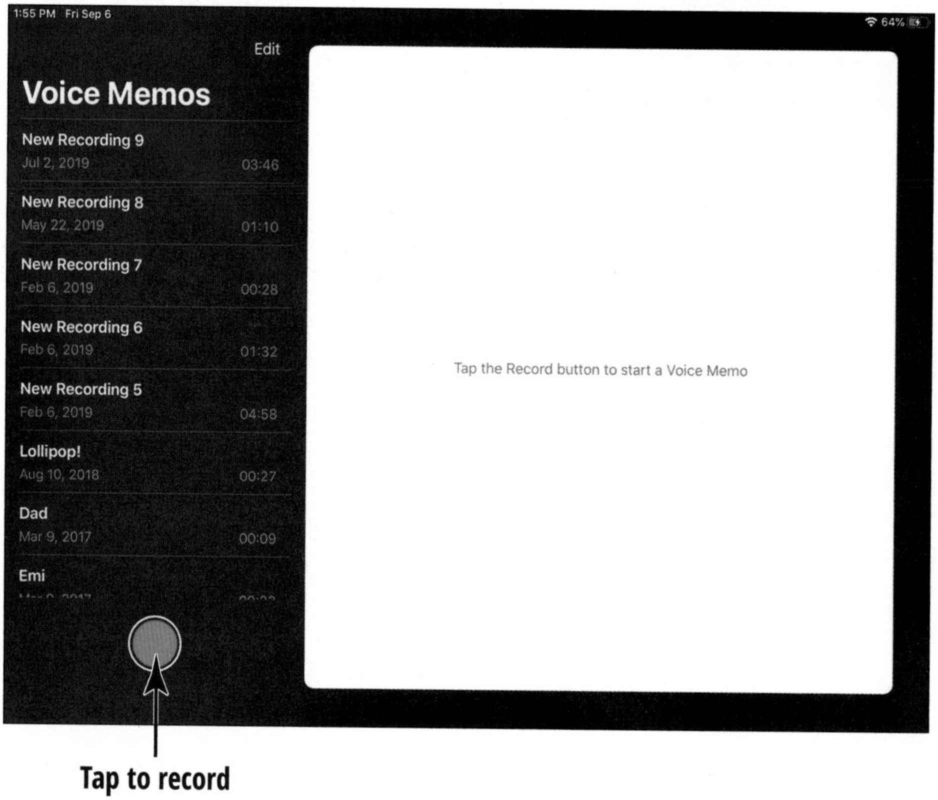

Tap to record

FIGURE 21-1

FIGURE 21-2

3. While recording, you can

   - Tap the name of the recording (called New Recording by default) to give it a new more descriptive name.

   - Tap the red Pause button to pause the recording; then tap Resume to continue recording.

   - While paused, drag the waveform to a place in the recording you'd like to record over and then tap the Replace button to begin recording from there.

   - Tap Done to stop recording, and the new recording appears in the Voice Memos list.

4. Tap a memo in the list to open its window. Tap the play button to play it back, tap the Forward or Reverse buttons to move forward or backward 15 seconds in the recording, or tap the Trash icon to delete it. You can also tap the name of the memo to rename it.

TIP

Deleted voice memos are kept for 30 days in a folder at the bottom of the Voice Memos list called Recently Deleted. You can retrieve a deleted memo by tapping the Recently Deleted button, tapping the name of the memo you want to retrieve, and then tapping Recover at the upper-center of the screen.

Measure Distances

iPadOS uses the latest advancements in AR (augmented reality) and your iPad's camera to offer you a cool new way to ditch your measuring tape: the Measure app! This app allows you to use your iPad to measure distances and objects simply by pointing your iPad at it. This app's fun to play with and surprisingly accurate to boot.

TECHNICAL
STUFF

As of this writing, the Measure app can only measure in straight lines, but Apple is working to allow more flexibility in upcoming iPadOS updates.

TIP

Make sure you have plenty of light when using the Measure app, which increases the accuracy of your measurements.

1. Open the Measure app by tapping its icon.

2. Your iPad will prompt you to calibrate the Measure app by panning your iPad around so the camera gets a good look at your surroundings, as illustrated in **Figure 21-3**.

3. Once calibrated, you'll need to add the first reference point for your measurement. Do so by aiming the white targeting dot in the center of the screen to the location of your first reference point, as shown in **Figure 21-4**. Tap the Add a Point button (white button containing the +) to mark the point.

4. Next, mark the second reference point by placing the targeting dot on the location and tapping the Add a Point button again.

TIP

Should you make a mistake or simply want to start afresh, tap the Clear button in the upper-right corner to clear your reference points and begin again.

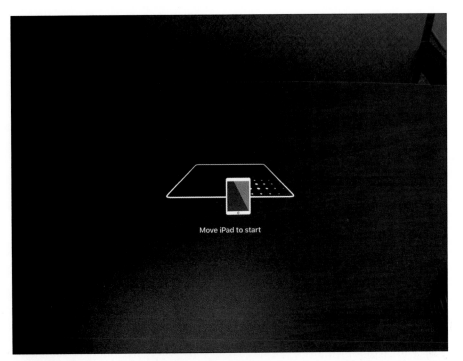

FIGURE 21-3

FIGURE 21-4

5. The length of your measurement is displayed as a white line, and the distance is shown in the middle of it (see **Figure 21-5**).

FIGURE 21-5

6. You can continue to make measurements by aiming the targeting dot at a previous reference point, tapping the Add a Point button, and moving your iPad to the next reference point, where you again tap the Add a Point button to make a new measurement (as shown in **Figure 21-6**).

7. When you're finished measuring, tap the white Capture button (just above the Add a Point button) to save an image of your measurements to the Camera Roll in the Photos app.

Measure is a very handy app and is only going to get more useful as Apple updates it.

FIGURE 21-6

Find a Missing Apple Device

iPadOS pairs the Find My iPhone app (even though you have an iPad, the app was still called Find My iPhone) and the Find My Friends app, combining their functionalities to make a single easy-to-use app called Find My. Find My can pinpoint the location of your Apple devices and your Apple-using friends. This app is extremely handy if you forget where you left your iPad or someone steals it. Find My not only lets you track down the critter but also lets you wipe out the data contained in it if you have no way to get the iPad (or other Apple device) back.

REMEMBER

You must have an iCloud account to use Find My. If you don't have an iCloud account, see Chapter 3 to find out how to set one up.

TIP

If you're using Family Sharing, someone in your family can find your device and play a sound. This works even if the volume on the device is turned down. See Chapter 12 for more about Family Sharing. Also, see Apple's support article called "Share your location with your family" at https://support.apple.com/en-us/HT201087 (as of this writing) for help with this service.

Follow these steps to set up the Find My feature for your iPad:

1. Tap Settings on the Home screen.

2. In Settings, tap your Apple ID at the top of the screen and then tap Find My.

3. In the Find My settings, tap Find My iPad and then tap the On/Off switch for Find My iPad to turn the feature on (see **Figure 21-7**).

Tap here to enable Find My iPad

2:46 PM Fri Sep 6		🛜 70% 🔋
Settings	**‹** Find My	**Find My iPad**

Finish Setting Up Your iPad ① ›	**Find My iPad** ⬜
	Locate, lock, or erase your iPad and supported accessories. Your iPad cannot be erased and reactivated without your password. About Find My iPad and Privacy...
✈️ Airplane Mode ⬜	
🛜 Wi-Fi computer	**Enable Offline Finding** 🔵
⚫ Bluetooth Off	Offline finding enables your devices to be found when not connected to Wi-Fi or cellular.
🔔 Notifications	**Send Last Location** ⬜
🔊 Sounds	Automatically send the location of this iPad to Apple when the battery is critically low.
🌙 Do Not Disturb	
⏳ Screen Time	
⚙️ General ①	
🎛️ Control Center	
🔠 Display & Brightness	
♿ Accessibility	
🌸 Wallpaper	

FIGURE 21-7

TIP

You may also want to turn on the Enable Offline Finding option. This is a new option that allows Apple devices to be found using their built-in Bluetooth technology, even when not connected to Wi-Fi or a cellular network. When you mark your device as missing on www.icloud.com and another Apple user is close by the device, the two devices connect anonymously via Bluetooth and you're notified of its location. It's pretty cool stuff and completely private for all involved parties.

4. From now on, if your iPad is lost or stolen, you can go to www.icloud. com from your computer, iPhone, or another iPad and enter your Apple ID and password.

5. In your computer's browser, the iCloud Launchpad screen appears. Click the Find iPhone button to display a map of your device's location and some helpful tools (see **Figure 21-8**).

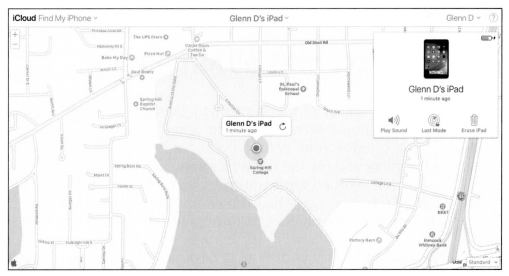

FIGURE 21-8

6. Click the All Devices option at the top of the window and click your iPad in the list. In the window that appears, choose one of three options:

- To wipe information from the iPad, click the Erase iPad button.
- To lock the iPad from access by others, click the Lost Mode button.

- Click Play Sound to have your iPad play a "ping" sound that might help you locate it if you're in its vicinity. If you choose to play a sound, it plays for two minutes, helping you track down your iPad in case it fell behind the couch or somebody holding your iPad is within earshot. You can also tap OK on your iPad (once you find it) to stop the sound before the two minutes is up.

TIP The Erase iPad option will delete all data from your iPad, including contact information and content (such as music and photos). However, even after you've erased your iPad, it will display your phone number on the Lock screen along with a message so that any Good Samaritan who finds it can contact you. If you've created an iTunes or iCloud backup, you can restore your iPad's contents from those sources.

TIP The Lost Mode feature allows you to send whomever has your iPad a note saying how to return it to you.

An Overview of the Home App

Since the smart home movement began a few years ago, controlling your home remotely meant juggling several apps: one for your lights, one for your garage doors, one for your thermostat, one for your oven, and on and on. While some developers have tried to create apps that worked with multiple smart home platforms by multiple manufacturers, none had the clout or the engineering manpower to pull things together — until Apple jumped in.

The Home app on your iPad is designed to work with multiple smart home platforms and devices, and you can control all of the smart devices in your home from one easy-to-use app.

Here's a list of the types of devices you can control with your iPad: lighting, locks, windows and window shades, heating and cooling systems, speakers, humidifiers and air purifiers, security systems, garage doors, electrical plugs and switches, motion sensors, video cameras, smoke and carbon monoxide detectors, and even more!

TIP

If you want to use the Home app with your smart home devices, make sure that you see the "Works with Apple HomeKit" symbol on packaging or on the website (if you purchase the device online). Apple has an ever-growing list of HomeKit-enabled devices at www.apple.com/ios/home/accessories. You can also buy HomeKit-enabled devices on Apple's website: www.apple.com/shop/accessories/all-accessories/homekit.

Because there are so many ways to configure and use the Home app and so many different accessories you can control with it, it's really beyond the scope of this book cover the app in detail. Apple offers a great overview at www.apple.com/ios/home.

IN THIS CHAPTER

» **Cleaning and protecting your iPad**

» **Fixing a nonresponsive iPad**

» **Updating the iOS software**

» **Getting support**

» **Backing up your iPad**

Chapter **22**

Troubleshooting and Maintaining Your iPad

Pads don't grow on trees — they cost a pretty penny. That's why you should learn how to take care of your iPad and troubleshoot any problems it might have so that you get the most out of it.

In this chapter, I provide some advice about the care and maintenance of your iPad, as well as tips about how to solve common problems, update iPad system software, and even reset the iPad if something goes seriously wrong. In case you lose your iPad, I even tell you about a feature that helps you find it, activate it remotely, or even disable it if it has fallen into the wrong hands. Finally, you get information about backing up your iPad settings and content using iCloud and the fingerprint reader feature, Touch ID.

Keep the iPad Screen Clean

If you've been playing with your iPad, you know (despite Apple's claim that the iPad has a fingerprint-resistant screen) that it's a fingerprint magnet. Here are some tips for cleaning your iPad screen:

» **Use a dry, soft cloth.** You can get most fingerprints off with a dry, soft cloth, such as the one you use to clean your eyeglasses or a cleaning tissue that's lint-and chemical-free. Or try products used to clean lenses in labs, such as Kimwipes (which you can get from several major retailers, such as Amazon, Walmart, and office supply stores).

» **Use a slightly dampened soft cloth.** This may sound counter-intuitive to the previous tip, but to get the surface even cleaner, very (and I stress, very) slightly dampen the soft cloth. Again, make sure that whatever cloth material you use is free of lint.

» **Remove the cables.** Turn off your iPad and unplug any cables from it before cleaning the screen with a moistened cloth, even a very slightly moistened one.

» **Avoid too much moisture.** Avoid getting too much moisture around the edges of the screen, where it can seep into the unit. It isn't so much the glass surface you should worry about, as it is the Home button (if your iPad is equipped with one) and the speaker holes on the top and bottom of the iPad.

» **Don't use your fingers!** That's right, by using a stylus (or an Apple Pencil, if your iPad supports it) rather than your finger, you entirely avoid smearing oil from your skin or cheese from your pizza on the screen. Besides the Apple Pencil, a number of top-notch styluses are out there; just search Amazon for "iPad stylus," and you'll be greeted with a multitude of them, most of which are priced quite reasonably.

» **Never use household cleaners.** They can degrade the coating that keeps the iPad screen from absorbing oil from your fingers. Plus, you simply don't need to go that far since the screen cleans very easily with little or no moisture at all.

TIP

Don't use premoistened lens-cleaning tissues to clean your iPad screen! Most brands of wipes contain alcohol, which can damage the screen's coating. Be sure whatever cleaner you do use states that it's compatible with your model iPad, as there are differences in screen technology between models.

Protect Your Gadget with a Case

Your screen isn't the only element on the iPad that can be damaged, so consider getting a case for it so that you can carry it around the house or travel with it safely. Besides providing a bit of padding if you drop the device, a case makes the iPad less slippery in your hands, offering a better grip when working with it.

Several types of covers and cases are available, but be sure to get one that will fit your model of iPad because their dimensions and button placements may differ, and some models have slightly different thicknesses. There are differences between covers and cases:

> » **Covers tend to be more for decoration than overall protection.** While they do provide some minimal protection, they're generally thin and not well-padded.

> » **Cases are more solid and protect most, if not all, of your iPad.** They're usually a bit bulky and provide more padding than covers.

Extend Your iPad's Battery Life

The much-touted battery life of the iPad is a wonderful feature, but you can do some things to extend it even further. Here are a few tips to consider:

> » **Keep tabs on remaining battery life.** You can estimate the amount of remaining battery life by looking at the Battery icon on the far-right end of the Status bar, at the top of your screen.

» **Use standard accessories to charge your iPad most effectively.** When connected to a recent-model Mac or Windows computer for charging, the iPad can slowly charge; however, the most effective way to charge your iPad is to plug it into a wall outlet using the Lightning-to-USB cable and the USB power adapter that come with your iPad.

Third-party charging cables usually work just fine, but some are less reliable than others. If you use a third-party cable and notice that your iPad is taking longer than usual to charge, it's a good idea to try another cable.

» **Use a case with an external battery pack.** These cases are very handy when you're traveling or unable to reach an electrical outlet easily. However, they're also a bit bulky and can be cumbersome in smaller hands.

» **The fastest way to charge your iPad is to turn it off while charging it.** If turning your iPad completely off doesn't sound like the best idea for you, you can disable Wi-Fi or Bluetooth to facilitate a faster recharge.

Activate Airplane Mode to turn both Wi-Fi and Bluetooth off at the same time.

» **The Battery icon on the Status bar indicates when the charging is complete.**

Be careful not to use your iPad in ambient temperatures higher than 95-degrees Farenheit (35-degrees Celcius), as doing so may damage your battery. Damage of this kind may also not be covered under warranty. Charging in high temperatures may damage the battery even more.

If you notice that you're battery won't charge more than 80%, it could be getting too warm. Unplug the iPad from the charger and try again after it's cooled down a bit.

Your iPad battery is sealed in the unit, so you can't replace it yourself the way you can with many laptops or other cellphones. If the battery is out of warranty, you have to fork over about $99 to have Apple install a new one with AppleCare coverage. See the "Get Support" section, later in this chapter, to find out where to get a replacement battery.

TIP

Apple offers AppleCare+. For $99, you get two years of coverage, which even covers you if you drop or spill liquids on your iPad. (Apple covers up to two incidents of accidental damage with a $49 service fee, plus tax) You can purchase AppleCare+ when you buy your iPad or within 60 days of the date of purchase. Visit `http://www.apple.com/support/products/ipad` for more details.

What to Do with a Nonresponsive iPad

If your iPad goes dead on you, it's most likely a power issue, so the first thing to do is to plug the Lightning-to-USB cable into the USB power adapter, plug the USB power adapter into a wall outlet, plug the other end of the cable into your iPad, and charge the battery.

Another thing to try — if you believe that an app is hanging up the iPad — is to press the Sleep/Wake button for a couple of seconds and then press and hold the Home button. The app you were using should close.

You can always use the tried-and-true reboot procedure: On iPads with Home buttons, you press the Sleep/Wake button until the power off slider appears. For iPads with no Home button, press the Top button and either Volume button until the power off slider appears. Drag the slider to the right to turn off your iPad. After a few moments, press the Sleep/Wake button to boot up the little guy again.

If the situation seems drastic and none of these ideas works, try to force restart your iPad. To do this, press and hold the Sleep/Wake button and the Home button at the same time (for iPads with Home buttons) for at least ten seconds until the Apple logo appears onscreen. For iPads without Home buttons, press the Volume Up button once, press the Volume Down button once, and then press and hold the Sleep/Wake (Power) button until the Apple logo appears.

TIP

If your iPad has this problem often, try closing out some active apps that may be running in the background and using up too much memory. To do this on iPads with Home buttons, press the Home button twice, and then from the screen showing active apps, tap and drag an app upward to close it. For iPads without Home buttons, swipe up from the bottom of the screen and pause momentarily until the active apps display. Then swipe an app upward to close it. Also check to see that you haven't loaded up your iPad with too much content, such as videos, which could be slowing down its performance.

Update the iPadOS Software

Apple occasionally updates the iPad system software, known as iPadOS (formerly iOS), to fix problems or offer enhanced features. You should occasionally check for an updated version (say, every month or so). You can check by connecting your iPad to a recognized computer (that is, a computer that you've used to sign into your Apple account before) with iTunes installed, but it's even easier to just update from your iPad Settings, though it can be just a tad slower:

1. Tap Settings from the Home screen.

2. Tap General and then tap Software Update (see **Figure 22-1**).

3. A message tells you whether your software is up-to-date. If it's not, tap Download and Install and follow the prompts to update to the latest iOS version.

TIP

If you're having problems with your iPad, you can use the Reset feature to try to restore the natural balance. Follow the preceding set of steps and then tap the Reset button instead of the Software Update button in Step 2.

Tap here to check for updates

12:30 PM Fri Sep 6	🖙 34%🔋
Settings	**General**

Settings		General	
✈ Airplane Mode	⬤	About	>
🛜 Wi-Fi	computer	Software Update	➊ >
ⓑ Bluetooth	Off		
		AirDrop	>
⬛ Notifications		Handoff	>
🔊 Sounds		Multitasking & Dock	>
🌙 Do Not Disturb			
⏳ Screen Time		iPad Storage	>
		Background App Refresh	>
⚙ General	➊		
⬛ Control Center		Date & Time	>
AA Display & Brightness		Keyboard	>
ⓘ Accessibility		Fonts	>
⬛ Wallpaper		Language & Region	>
⬛ Siri & Search		Dictionary	>
⬛ Touch ID & Passcode			

FIGURE 22-1

Restore the Sound

My wife frequently has trouble with the sound on her iPad, and sub-sequently we've learned quite a bit about troubleshooting sound issues, enabling us to pass our knowledge on to you. Make sure that:

WARNING

» **You haven't touched the volume control buttons on the side of your iPad.**

Be sure not to touch the volume down button and inadvertently lower the sound to a point where you can't hear it. Pushing the volume buttons will have no effect if the iPad is sleeping.

» **The speaker isn't covered up.** No, really — it may be covered in a way that muffles the sound.

» **A headset isn't plugged in.** Sound doesn't play over the speaker and the headset at the same time.

» **The volume limit is set to On.** You can set up the volume limit for the Music app to control how loudly your music can play (which is useful if you have teenagers around). Tap Settings on the Home screen and then, on the screen that displays, tap Music, then tap Volume Limit under the Playback section if it is set to On. Use the slider that appears (shown in **Figure 22-2**) to set the volume limit. If the slider button is all the way to the left, you've set your volume limit too low (all the way down, as a matter of fact).

When all else fails, reboot.

TIP

FIGURE 22-2

Get Support

Every new iPad comes with a year's coverage for repair of the hardware and 90 days of free technical support. Apple is known for its high level of customer support, so if you're stuck, I definitely recommend that you give them a try. Here are a few options that you can explore for getting help:

» **The Apple Store:** Go to your local Apple Store (if one's nearby) to see what the folks there might know about your problem. Call first and make an appointment with the Genius Bar to be sure you get prompt service.

» **The Apple support website:** It's at http://support.apple. com/ipad. You can find online manuals, discussion forums, and downloads, and you can use the Apple Expert feature to contact a live support person by phone.

» **The iPad User Guide:** You can download the free manual that is available through Apple Books from the Apple Books Store. Be sure to download the one for iPadOS! See Chapter 13 for more about Apple Books.

» **The Apple battery replacement service:** If you need repair or service for your battery, visit http://www.apple.com/ batteries/service-and-recycling and scroll down to the iPad Owners section. Note that your warranty provides free battery replacement if the battery is defective during the warranty period. If you purchase the AppleCare+ service agreement, this is extended to two years.

WARNING

Apple recommends that you have your iPad battery replaced only by an Apple Authorized Service Provider. Please don't take this warning lightly; you don't want to trust the inner workings of your iPad to just anyone who says they can work on it.

Back Up to iCloud

You used to be able to back up your iPad content using only iTunes, but since Apple's introduction of iCloud with iOS 5, you can back up via a Wi-Fi network to your iCloud storage. You get 5GB of storage for free or you can pay for increased storage (a total of 50GB for $0.99 per month, 200GB for $2.99 per month, or 2TB for $9.99 per month).

You must have an iCloud account to back up to iCloud. If you don't have an iCloud account, see Chapter 3 to find out more.

To perform a backup to iCloud:

1. Tap Settings from the Home screen and then tap your Apple ID at the top of the screen.

2. Tap iCloud and then tap iCloud Backup (see **Figure 22-3**).

3. In the pane that appears (see **Figure 22-4**), tap the iCloud Backup switch to enable automatic backups. To perform a manual backup, tap Back Up Now. A progress bar shows how your backup is moving along.

If you get your iPad back after it wanders and you've erased it, just enter your Apple ID and password, and you can reactivate it.

You can also back up your iPad using iTunes. This method actually saves more types of content than an iCloud backup, and if you have encryption turned on in iTunes, it can save your passwords as well. However, this method does require that you connect to a computer to perform the backup. If you do back up and get a new iPad at some point in the future, you can restore all your data from your computer to the new iPad easily.

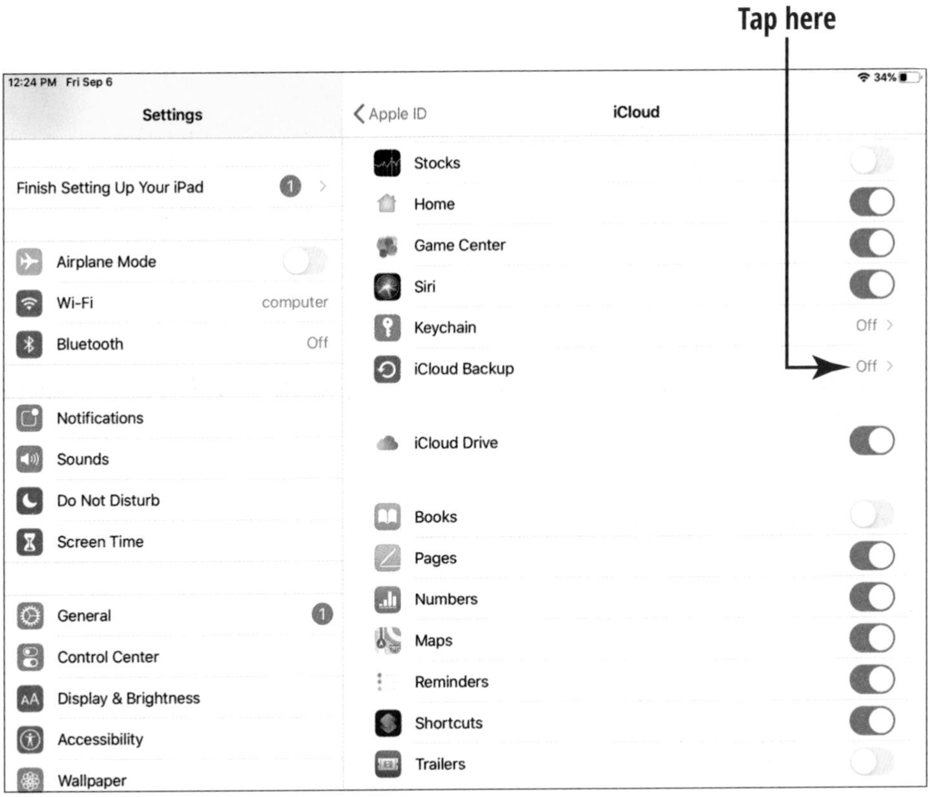

Tap here

FIGURE 22-3

APPLE ID AND PASSWORD SUPPORT

In today's technology-driven society, it seems you need a username and password to wake up in the morning! Remembering usernames and passwords can be a daunting task, and your Apple ID and password are no exceptions. Thankfully, Apple is at the ready with your solution, but it's not one-size-fits-all; situations differ, but they're ready in every case. Whether you've forgotten your Apple ID, can't remember your password, your Apple ID account is locked, or just about any other issue you can come up with, Apple's got your answer at `https://support.apple.com/apple-id`. If you can't find what you're looking for by using any of the links on the site, scroll down to the bottom and click the blue Get Support button under the "Tell us how we can help" section to connect with Apple's stellar support team.

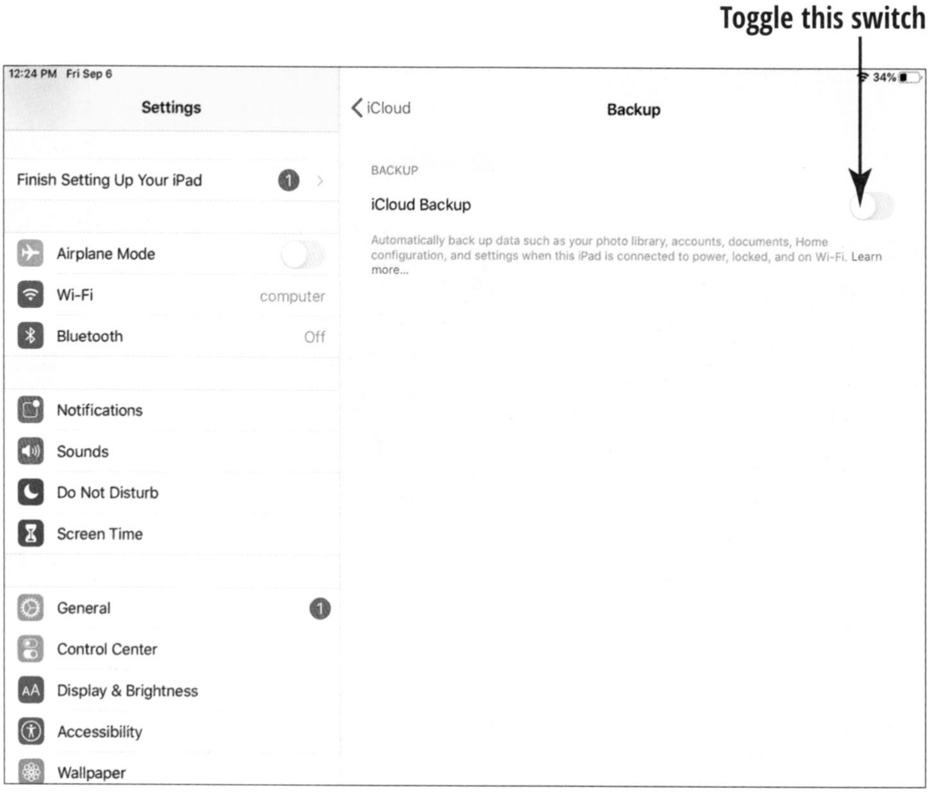
Toggle this switch
12:24 PM Fri Sep 6
34%
Settings
Finish Setting Up Your iPad
Airplane Mode
Wi-Fi
computer
Bluetooth
Off
Notifications
Sounds
Do Not Disturb
Screen Time
General
Control Center
Display & Brightness
Accessibility
Wallpaper
iCloud
Backup
BACKUP
iCloud Backup
Automatically back up data such as your photo library, accounts, documents, Home configuration, and settings when this iPad is connected to power, locked, and on Wi-Fi. Learn more...

FIGURE 22-4

Index

M

vision settings
Apple Books app display settings, 254–257
brightness, 94–96, 254–255
label settings, 104
Magnifier, 92–94
Night Shift, 96
reduce motion, 104
text appearance, 103
wallpaper, 96–98
zoom setting, 102
Voice Control, 113–116
Voice Memos, 379–382
VoiceOver, 98–101
volume
controls, 21, 273
hearing settings, 104–106
muting FaceTime, 168
troubleshooting, 397–398
volume rocker, as camera control, 284

W

Wallet, 242–243
wallpaper, changing, 96–98
Warning icon, 2
web browsing
bookmarks, 201–204
features, 191
gestures, 193–194
history, 198–200
navigating, 194–196
privacy settings, 206

Reading List, 204–206
tabbed browsing, 196–198
web searches, 200–201
Web searches, with Siri, 130–131
websites
Apple, 25
Apple iPad, 3
Apple support, 395, 399
Cheat Sheet, 2
Home Sharing, iTunes, 272
HomePod, 276
iPad For Seniors For Dummies Cheat Sheet, 2
iTunes Match, 268
Wi-Fi
features, 12
hotspots, 16, 192–193
options, 15–16
Wi-Fi icon, 52
Wi-Fi-only iPad, 15–16
Wikipedia, 259
wireless networking. *See* Wi-Fi
World Clock, 330

Y

Yahoo! Mail, 210–212

Z

zoom
accessibility settings, 102
double-tap gesture, 28

About the Author

Dwight Spivey has been a technical author and editor for over a decade, but he has been a bona fide technophile for more than three of them. He's the author of *iPad For Seniors For Dummies,* 11th Edition (Wiley), *iPhone For Seniors For Dummies,* 9th Edition (Wiley), *Idiot's Guide to Apple Watch* (Alpha), *Home Automation For Dummies* (Wiley), *How to Do Everything Pages, Keynote & Numbers* (McGraw-Hill), and many more books covering the tech gamut.

Dwight is also the Educational Technology Administrator at Spring Hill College. His technology experience is extensive, consisting of macOS, iOS, Android, Linux, and Windows operating systems in general, educational technology, desktop publishing software, laser printers and drivers, color and color management, and networking.

Dwight lives on the Gulf Coast of Alabama with his wife, Cindy, their four children, Victoria, Devyn, Emi, and Reid, and their dog, Rocky (RIP Indy and Rosie).

Dedication

To my nephews, Keaton, Kooper, and Paul, and my great-nephew, Porter.

I love you, guys!

Author's Acknowledgments

Carole Jelen, my superb agent, is always first on this list. Thank you, Carole!

Next, the awesome editors, designers, and other professionals at Wiley are absolutely critical to the completion of these books I'm so blessed to write. I hope every individual involved at every level knows that I'm truly grateful for their dedication, hard work, and patience in putting together this book. As always, extra-special gratitude to Ashley Coffey, Tim Gallan, and Tom Egan.

Publisher's Acknowledgments

Acquisitions Editor: Ashley Coffey
Project Editor: Tim Gallan
Technical Reviewer: Thomas Egan

Production Editor: Mohammed Zafar Ali
Cover Image: © DragonImages/ Getty Images